Understanding Legitimacy

Understanding Legitimacy

Political Theory and Neo-Calvinist Social Thought

Philip D. Shadd

LEXINGTON BOOKS
Lanham • Boulder • New York • London

Published by Lexington Books
An imprint of The Rowman & Littlefield Publishing Group, Inc.
4501 Forbes Boulevard, Suite 200, Lanham, Maryland 20706
www.rowman.com

Unit A, Whitacre Mews, 26-34 Stannary Street, London SE11 4AB

Copyright © 2017 by Lexington Books

All rights reserved. No part of this book may be reproduced in any form or by any electronic or mechanical means, including information storage and retrieval systems, without written permission from the publisher, except by a reviewer who may quote passages in a review.

British Library Cataloguing in Publication Information Available

Library of Congress Cataloging-in-Publication Data

Library of Congress Control Number: 2016952269

ISBN 9781498518963 (cloth : alk. paper)
ISBN 9781498518970 (electronic)

∞™ The paper used in this publication meets the minimum requirements of American National Standard for Information Sciences Permanence of Paper for Printed Library Materials, ANSI/NISO Z39.48-1992.

Printed in the United States of America

Contents

Acknowledgments — vii

1 Introduction — 1

Part I: JL Legitimacy — **13**
2 Clarifying the Question and Surveying the JL Answer — 15
3 A First Unacceptable Consequence of JL — 35
4 A Second Unacceptable Consequence of JL — 53
5 A Third Worry about JL — 67

Part II: The Neo-Calvinist Alternative — **79**
6 An Outline of Neo-Calvinist Thought — 81
7 A Neo-Calvinist Theory of Legitimacy — 115

Part III: JL and Neo-Calvinist Legitimacy in Dialogue — **135**
8 Is Consent Needed to Justify Coercion? — 137
9 The Human Flourishing Tie — 153
10 How to Steer Clear of Paternalism — 169
11 Conclusion — 181

Bibliography — 195
Index — 201
About the Author — 207

Acknowledgments

There are many persons who in some way contributed to completion of this project, and I especially wish to acknowledge the following among them.

First, I would like to thank Prof. Will Kymlicka, who was essential to this research in its formative stages. I am especially grateful for his consistent support of my suggestion that Christian political thought is worthy of attention, even that of secular thinkers. I have discussed not every, but most, aspects of this work with him, and have benefited from his gift for clarity in analyzing complex philosophical problems. I am also grateful to Prof. Andrew Lister who extensively read, and gave feedback on, earlier drafts of much of this work. I benefited in particular from his expertise on justificatory liberalism. My concerns with justificatory liberalism do not discount all that I have learned from his nuanced, insightful, and even-handed defence of that view.

I would like to thank the Institute for Christian Studies (ICS) community, which welcomed me as a research associate of the Centre for Philosophy, Religion, and Social Ethics at ICS in summer 2015. ICS nurtured my particular interest in neo-Calvinism. The shift that occurred from an earlier draft of the manuscript focusing on Reformed thought more broadly to the current book focusing specifically on neo-Calvinism would not have been possible without ICS.

I would like to thank as well the various staff at Lexington/Rowman & Littlefield with whom I have worked at various stages in the publishing process, especially Ms. Jana Hodges-Kluck, senior acquisitions editor. Thanks also to Ms. Rachel Weydert, assistant acquisitions editor. I am indebted, too, to an anonymous reviewer whose comments were helpful, among other ways, in narrowing my focus to neo-Calvinism.

Chapter 3 was originally published in a slightly different form as Philip Shadd, "Why Nothing Is Justified by Justificatory Liberalism," *Public Reason: Journal of Political and Moral Philosophy* 6, no. 1 (2014): 3–19. I thank *Public Reason* for permission to reprint that essay here.

In terms of those for whom I am grateful, I must especially single out my wife. Her support for this work has been outstanding. She has patiently endured my long hours of research, writing, and editing. She has been gracious and flexible, and a constant source of encouragement. Thank you, Jessica.

Finally, it is my belief that none of this work would have been possible without God's enabling. If so, my greatest debt of all is undoubtedly owed to Him.

Chapter One

Introduction

THE FAMILIAR FACTS OF POLITICAL LEGITIMACY

Governments are imperfect. Some degree of imperfection attends legal coercion whenever and wherever it is used. People will disagree about exactly where governments go wrong, and about how far short of perfection legal coercion falls. But we all agree that actual governments and legal coercion fall short of being perfectly just.

Yet this doesn't mean that governments are morally unjustified in coercively enforcing laws and criminal codes. We shouldn't expect quite as much agreement on this point as on the last, but here, too, I think most of us will agree. Despite its imperfections, much legal coercion is justified and it seems we are normally under a moral obligation to respect it.

These are the familiar facts in view when political theorists refer to and debate the topic of political legitimacy. The question of political legitimacy asks: what makes legal coercion legitimate even if imperfectly exercised? Legitimacy is the characteristic possessed by legal coercion that, while being imperfect, is nonetheless morally justified. In addressing this topic, then, political theorists try to illuminate such issues as the conditions legitimate legal coercion must satisfy, the gap that exists between legitimate and perfectly just governments, and the legitimacy or illegitimacy of specific uses of legal coercion.

MY GUIDING QUESTION

The topic of political legitimacy raises another issue as well. It may escape our attention given its relatively high degree of abstraction, yet it inevitably factors into our deliberations about legitimacy and warrants philosophical attention. Simply put, the issue is this: what is legitimacy even about? This is my guiding question.

The impetus for this question is my wondering how we ought go about developing answers to any of the more specific questions regarding legitimacy. How ought we go about explaining and justifying legitimate legal coercion? How ought we go about setting the threshold past which legitimacy obtains, and how to understand the relationship between this level and that of full justice? How ought we go about discriminating between legitimate and illegitimate instances of legal coercion?

Given my question, it's been suggested that my particular concern isn't so much legitimacy as it is the justification of legitimacy.[1] This is correct. My concern is not to elaborate a list of specific conditions for legitimate legal coercion, much less to evaluate the legitimacy of specific laws. Instead, my concern is to develop a more general philosophical framework that will illuminate the type of conditions that legitimate coercion satisfies, the type of reasons by which it is justified. Doing so, I take it, is tantamount to elucidating what legitimacy is about. For understanding what legitimacy is generally about is a prerequisite for addressing more specific legitimacy-related issues in the appropriate terms.

My project is a philosophical one. The objects under investigation are drawn from the real world of practical politics, but it is a philosophical explanation of these objects that I'm after. In other words, my project is not a call to any particular political actions. Rather, it is an attempt to understand the philosophical presuppositions in terms of which we must understand legitimacy if we are to make sense of the convictions about real-world legitimacy that we hold. Those are the objects under investigation: certain common convictions about legitimate coercion, which have been forged by real-world political experience. What I seek is a philosophical framework that would enable us to explain the content of these convictions in a consistent and unified way.

THE JUSTIFICATORY LIBERAL ANSWER

There is one such framework currently on offer that forms the dominant approach to legitimacy among contemporary, mainstream political theorists. This approach is justificatory liberalism (JL).[2] It was largely pioneered by John Rawls,[3] and has been refined by subsequent theorists into several variants. But all JL theorists share a set of core ideas in terms of which they would have us conceptualize and evaluate legitimacy. These categories represent, according to JL, what legitimacy is about.

The central idea of JL is this: legitimate legal coercion is based on reasons that all reasonable persons can accept. This is a general framework for legitimacy of the type I seek, as it sets out a vision of how legitimate legal coercion might be justified. Hence, *justificatory* liberalism.

But who counts as reasonable? What reasons would they accept? In the end, what legal coercion is and isn't legitimate? To answer such questions, JLs explicate their central idea in terms of a hypothetical procedure. In doing so, they build upon the social contract tradition of political philosophy. Broadly speaking, JLs answer these questions as follows. The envisaged procedure is carried out in idealized circumstances that correct for deficits of character, rationality, and political equality such as are faced by real-world persons. Reasonable persons are persons as represented by the parties to the hypothetical procedure. The reasons on which legitimate coercion is based are those which the idealized parties would find acceptable. Legitimate legal coercion is coercion all idealized parties would support as part of a social agreement.

In sum, JL theorists would have us ask: what reasons and forms of legal coercion based on these reasons would all agree to in such a procedure? This is what legitimacy is about. Such are the terms JL proposes for theorizing and debating more specific legitimacy-related issues.

THE PROBLEMS JL FACES

Alas, the JL understanding of legitimacy is not without its difficulties. Among the well-known objections to JL is that it places unfair burdens on religious citizens. Another is that the set of reasons that all can accept is empty. According to yet another, even if the set isn't empty, what reasons it does contain are too meager to settle any substantive political disagreement. In fact, such are the difficulties JL faces that even JL theorists such as James Bohman and Henry Richardson are rejecting the very idea of "reasons that all can accept" and are salvaging JL only by taking it in a very different direction.[4]

In addition to these well-known objections, I will present three additional concerns with JL as a framework for legitimacy. First, I argue that JL would de-legitimize all, not just some, legal coercion. Second, I argue that the JL framework undercuts the view that there are certain basic rights which must be protected as a condition of legitimacy. I present a third concern as well, though more cautiously. I suggest that the JL framework structurally involves an objectionable form of paternalism. What exactly this third critique amounts to is somewhat unclear. But it is cause enough for concern that I present it here as yet one more reason for seriously doubting the JL approach.

In light of the problems raised both by me and others, there is evident need for an alternative approach to legitimacy. On my analysis of the JL framework, JL would have us conceptualize legitimacy in terms of consent, procedures, and self-legislation: consent, in that legitimate coercion must be supported by all; procedures, in that JLs explicate their central idea in terms of proceduralism and claim that the policy conclusions of JL result from such procedures; and self-legislation, in that JLs aim to respect persons' free-and-equal status by representing legitimate coercion as norms that citizens legislate for themselves. However, the problems besetting JL suggest that legitimacy ought be understood in terms of a different set of categories.

TURNING TO NEO-CALVINISM

To develop an alternative, where should political theorists turn? My proposal, which I suspect will come as a surprise, is that they turn to the tradition of Christian social thought known as neo-Calvinism. Historically, figures such as Abraham Kuyper and Herman Dooyeweerd represent this tradition, as do, at present, thinkers such as David T. Koyzis, Jonathan Chaplin, Lambert Zuidervaart, and, to a limited extent, Nicholas Wolterstorff. It is a tradition replete with conceptual resources that can be brought to bear on any number of issues within political theory, including that of political legitimacy.

My suggestion may surprise for the following reasons. Mainstream political theory nowadays largely proceeds on a secular basis, in secular terms. Not only so, but specifically in regard to the topic of legitimacy, religious argument is often thought to be part of the problem rather than the solution. The question of legitimacy, as influentially conceived by Rawls, arises in pluralistic contexts where citizens who hold otherwise conflicting worldviews nonetheless seek a fair basis for social cooperation. And religions are paradigmatic of worldviews that conflict.

Actually, though, my suggestion shouldn't be altogether surprising. For neo-Calvinism, its seminal statements having been formulated amidst the rising tides of secularism in the Netherlands in the early twentieth century, has long been keenly interested in the proper limits of coercive state power. It has long theorized freedom of religion and church-state separation, and wrestled with pluralism and its implications for society and politics.

I propose, then, that political theorists—even secular ones—mine neo-Calvinist thought for conceptual insights that might help us develop an alternative to the failed JL framework for legitimacy.

THE NEO-CALVINIST ALTERNATIVE

This is exactly what I set out to do: out of the resources offered by neo-Calvinism, I reconstruct an alternative framework for legitimacy. It is not the only such theory that could be built up out of a neo-Calvinist background.

But it is one which, I believe, represents some of the best insights of the tradition, and which succeeds at those very points where I show JL to be inadequate.

The central neo-Calvinist insight on which I base my framework is this: legitimacy is a function of preventing basic wrongs. As Kuyper says, the coercive state is only necessary "by reason of sin." What is legitimacy fundamentally about? Not proposals that all might agree to (as JL would have it), but about basic wrongs that must be prevented and basic rights that must be protected.

I explicate this central insight in terms of three big ideas, placing special emphasis on the first two. First, legitimacy-conditional wrongs are violations of natural rights. As natural rights, these are objective rights. That is, individuals, as well as institutions, possess such rights whether or not societies recognize them. Recognizing that institutions, not just individuals, possess natural rights is a distinguishing insight of neo-Calvinism. Legitimacy-conditional wrongs[5] are violations of the natural rights of either. Second, legitimacy-conditional rights and wrongs presuppose some or another view of basic human flourishing. Both parts of this second idea are crucial. Some or another view of human flourishing is needed to generate a list of contentful, legitimacy-conditional basic rights in a non-arbitrary way. But we need to understand these rights only in terms of basic flourishing because, as neo-Calvinists point out, full-orbed human flourishing requires not only government but a wide array of healthy social institutions. We also focus only on basic flourishing because it is the fundamental importance of the interests and dignity protected by basic rights which distinguishes them as demanding legal enforcement. A further reason for restricting ourselves to basic flourishing is that it is clearly illegitimate to impose a full-blown conception of the good on others. As I say, neo-Calvinist thought has long been concerned to uphold religious freedom and church-state separation. It is no part either of neo-Calvinism or my neo-Calvinist account that political institutions be religiously or ideologically partial.

In addition to these first two ideas, the third is that we ought understand the normative standard represented by legitimacy-conditional wrongs as being exogenous. Such a standard is one we understand as originating from outside humans, as not being the product of self-legislation. While this third idea raises a certain philosophical puzzle that I admittedly leave incomplete, I present the idea nonetheless believing that it makes at least some headway in redressing the problems caused by JL's emphasis on self-legislation.

The neo-Calvinist approach to legitimacy can be summarized as follows. Legitimacy is a function of preventing basic wrongs: that is, preventing a) violations of individual and institutional natural rights, that are b) tied to a view of basic human flourishing, and that c) represent an exogenous normative standard. *Pace* JL, legitimacy isn't about consent, procedures, and self-legislation. Rather, it is about preventing basic wrongs—about natural rights, basic human flourishing, and exogenous norms. Note in advance that my neo-Calvinist account will not elaborate a list of specific legitimacy conditions. As per the level of abstraction at which my guiding question is pitched—what is legitimacy about?—the neo-Calvinist alternative outlined here instead sets out the general conceptual categories we need if we are to make philosophical sense of the convictions we hold concerning legitimacy.

CLARIFYING MY AIMS

Let me emphasize that neo-Calvinist legitimacy as I present it is a philosophical account. What it seeks to do is make philosophical sense of the convictions we hold about real-world legitimacy, to illuminate the philosophical presuppositions they involve if they are to be integrated in a unified, consistent, transparent way. My argument is that whether we judge a given use of legal coercion to be legitimate or illegitimate, we should understand the considerations bearing on its legitimacy in terms of natural rights that are tied to basic human flourishing. We might disagree over the legitimacy of a particular law, yet—in light of certain convictions widely shared—it seems we're committed to the general categories identified by my neo-Calvinist framework.

I worry that the conclusions I advance are at once too familiar and too exotic. On the one hand, JL has already been thoroughly critiqued, and claiming that basic rights are natural and objective and that they require some account of human interests might seem uncontroversial. On the other hand, my appeal to a religious tradition of thought may seem exotic, idiosyncratic, alienating, or misplaced in a field that proceeds on a thoroughly secular basis. So I see myself running both these risks.

Nonetheless, I count them worth running inasmuch as they're needed to accomplish my primary goal of helping us think about legitimacy in terms other than those proffered by JL. My broad complaint against JL is that the way it conceptualizes legitimacy—emphasizing categories such as consent and procedures—just doesn't seem to fit what legitimacy is about in the real world, as reflected by common legitimacy-related convictions. It is not that JL is without its attractions. Consent, procedures, and self-legislation all have important roles to play both in political theory and practice. But they are relatively unimportant when it comes to the issue of legitimacy, or so it seems to me. For in our actual political experience, we're quite unwilling to yield on what we take to be justice's most basic demands, and when such demands are at stake—as when human rights are violated—we also seem quite willing to coerce others whether or not they agree with us. Moreover, these are just the sort of basic demands we seem most inclined to view as legitimacy-conditional. Such realities suggest that JL conceptualizes legitimacy in altogether the wrong terms. And so each of the ideas that I advance—both the familiar and unfamiliar—are part of my best attempt to generally move us away from the JL framework and onto different philosophical terrain. If, taken together, the package of ideas I present makes any progress in this general direction, I will consider myself successful despite the questions that will surely remain concerning various parts of this package.

If not already clear, my primary goal is progress on a substantive normative question of political theory—the question of political legitimacy. To this end, I develop my account of neo-Calvinist legitimacy and defend it against its JL counterpart. I do have two secondary goals as well, though, which are rather distinct from the first. One concerns comparative political theory more than normative political theory. This goal is to advance the neo-Calvinist tradition as a reservoir of conceptual insights and resources from which political theorists can, and should, draw. The relationship between my primary goal and this secondary goal is as follows: neo-Calvinist thought—as represented by my neo-Calvinist account—helps us make progress toward understanding legitimacy, progress which also thereby vindicates the neo-Calvinist tradition as one worthy of further investigation. Another secondary goal is to extend the neo-Calvinist tradition itself. While neo-Calvinists have fruitfully analyzed issues such as pluralism, education, markets, and the role of government in the provision of social services,[6] among others, the neo-Calvinist approach has not been brought to bear on the question of political legitimacy as formulated in contemporary political theory. Thus, I hope to extend the tradition itself by a new application of it.

The main goal, then, is to advance discussion of an important normative question. In the process of doing so, I also hope to commend and extend neo-Calvinist thought.

A CHAPTER-BY-CHAPTER OVERVIEW

Part I: JL Legitimacy

The following is a summary of the contents of each chapter.

The project is broken into three parts. Broadly speaking, the first exclusively engages JL legitimacy; the second exclusively engages neo-Calvinism; the third brings the two into dialogue with one another.

In chapter 2, I begin by setting up my guiding question, and by laying out the criteria for a successful answer. As to the latter, our best framework for legitimacy will be one that makes sense of the considered convictions (CCs) we hold concerning legitimate and illegitimate real-world uses of legal coercion. In particular, I highlight three such convictions:

- the conviction that much actual legal coercion is legitimate, even amidst disagreement between seemingly reasonable persons
- the conviction that there exist certain basic rights which must be protected as conditions of legitimacy
- the conviction that it is illegitimate to legally coerce free-and-equal persons on paternalistic grounds

While we may hold other convictions as well, these three are hardly peripheral to our views on legitimacy. Quite the contrary, I think these are among our most important legitimacy-related CCs, and any framework that doesn't make good sense of them is inadequate as a framework for legitimacy.

Chapter 2 also includes an introductory exegesis of JL. I isolate what I mean by "justificatory liberalism" and I explain my focus on a Rawlsian version of JL. Acknowledging that JL accounts differ from one another along various dimensions, I nonetheless identify certain core concepts widely shared by JL theorists. These include the concepts of public reasons and reasonable persons.

Chapters 3–5 are then devoted to an internal critique of JL. This critique is internal to JL insofar as each of these chapters proceeds by arguing that JL leads to some or another consequence that is unacceptable by JLs' own lights. I take it that JLs themselves share the three aforementioned CCs on which I focus. So each of chapters 3–5 proceeds by arguing that JL leads to consequences that conflict with one of these CCs.

Chapter 3 argues that JL would de-legitimize all, not just some, legal coercion. It would do so by combining a unanimity condition with its permissive criteria for reasonable persons. In light of the latter, there are persons who would reject all legal coercion but nonetheless qualify as reasonable. Chapter 4 argues that JL undercuts legitimacy-conditional basic rights. It does so in virtue of three asymmetries that exist between the sort of rights JL can deliver and characteristics real-world basic rights possess. We view legitimacy-conditional rights as procedure-independent, contentful, and objective. But the rights JL affords are presented as procedure-dependent, the product of a contentless proceduralism, and a function of group consensus. Thus, these first two consequences to which JL leads are unacceptable by conflicting, respectively, with our CC that much actual legal coercion is legitimate and our CC that legitimacy is conditional upon protecting certain basic rights.

Chapter 5 offers up another unacceptable consequence to which JL seems to lead, namely, to paternalistic justifications of legal coercion. If guilty, JL would thereby conflict with the third aforementioned CC as well. That said, the motivation for this argument is the important difference that seems to exist between coercion for someone's good and coercion for the sake of justice, but it is difficult to articulate exactly what this distinction consists in.

Also, while JL seems implicated in paternalism of a certain sort, it is admittedly an unusual sort, and perhaps not one of great concern even if JL is guilty of it. Nevertheless, given how firmly we hold the CC that paternalistic coercion is illegitimate, even the mere possibility that JL involves paternalism is cause for concern. Moreover, I believe a compelling case can be made that JL does, in fact, realize this possibility, and this is the case I try to set forth in chapter 5.

Part II: The Neo-Calvinist Alternative

I switch gears in chapter 6. I leave behind the secular background of JL, and enter the very different conceptual world of neo-Calvinism. In this chapter, I do not specifically broach the topic of political legitimacy. Rather, I set forth the neo-Calvinist tradition by way of nine tenets that outline the tradition as a whole. That all people are equal and ultimately accountable only to God, and that society properly divides into separate spheres, are among these tenets. As general tenets, they can be applied to any number of issues within political theory, not just legitimacy. This chapter, then, more than any other, serves the secondary goal of advancing neo-Calvinist thought as a general resource on which political theorists can, and should, draw. For the most part, here neo-Calvinism is presented in its own terms.

In chapter 7, I then bring neo-Calvinist insights to bear on the topic of political legitimacy. Given my guiding question, I develop a general philosophical framework for understanding legitimacy. The reader should not expect a list of specific legitimacy conditions or pronouncements regarding the legitimacy of specific laws, but rather a framework for making sense of these more specific legitimacy-related judgments. In this chapter I identify the neo-Calvinist insight most relevant to the issue of legitimacy as being that legitimacy is about the prevention of basic wrongs. As per tenet 3 presented in chapter 6, the coercive state is only needed "by reason of sin." It is also here that I introduce the three big ideas I use in explicating this central insight. First, legitimacy-conditional wrongs are natural rights violations. Second, these rights and wrongs are tied to basic human flourishing. In addition to these two, I touch on the idea of an exogenous normative standard.

Chapter 7 proceeds without reference to JL, yet compared to chapter 6 its ideas should be more readily accessible to secular readers. For in addition to explaining the key ideas of neo-Calvinist legitimacy, I seek to corroborate them with some argumentation not based on neo-Calvinist grounds. This argumentation is only a first attempt to illustrate the plausibility of my neo-Calvinist account.

Part III: JL and Neo-Calvinist Legitimacy in Dialogue

JL reenters the discussion in chapter 8. The purpose of this chapter, and the two that follow it, is to explicitly compare and contrast JL and neo-Calvinist legitimacy. It is ultimately on these arguments that I rest my case, for in each of these three chapters I try to show that neo-Calvinist legitimacy succeeds at a specific point where JL fails. I ultimately conclude that since neo-Calvinist legitimacy makes better sense of the three key CCs under consideration, it is a superior framework for legitimacy.

In chapter 8, I explain how neo-Calvinist legitimacy avoids the de-legitimization of all legal coercion and restores the legitimacy of much coercion that exists amidst disagreement. It does so by understanding legitimacy in terms of natural rights, and in terms of the objectivity such rights involve, as opposed to consent. Appropriating David Estlund's notion of null nonconsent, I highlight the inescapability of justice's basic demands and explain how neo-Calvinist legitimacy saves coercion amidst disagreement by preventing withheld consent from relieving parties of legitimacy-conditional duties. Natural, objective rights help make sense of such coercion, but consent does not.

Chapter 9 explains how appreciating the role of basic human flourishing redresses the problems caused by JL's proceduralism. By virtue of its contentless proceduralism, JL undercuts basic rights which we experience as having certain definite content. Thinking in terms of human flourishing, however, makes available just this sort of content. Moreover, thinking in terms of basic flourishing ensures that we understand legitimacy-conditional rights and wrongs in a way appropriate to the fundamentally important interests such rights and wrongs represent. Thus, basic human flourishing provides content of the substantive, definite, basic sort appropriate to our CC in the existence of certain legitimacy-conditional basic rights.

Then in chapter 10, I explore how the neo-Calvinist idea of exogenous norms might avoid the sort of paternalism that lurks within JL. The suggestion is as follows: being exogenous, the norms represented by legitimacy-conditional rights do not prompt us to ask a question of self-interest in justifying these rights. Absent a question of self-interest, the threat of paternalism is averted. In particular, chapter 10 takes up at greater length the apparent distinction between coercion for people's good and coercion for the sake of justice. Though my reflections on how these two types of justifications differ are incomplete, I do think they make at least some progress. And whereas JL would seem to fall on the wrong side of this divide, my proposal is that neo-Calvinist legitimacy does not.

In sum, the conclusion of part III is that neo-Calvinist legitimacy provides a framework that makes better sense of political legitimacy than its JL counterpart. I think the first two weaknesses of JL, and the first two corresponding strengths of neo-Calvinist legitimacy, go far in showing this. I also suggest that the third weakness of JL, and the third strength of neo-Calvinist legitimacy that corresponds to it, reinforce this conclusion.

I end part III by responding to some lingering objections and by sketching out directions in which further work on neo-Calvinist legitimacy might go. Among the former is the question of why, if neo-Calvinist insights can seemingly be translated into secular terms, we should hold onto neo-Calvinist thought more broadly at all.

TOWARD CLEARER THINKING ABOUT LEGITIMACY

We all know that governments are imperfect. Yet we usually have neither a clear sense of why these imperfect governments are nonetheless justified in their use of legal coercion, nor a clear framework in our minds for evaluating when governments might become so flawed as to be unjustified in their use of legal coercion. In a word, we lack clear thinking on what legitimacy is about. I don't think JL helps much in this regard. But I hope that neo-Calvinist legitimacy does.

NOTES

1. I thank Rahul Kumar for this insight.
2. Depending upon context, I will variously use the acronym "JL" to mean "justificatory liberalism," "justificatory liberal" (as an adjective), and "justificatory liberal" (as in an advocate of this view).
3. John Rawls, *Political Liberalism*, Expanded Edition (New York: Columbia University Press, 2005).
4. James Bohman and Henry S. Richardson, "Liberalism, Deliberative Democracy, and 'Reasons That All Can Accept,'" *The Journal of Political Philosophy* 17, no. 3 (2009): 253–74.
5. Throughout, the phrase "legitimacy-conditional wrongs" is simply shorthand for wrongs that must be prevented for a political regime to be legitimate. Similarly, throughout the phrase "legitimacy-conditional rights" will be used as shorthand for rights that must be protected for a regime to be legitimate.
6. E.g., Rockne M. McCarthy, James W. Skillen, and William A. Harper, *Disestablishment a Second Time: Genuine Pluralism for American Schools* (Grand Rapids, MI: Christian University Press, 1982);Bob Goudzwaard, *Globalization and the Kingdom of God*, ed. James W. Skillen (Grand Rapids, MI: Baker Books, 2001).

Part I

JL Legitimacy

Chapter Two

Clarifying the Question and Surveying the JL Answer

The present chapter sets the stage for the rest of the book. It does this by first clarifying the issue at hand. I then lay out criteria for the best answer to my guiding question. I provide an overview of JL, and this exegesis leads to an argument I make at the end of this chapter. I will argue that the legitimacy of which JL theorists speak cannot be restricted to liberal democratic contexts. It applies wherever persons, morally speaking, are free and equal. As such, JL does indeed provide one candidate answer to my guiding question, and it can profitably and appropriately be contrasted with the neo-Calvinist alternative I later present.

By the end of this chapter, then, I hope both that the issue at hand, and the relevance of JL to this issue, will be clear.[1]

CLARIFYING MY QUESTION

What the Question Is

To clarify the issue I wish to address, I must distinguish between two questions. The first is this: what makes the use of coercive political power legitimate even if imperfectly exercised? This is the main question of political legitimacy. Rawls is widely credited for bringing this issue to the fore in contemporary political philosophy. He notes, "Legitimacy allows an undetermined range of injustice that justice might not permit."[2]

By contrast, the related yet distinct question I hope to answer is this: what is even the right framework for thinking about legitimacy? Put another way, what are the most apt categories for thinking about legitimacy, for conceptualizing and debating the legitimacy of legal coercion?

Given what my question is, my discussion of legitimacy will proceed at a higher level of abstraction than one might expect. I take it there exists a distinction between first-order judgments of legitimacy and the higher-order justifications of those first-order judgments. At issue in this book is what form these justifications should take. Examples of first-order judgments include: that it is illegitimate to violate freedom of religion; that undemocratic regimes are illegitimate; that legislation issuing from a real-world democratic procedure is legitimate; that a failure to optimize the public good, in terms of such things as healthcare, education, and job creation, jeopardizes a regime's legitimacy; that taxes are illegitimate; and so on. These judgments vary somewhat in their degree of specificity, but all enable us to readily, directly evaluate specific uses of legal coercion, or are themselves direct evaluations. But what makes these judgments either good or bad? In contrast to these first-order judgments, we must evaluate the higher-order grounds on which they are putatively justified. For this latter task, we need to query the appropriate terms for formulating and justifying such judgments. It may be helpful to think of my project not as concerned with legitimacy itself, but as concerned with the justification of legitimacy.

It may be helpful here to understand my question in light of a distinction drawn by T. M. Scanlon. Scanlon distinguishes between a normative theory of morality and a philosophical theory of morality.[3] A normative theory proposes a decision-procedure for making moral choices. In terms of their level of abstraction, first-order legitimacy judgments correspond to normative moral theories. By contrast, a philosophical theory addresses the nature of the very subject matter of morality. In Scanlon's terms, then, my intention is to develop a philosophical theory of legitimacy rather than a normative one. The neo-Calvinist legitimacy I defend is of the philosophical order. In drawing his distinction, Scanlon characterizes a philosophical theory in a variety of complementary ways. A philosophical theory concerns what moral judgments "can be about"; it concerns the "nature" and "subject matter" of morality; it explores "the kind of property" that moral rightness is; and it informs what "the best forms of moral argument amount to."[4] I find these all helpful ways of conceiving the level at which my discussion of legitimacy is pitched. Given my question, candidate answers will illuminate what our legitimacy judgments are about, what their subject matter is, what the property of legitimacy consists in, and what the terms of debate should be in evaluating the legitimacy of specific coercive measures.

Granted, the line between the main question of legitimacy and my related question is somewhat fuzzy. Nonetheless, it is certainly true that discussions of legitimacy can operate at varying levels of abstraction. With this latter point in mind, I hope to have made clear that my discussion of legitimacy will be pitched at a higher level of abstraction than many more familiar discussions. My question again: what is the right framework for thinking about legitimacy? In what terms should we conceptualize the legitimacy of coercive political power?

What the Question Is Not

If not already clear, let me emphasize that I am concerned with legitimacy in a normative rather than descriptive sense. My concern is not with what coercive institutions people actually do accept as legitimate, but with what institutions people ought to recognize as legitimate. As such, normative legitimacy contrasts with "the positivist or Weberian account of legitimacy typically used in the social sciences—according to which general acceptance *de facto* by the majority of people of social and political institutions and officials' actions is sufficient for the legitimate exercise of political power."[5] Rawls' and other JLs' concern is with normative rather than merely descriptive legitimacy. So is mine.

Similarly, I do not understand legitimacy in terms of a distinction between "external" and "internal" legitimacy. For such a distinction presupposes a descriptive account of the sort rejected in the previous paragraph. Using these categories, it is possible for a regime to be legitimate in one way while illegitimate in the other. For instance, an "internally" legitimate regime may be "externally" illegitimate as when a population comes to accept (perhaps for ideological or religious reasons) severely unjust social arrangements. But, as I use the term, mere acceptance of coercion does not guarantee its normative legitimacy.

I also do not understand legitimacy to be merely a context-relative phenomenon. Rather, I understand normative legitimacy to have universal implications, applying in diverse socio-historical contexts.[6] Why might we believe that such a context-transcendent standard of legitimacy exists? I don't mean to simply presume its existence, and in due course I will provide further defense of its existence. For now, though, the fact that we do, as a matter of course, make legitimacy judgments across different times and places, and regard ourselves as morally justified in doing so, is at least provisional evidence that a context-transcendent standard of legitimacy exists. Certain well-known cases are obvious: the Nazi regime was illegitimate, as was apartheid South Africa. Moving further back in history we may become somewhat less sure in our judgments. But we nonetheless judge as illegitimate the intolerant regimes driving the European Wars of Religion, don't we? So, too, was the execution of Servetus, wasn't it?[7] I assume we are right in denouncing such measures as illegitimate. As such, seeking to understand legitimacy as a context-transcendent normative phenomenon seems a worthwhile pursuit. Perhaps our investigation will ultimately leave us unconvinced that such a legitimacy standard exists, but I aim, should it exist, at legitimacy so understood.

Now to preempt a different sort of issue. As I understand it, there is no important asymmetry between the concept of legitimacy and those of obligation and authority.[8] Since theorists not uncommonly think it important to separate these concepts,[9] let me clarify my understanding of their interrelationship.

The legitimacy threshold has at least three significant implications, appreciation of which explains the relationship between legitimacy and the related concepts of political authority and obligation. First, the legitimacy threshold informs the question of what, in principle, makes any legal coercion permissible. What justifies the very existence of legally coercive institutions? For any set of laws that falls below the threshold, that set of laws is illegitimate and ought not be coercively enforced. This also means that if no set of laws meets the threshold, then no set of laws can be legitimately enforced. Therefore, below the threshold, no state is justified. Above, at least some coercive state is justified. Second, insofar as we are subject to legal coercion, legitimacy identifies a threshold above which we have a moral obligation to support the extant regime and below which no such obligation exists. Here the question is: what minimal moral criteria make laws legitimate such that citizens have an obligation to respect them? Third, insofar as we exercise legal coercion, the legitimacy threshold helps clarify when we are and are not justified in legally coercing our fellow citizens. Below the threshold, legal coercion is a morally impermissible way of discouraging a behaviour with which I disagree. But above the threshold, it is not. So the concept of legitimacy also informs this question: when are some citizens justified in using legal coercion against other citizens even if they do so imperfectly?

Conceptually, these three issues are distinct. Practically, however, I regard them as equivalent. For in each case it is the same moral considerations that trigger a change regarding the morality of coercive political power—whether legitimating its existence, obligating those under it, or investing those exercising it with authority. The latter two implications speak to the issues of obligation and authority, respectively. I hope it is clear, then, how on my view all three concepts are interrelated, and especially how the latter two relate to the legitimacy threshold.

At this point let me head off just one more potential misunderstanding. My question is not that of the role of religion in liberal democracies. This clarification is needed since for many of the authors and texts I'll draw upon, this is their primary question. May laws permissibly be enacted on religious grounds? Is it morally appropriate for citizens to invoke their religious beliefs in the public square and in their voting? These questions are of prime importance in much JL work,[10] as well as in that of JL's critics,[11] yet not in the present work. This clarification is also especially important in light of my suggestion that we turn to a religious tradition of political theory, namely, neo-Calvinism. Readers might take my invocation of religious premises in political theorizing to mean that I endorse the invocation of religious premises in the public square. Not necessarily, and, in any case, the propriety of the latter is not my question.

Rather, my issue is that of legitimacy—what the right framework is for thinking about the conditions that make coercive political power legitimate even if imperfect. JL is an appropriate interlocutor in this discussion as JL addresses not only the issue of religion's place in politics but also the issue of legitimacy. In my discussion of legitimacy, I may find it necessary to invoke religious premises—say, premises involving God, creation order, or divine norms. But if I do, I do so to the end of giving a philosophical account of legitimacy. Philosophically, religious premises may be required to account for our legitimacy-related convictions, even while, on a practical level, we may remain convinced that it is improper to base laws on sectarian religious beliefs. I hope the philosophical orientation of my project will be made clearer by the methodological points to which I now turn.

WHAT WILL SETTLE THE ISSUE?

How will we know which framework for legitimacy is best, whether JL, neo-Calvinist, or otherwise?

According to the desideratum I will use, the best account will be that which makes best sense of the CCs we hold concerning legitimacy in the real world. While I will disagree with Rawls on many points, I largely follow him in his method. According to Rawls, we must start by taking certain bedrock moral convictions as given; "considered convictions" is Rawls' term.[12] This doesn't mean they cannot be altered in due course, but they form our starting point and the initial parameters within which we assess competing accounts. These bedrock convictions are primarily given us through political experience, not abstract philosophy. The wrongness of slavery is a paradigm CC, as is the justness of religious toleration.[13] The role of philosophical reflection is then to systematize and clarify these convictions, and to illuminate how the principles underlying our CCs ought be applied in new contexts.[14] My desideratum adapts this approach to the issue of legitimacy.

Since our topic is legitimacy, it is our CCs concerning legitimacy in which I am specifically interested. Just as legitimacy is conceptually distinct from justice, so we should be careful to distinguish between our justice-related CCs and our specifically legitimacy-related CCs. We operate in the real world with certain CCs about legitimate and illegitimate legal coercion, and the CCs on which I focus are ones that I expect all of us—as citizens and partisans of modern liberal democracies—will share. Both JL and neo-Calvinist theorists share them also.

The legitimacy-related CCs on which I focus are these:

- the conviction that many real-world uses of legal coercion are, indeed, legitimate, even when they occur amidst disagreement between epistemic peers
- the conviction that real-world legitimacy is conditional upon protecting certain basic rights, such as those often constitutionally entrenched in liberal democracies
- the conviction that it is illegitimate to legally coerce others on paternalistic grounds

We may hold other legitimacy-related CCs as well—for instance, that laws aren't necessarily legitimate simply because they are popular. I especially focus, though, on these three.

In short, the account of legitimacy I seek is the one that makes best sense of our CCs. Doing so means achieving what Rawls calls "reflective equilibrium," where "our principles and judgments coincide."[15] In the present case, the relevant judgments are our legitimacy-related CCs and the relevant principles are those key ideas that constitute either the JL or neo-Calvinist framework for legitimacy. Remember our question: what is the right framework for thinking about legitimacy? To settle the issue, then, we must ask whether the JL framework or its neo-Calvinist counterpart better matches with and explains the relevant CCs.

AN OVERVIEW OF JL

JL explains legitimate legal coercion in terms of reasons that all reasonable persons can accept. To explicate this core principle, they represent legitimate coercion as issuing from a hypothetical procedure in which coercion is justified by reasons that idealized citizens all find acceptable. I will start with a few points about nomenclature and then return to this core principle.

The term "justificatory liberalism" was coined by Gerald Gaus in his book by that same name.[16] In that book, Gaus distinguishes between justificatory liberalism and political liberalism, identifying himself as the former and Rawls as paradigmatic of the latter. I follow Christopher Eberle, however, in regarding the commonalities between the two as more important than their differences.[17] Thus, although my main JL interlocutors will be Rawlsian JLs, I will simply refer to them as "JL" theorists.

Why focus on Rawlsian JL rather than some other type? For one, Rawlsian JL is the most influential and widely-held version. Kevin Vallier and

Fred D'Agostino note that the "consensus approach"[18] exemplified by Rawlsian JL is "by far the dominant conception of public justification."[19] Another reason for focusing on Rawlsian JL is that it is more consonant with the general tenor of public justification than its non-Rawlsian counterparts, such as Gaus' convergence JL.[20] Not all of the reasons allowed by convergence approaches would be acceptable to all citizens, but all allowed by consensus approaches would. In this sense, Rawlsian or consensus JL is more consonant with the notion of justifications that are public. Indeed it strikes me that convergence accounts might be more aptly named "acceptance liberalism" than "justificatory liberalism," given that such accounts only regard mere acceptance of coercion as relevant with little regard for the quality or nature of the reasons for which coercion is accepted. A third and related reason for favoring Rawlsian JL is that it seems to better satisfy the sincerity requirement.[21] This is the requirement that citizens offer reasons they sincerely believe to be sufficient as a justification. Far from satisfying this requirement, convergence JL would allow, if not positively encourage, citizens to simply offer reasons they think others will find persuasive, even if they themselves think the reasons to be deficient as a justification. In any case, my major critiques of JL apply equally to consensus and convergence versions of JL: my argument in chapter 3 applies equally due to the reasonable objections of anarchists; my argument in chapter 4 applies to both given that both emphasize proceduralism; my chapter 5 argument more obviously indicts Rawlsian JL, but applies to Gaus' JL as well insofar as convergence JL still idealizes citizens in certain ways. So while focusing on Rawlsian JL, what I say will also bear on non-Rawlsian JLs.

Rawls is the archetype JL,[22] but my JL interlocutors will be several. They include Thomas Nagel, Andrew Lister, Jonathan Quong, Stephen Macedo, and Corey Brettschneider.[23] I will also interact with Joshua Cohen, whose deliberative democratic theory gives institutional expression to Rawls' idea of public reasoning.[24]

JL distinguishes itself from other liberal political philosophies, such as those of John Stuart Mill, Ronald Dworkin, Will Kymlicka, or Joseph Raz, by its distinctive mode of justifying legal coercion. According to this view, coercive political power is legitimately exercised only when exercised on the basis of reasons that all reasonable persons can accept. By contrast, the likes of Mill, Dworkin, Kymlicka, and Raz base liberal institutions and the coercion they involve on values such as individuality or autonomy. As such, they are perfectionist liberals. The supreme importance they accord to individual freedom, though, can be reasonably disputed, which is why JLs part ways with them. They offer different answers to the question, "Must liberal political philosophy be based in some particular ideal of what constitutes a valuable or worthwhile human life, or other metaphysical beliefs?"[25] Perfectionist liberals answer yes. But JLs answer no, convinced it is both possible and only appropriate to base coercive liberal institutions on principles that all persons can accept.

Alternatively, JL can be stated as the view that political power is legitimately exercised only when exercised on the basis of reasons that no one can reasonably reject. But either way JL involves a unanimity condition[26]: either universal acceptability, or universal nonrejectability.[27] Either way, JL is the view that legitimate legal coercion is based on reasons that all reasonable persons, in some sense, endorse.

Let us have a few representative statements of JL's central idea before us. Rawls' liberal principle of legitimacy is the most famous: "To this political liberalism says: our exercise of political power is fully proper only when it is exercised in accordance with a constitution the essentials of which all citizens as free and equal may reasonably be expected to endorse in the light of principles and ideals acceptable to their common human reason. This is the liberal principle of legitimacy."[28] Amy Gutmann and Dennis Thompson give voice to the idea in this way: we ought "aspire[] to a politics in which citizens and their accountable representatives, along with other public officials, are committed to making decisions *that they can justify to everyone bound by them.*"[29] And Lister provides the following clear summary statement: "The exercise of political power is justified only if it is justifiable to all those subject to it, that is, only if it is acceptable to all suitably rational and moral individuals without them having to give up the religious or philosophical doctrine they reasonably espouse."[30]

At its heart, we should understand JL as a concerted response to "the traditional liberal demand to justify the social world in a manner acceptable 'at the tribunal of each person's understanding.'"[31] JL attempts to meet this demand by identifying legitimate legal coercion only as that based on reasons to which all reasonable persons can agree. JL's unanimity condition is that legal coercion pass "at the tribunal of *each* person's understanding" (emphasis mine).

Having set forth the core tenet of JL, let us now sample a few, though certainly not all,[32] of the dimensions along which it needs to be specified. Here I focus on aspects of JL especially relevant to later stages of my argument. In considering the questions to follow, we will only survey JL's general answers to them. We can draw a more useful sketch of JL as a whole by focusing on broad areas of agreement than on fine-grained points of disagreement between JLs.

What count as reasons all can accept? In other words, what count as suitably "public" reasons on which legitimate uses of legal coercion are based?

This is a vexing question to which JLs have given varying answers. While JLs deploy certain standard examples of nonpublic reasons—such as the "salvation of souls" or "religious truth"[33]—various attempts have been made at capturing the general nature of public reasons. These attempts proceed by identifying a public reason with a particular characteristic or bundle of characteristics that all such reasons supposedly share. Rawls' conception of a public reason comes in a bundle: being "reasons that are responsive to the fundamental interests of democratic citizens, in their capacity as free and equal moral persons,"[34] public reasons do not presuppose the acceptance of any one particular comprehensive view, but are already implicit in publicly accepted liberal democratic institutions; they accord with the well-established findings of the sciences; they do not rest on overly technical or controversial economic theories[35]; and they are responsive to normal, commonly accepted rules of logic and inference.[36] Meanwhile other theorists try to capture the nature of public reasons with qualities such as intelligibility, replicability, or fallibility.[37]

However, I believe it to be beyond dispute that JLs have failed to successfully characterize public reasons. For Eberle provides a compelling critique that is applicable to all such attempts.[38] In all attempts, the clear motivation of JL theorists is to distance themselves from religious ways of thinking—from what William Alston would refer to as a religious "doxastic practice"[39]—that seem to be ultimately founded on nothing more than an adherent's personal faith.[40] Eberle's devastating conclusion, though, is that there is no doxastic practice that isn't ultimately self-referential. For consider that epistemic source which JL theorists themselves would regard as the most "public" of all, namely, sense perception: the only way to check questionable sense perceptions is by relying, paradoxically and self-referentially, on other sense perceptions.[41]

Despite this failure, though, even as a critic of JL I am not quite ready to dismiss as irrelevant the distinction between public and nonpublic reasons. I hesitate to do so because difficulty in distinguishing them seems mainly a theoretical issue, while in practice I admit we can readily categorize many reasons either as public or nonpublic in an intuitive sense. This intuitiveness makes it difficult to weigh the significance of JL's failure to capture public reasons' general nature. This much is clear: in contemporary real-world democracies, there are certain kinds of reasons that enjoy widespread, virtually unanimous, acceptance among citizens who disagree on much else. Such reasons include many scientific findings, empirical observations, much sociological data, as well as many basic moral considerations and moral prohibitions. What is unclear is whether these reasons emerge from epistemic sources that really are different in kind from those on which particular religious traditions rely.[42]

JL theorists are clear that the reasons they have in mind must not be acceptable to just anyone. Rather, they are reasons that must be acceptable to reasonable persons. Now we ask: who counts as reasonable?

In coming to grips with JL, one runs up against a recurrent tension between procedure and substance, and the tension arises here as well. In an illuminating essay, Martha Nussbaum shows how Rawls equivocates between what are essentially procedural and substantive conceptions of the reasonable person. These correspond to Nussbaum's "ethical" and "epistemic" conceptions, respectively.[43] According to the procedural (or ethical) conception, the reasonable person is simply the citizen who is willing to cooperate with others on the basis of fair terms of cooperation.[44] According to the substantive (or epistemic) conception, the reasonable person is the citizen who lives according to a comprehensive view that meets certain theoretical criteria. Nussbaum summarizes Rawls' theoretical criteria:

> His definition includes three features, all of them theoretical rather than ethical. First, a reasonable doctrine is "an exercise of theoretical reason" that "covers the major religious, philosophical, and moral aspects of human life in a more or less consistent and coherent manner. It organizes and characterizes recognized values so that they are compatible with one another and express an intelligible view of the world." Second, the doctrine is also an "exercise of practical reason" that gives instruction on how to weigh values and what to do when they conflict. Third, such a doctrine, while not necessarily fixed and unchanging, "normally belongs to, or draws upon, a tradition of thought and doctrine" and therefore tends to evolve "slowly in the light of what from its point of view, it sees as good and sufficient reasons."[45]

Substantively (or epistemically), the reasonable person deliberates with consistency and coherence, eliminating contradictions within their view and systematically ordering elements within the view. As Bohman and Richardson might say, the reasonable person is simply the person who meets the "constitutive commitments of reasonableness" and the "substantive norms of reasonableness."[46] I believe that Nussbaum's critique of Rawls is on target, that there is slippage between these two conceptions of the reasonable person in Rawls' work.

Rawls' official stance favors the procedural conception. Reasonable citizens share two characteristics. First, they are willing to "propose and honour fair terms of cooperation." Second, they recognize the burdens of judgment and "accept their consequences" for the regulation of public life.[47] The burdens of judgment are the normal epistemic difficulties we face when considering a complicated issue, such as the difficulty of weighing complex evidence, of screening out biases, of giving specific shape to vague concepts, and so on. Recognizing these burdens means that when citizens disagree over philosophical, moral, or religious matters, they attribute their disagreement to these burdens rather than believe others to suffer from moral or cognitive shortcomings. Moreover, the burdens of judgment give rise to the fact of reasonable pluralism, the fact that people will inevitably and reasonably come to different conclusions on philosophical, religious, and moral issues when they are permitted freedom of thought. So the reasonable person acknowledges that these burdens have implications for the "regulation of public life," but notice that neither of Rawls' two official characteristics says much about the substance of reasonable persons' beliefs.

I also agree with Nussbaum that the procedural (or ethical) conception is more in keeping with the general aims of Rawlsian JL.[48] Identifying reasonable citizens in this way is part and parcel of the broader JL ambition to respect citizens' free-and-equal status by representing political norms as the outcome of a procedure of self-legislation. Any substantive conception of a reasonable citizen, even a relatively modest one, will likely disqualify many citizens of liberal democracies as unreasonable, thereby excluding them from the self-legislating procedure. So unsurprisingly, there is a trend in the public justification literature since the time of Rawls toward ever-more procedural, ever-less substantive, conceptions of the reasonable citizen.[49]

In light of these considerations and taking Rawls as representative of JL, the basic JL answer to the question of who counts as a reasonable citizen consists of just two procedurally-oriented conditions.[50] First, the reasonable citizen is willing to fairly cooperate with others. Second, the reasonable citizen acknowledges the burdens of judgment and the fact of reasonable pluralism. So long as they meet these two conditions, citizens are certified as reasonable by JLs.

Concerning who counts as a reasonable citizen, another question is this: are the persons JLs have in mind actual or idealized, and, if the latter, idealized how?

The short answer is both, but it is also a complicated answer. For while JLs have actual persons in mind in some sense, upon inspection it is idealized persons who play the far more important role in JL theorizing.

On the one hand, it is the phenomenon of real-world pluralism that is largely the impetus for JL.[51] I've also pointed out that JLs have shifted more and more toward taking real-world citizens, religious or not, as they actually are. It's noteworthy, too, that JLs draw upon norms they believe are implicit in real-world institutions and actual political discourse.[52] So there is a definite sense in which JLs do have in mind real-world people when formulating their accounts.

On the other hand, no JL theorist is prepared to make their account actually depend on what real-world citizens, at a given time or place, believe. I believe there is a clear reason for this caveat: real-world citizens can be given to all sorts of irrational and morally repugnant ideas, individually and collectively. Regrettably history bears witness to this fact all too often. (For starters, consider the widespread acceptance which chattel slavery, apartheid, the oppression of women, and India's caste system have each enjoyed for periods—or most—of history, sometimes even being accepted by the very persons victimized under these systems).

Therefore, to avoid making their theories captive to the prejudices and otherwise misguided views of actual people, JL accounts abstract away from the profiles of real-world persons in various ways. For instance, Brian Barry envisages hypothetical contractors in what he calls the "circumstances of impartiality." These idealized persons are able to successfully "weigh all reasons in the same balance," having a "willingness to accept reasonable objections to a proposal regardless of the quarter from which they come." They are also well informed.[53] Rather than justifying liberal principles "to a subset of the real people we find in contemporary liberal democracies," Quong's "constituency of reasonable persons" to whom legitimate coercion must be unanimously acceptable "is an idealization."[54] As denizens of a well-ordered society,[55] they exhibit Quong's characteristics of reasonableness and regulate their corporate life according to a publicly justified conception of justice. The way in which the contracting scenario is conceived differs somewhat from JL account to JL account, but the objective behind all such scenarios is similar: they idealize real-world citizens in various ways in order to compensate for the limitations that jeopardize real-world persons' ability to adequately evaluate what social agreements they should accept or reject.

Three notable types of adjustments are made to real-world persons. They are idealized morally—to compensate for prejudices real persons often possess. They are idealized cognitively—to remedy the imperfect information that is available to real persons and to rectify their inability to properly process what information is available. They are also idealized materially—since, in the real world, unequal economic positions bias parties toward their social class and jeopardize fair agreements by making it possible for wealthier parties to exploit poorer parties. To the question of whether JLs have actual or hypothetical persons in mind, the answer is the latter much more than the former.

Consider now a third dimension along which JL accounts vary one from another. We've seen that JL involves a unanimity condition, but what does JL presume is the default should this condition not be met?

This is a question to which Lister draws our attention, distinguishing as he does between two "frames" in which JL can be understood.[56] These competing frames offer differing answers to the question of JL's default position. Within one of these frames, JL's unanimity condition applies to reasons—a reason must be acceptable to all—and the default is said to be exclusion—exclusion of the reason as a possible basis for legal coercion. Within the other, the condition applies to decisions—discrete laws or uses of political power must be acceptable to all—and the default is said to be state inaction. The default presumed by the second frame would seem to have rather libertarian implications, and it is ostensibly largely for this reason that Lister prefers interpreting JL within the first.[57]

I will engage Lister at greater length in the following chapter. For now, I raise the question of JL's default position simply to help clarify JL as I understand it. I agree with Lister that JL is concerned with reasons and not merely with decisions. It is, as Macedo says, about "reason-giving and reason-demanding, and the insistence that power be backed by reasons."[58] That said, I think Lister misrepresents the contrast between the defaults of "exclusion" and "state inaction." For even within the reasons/exclusion framing, lack of unanimity would seem to prevent state action even if there is also disagreement over state inaction. After all, given JL's core principle—that legitimate coercion is based on reasons that all reasonable persons can accept—what coercive measures could be legitimate if there are no reasons that all can accept? Whether or not there are unanimous reasons for inaction seems beside the point. So rather than either a reasons/exclusion or decisions/inaction framing, I actually think JL is rightly understood in terms of a reasons/inaction framing.[59]

Let me summarize our review of JL so far. According to JL, coercive political power is legitimate if it is based on reasons that all reasonable persons can accept. This is JL at its core. This is JL's principle of public justification. We reviewed the kind of reasons JL calls for: basic moral and empirical premises that are suitably general so as to command widespread assent amongst persons who otherwise disagree. We reviewed the kind of reasonable persons to whom these reasons must be acceptable: hypothetical persons who are both willing to honor fair terms of social cooperation and who recognize the fact of reasonable pluralism as having implications for social arrangements. Finally, we considered the default assumed by JL should its unanimity condition go unmet: JL is certainly concerned with reasons, not just decisions. But its default position involves both exclusion of disqualified reasons as well as prohibition of unjustified state actions.

There are further dimensions of JL we might consider, but the foregoing are especially important for the purposes of my project. Remember my question: what are the most apt categories for conceptualizing and debating legitimacy? As will become apparent over the course of our discussion, JL gives us the categories of consent, procedures, and self-legislation as a framework. The foregoing dimensions of JL will prove pertinent to my critique of these categories, and I will exposit other relevant aspects of JL as we go.

For now, I will make one argument regarding the scope of JL before concluding this chapter.

AN ARGUMENT ABOUT JL

Consider this question: in light of their foundational premise of free-and-equal citizens, can JL theorists be committed to anything less than a universal account of legitimacy? To anything less than an account of legitimacy that applies universally? I said above that I do not understand legitimacy to be merely context-relative. Legitimacy *qua* normative concept has universal implications. I suggested that our practice of denouncing regimes of times and places not our own gives us reason, at least provisionally, to regard legitimacy as context-transcendent. The neo-Calvinist account I'll develop gives us one possible framework for making sense of legitimacy understood in this universal way.

But does JL understand legitimacy in this universal way? Even if I am right to portray JL as operating at the higher level of abstraction with which my guiding question is concerned, mightn't it only provide a framework that applies to particular political contexts?

At first blush, we might think so, for JLs are often found characterizing their theories simply as theories of democratic legitimacy. Robert Audi says that he has "liberal democracy in mind as the context" for his JL theory,[60] and Rawls is explicit in *Political Liberalism* that he is concerned with two fundamental questions concerning "democratic society."[61] Samuel Freeman is right to comment that, "for Rawls the idea of public reason is essentially a feature of a *democratic society*,"[62] and likewise Cohen views his own discussion as one of "democratic, political legitimacy."[63] Furthermore, we've seen that JLs take themselves to simply be developing ideas already implicit in liberal democratic institutions. Democracies, then, are clearly at the forefront of JLs' minds, and liberal democracies in particular, wherein individuals enjoy standard basic rights.

Within these JL accounts of legitimacy, then, how ought we interpret judgments of legitimacy or illegitimacy? It seems that JL theorists want only to address a particular dimension of legitimacy, only a particular way in which coercion can be legitimate or illegitimate. They want only to assess the democratic credentials, or democratic pedigree, of proposed coercion. On this basis, they pronounce laws to be legitimate or illegitimate. This restricted sense of legitimacy is very much on display, for example, in Brettschneider's analysis of a regime whose laws formally protect basic rights and reflect the liberal values of freedom and equality, yet who presides over a society in which the comprehensive views prevalent in civil society do not share these values. Brettschneider describes such laws as lacking democratic legitimacy even though they are substantively just according to liberal ideals.[64]

But while JL theorists may want to restrict themselves only to democratic contexts, can do they do so? I argue they cannot.

For consider that one of JL's foundational premises is that citizens are free and equal. In Rawls' account, the idea of free-and-equal citizens—along with those of a well-ordered society and society as a fair system of cooperation—is foundational to everything else,[65] everything including his JL principle of public justification. Audi says that JL "best accords with treating citizens as free and equal."[66] And in Brettschneider, the ideal of free and equal citizenship is the basis of those public reasons which alone can justify legitimate coercion.[67] Citizens are free in being responsible moral agents having a capacity and right to lead their lives as they see fit,[68] and they are equal in that all have equal claim to freedom and none have a natural right to rule over others.

We can better understand how this premise of free-and-equal citizens has led to JL, both historically and conceptually, by reviewing some ideas of Jean-Jacques Rousseau. As Rousseau clearly saw, affirming both the freedom and equality of real-world citizens produces a problem for democratic theory. How can people who are coerced against their wills be regarded as free? By giving equal weight to every citizen's view, the liberty of those in the minority is jeopardized. I will refer to this as Rousseau's problem. Rousseau's solution was his concept of the "general will." When citizens act for what is truly the common good, they align their wills with those of their fellow citizens and law simultaneously represents both citizens' equality—in its concern for the common good—and freedom—as an expression of citizens' wills. JL's principle of public justification is addressed to essentially the same problem, still generated by citizens' twin characteristics of freedom and equality, and now also adjusted to the fact of reasonable pluralism. How can diverse real-world citizens who are coerced against their wills be genuinely respected as free and equal? In short, the JL answer is: by basing laws upon reasons that all persons, including the coerced themselves, could accept when represented as idealized parties to a fair hypothetical agreement.

But the premise of free-and-equal citizens also raises this question: from a moral point of view, wouldn't JLs recognize all persons everywhere as free and equal, regardless of the political culture in which they live? Surely they would. JLs are clear that the conception of persons with which they begin is a moral conception, even if only a political conception. That is, it is a moral conception even if they are only concerned with the moral rights and duties people have in public, political contexts. And crucially, from the moral point of view all persons have an equal right to lead their lives autonomously.

As such, wouldn't, morally speaking, the same standard of legitimacy JLs derive from free-and-equal personhood apply equally to both democratic and nondemocratic contexts? If JLs are right that free-and-equal personhood requires the JL standard of legitimacy in democratic contexts, it follows that JL applies wherever free-and-equal persons form societies. Rousseau's problem will surely arise wherever free-and-equal persons form societies, and so the JL response to this problem should apply universally as well.

CONCLUSION

The stage is now set for the rest of my project. I've set out the question: what is the best philosophical framework for understanding political legitimacy? In other words, what is the best framework for understanding legal coercion that is legitimate even if imperfectly exercised? I've also laid out the criteria for our best answer. We hold certain CCs concerning legitimacy in the real world, and our best approach to legitimacy will be the one that best fits and philosophically illuminates these convictions. Of particular interest are our convictions that much real-world coercion is legitimate even amidst disagreement, that legitimacy is conditional on protecting certain basic rights, and that legal coercion on paternalistic grounds is illegitimate.

I hope it is also now clear how JL is an appropriate interlocutor in this investigation. While JLs and I share many legitimacy-related CCs, such as the three just mentioned, JL isn't simply about judging specific laws to be legitimate or illegitimate. Instead JL gives us a philosophically rich proposal for making sense of our convictions, for understanding their presuppositions and seeing how they fit together. It does so with ideas such as public reasons, reasonable persons, and idealized agreements, as well as with categories of consent, proceduralism, and self-legislation that I will explore in greater depth later. Furthermore, JL calls us to a moral point of view and, as such, JL constitutes a universal theory of legitimacy given its foundational premise of free-and-equal persons. JL is thus an appropriate counterpart to the neo-Calvinist account of legitimacy I'll develop, which also seeks to make sense of legitimacy understood to be a context-transcendent normative reality.

In the following chapters I examine how JL fares on its own terms (chapters 3–5), only later to assess it in relation to its neo-Calvinist counterpart (part III).

NOTES

1. Note that JL has been put to various uses. It is sometimes discussed as an ethic of citizenship, as in the exchange between Robert Audi and Wolterstorff. It is also deployed in democratic theory, where both Joshua Cohen as well as Amy Gutmann and Dennis Thompson make the JL principle of public justification central to their respective conceptions of deliberative democracy. Moreover, JL may be used to address meta-ethical issues surrounding moral contractarianism, as Samuel Freeman does, or to develop a full-blown theory of justice, as Brian Barry does. See Robert Audi and Nicholas Wolterstorff, *Religion in the Public Square: The Place of Religious Convictions in Political Debate* (Lanham, MD: Rowman and Littlefield Publishers, Inc., 1997), 10, 129; Joshua Cohen, "Democracy and Liberty," in *Deliberative Democracy*, ed. Jon Elster (New York: Cambridge University Press, 1998), 185–231; Amy Gutmann and Dennis Thompson, *Democracy and Disagreement* (Cambridge, MA: The Bel-

knap Press of Harvard University Press, 1996); Samuel Freeman, "Moral Contractarianism as a Foundation for Interpersonal Morality," in *Contemporary Debates in Moral Theory*, ed. James Dreier (Hoboken, NJ: Blackwell Publishing Ltd., 2006), 57–76; Brian Barry, *Justice as Impartiality* (New York: Oxford University Press, 1995). By contrast, my interest is in JL as a possible explanation of political legitimacy. Rawls calls the most famous formulation of JL's core principle the "liberal principle of *legitimacy*" (emphasis mine).

2. Rawls, *Political Liberalism*, 428.

3. T. M. Scanlon, "Contractualism and Utilitarianism," in *Utilitarianism and Beyond*, ed. Amartya Sen and Bernard Williams (Cambridge: Cambridge University Press, 1982), 103–28.

4. Ibid., 104, 107, 108, 110, 107.

5. Samuel Freeman, *Rawls* (New York: Routledge, 2007), 376.

6. I do somewhat oversimplify here. For instance, I expect that the legitimacy conditions that apply to contexts of material abundance and advanced technology will be somewhat different than those that apply to impoverished, technologically primitive ones. However, the underlying principles of legitimacy—that is, the general framework for legitimacy—will remain invariant across contexts.

7. John Rawls, *Political Liberalism*, xlix.

8. In a survey article on the topic of legitimacy, Flathman aptly refers to these three concepts as "kissing cousins." See Richard E. Flathman, "Legitimacy," ed. Robert E. Goodin, Philip Pettit, and Thomas Pogge, *A Companion to Contemporary Political Philosophy*, 2007, Blackwell Reference Online.

9. E.g., Allen Buchanan, "Political Legitimacy and Democracy," *Ethics* 112 (July 2002): 689–719. In fact, Buchanan also introduces a fourth concept, authoritativeness, but I do not address it here.

10. For example, in the work of Rawls, Robert Audi, and Gerald Gaus. See John Rawls, "The Idea of Public Reason Revisited," in *Political Liberalism*, Expanded Edition (New York: Columbia University Press, 2005), 440–90; Robert Audi and Nicholas Wolterstorff, *Religion in the Public Square*; Robert Audi, "The Place of Religious Argument in a Free and Democratic Society," *San Diego Law Review* 30, no. 4 (1993): 677–702; Gerald Gaus and Kevin Vallier, "The Roles of Religious Conviction in a Publicly Justified Polity: The Implications of Convergence, Asymmetry and Political Institutions," *Philosophy and Social Criticism* 35, no. 1–2 (January 2009): 51–76.

11. As in Christopher Eberle's and Wolterstorff's work. See Christopher J. Eberle, *Religious Conviction in Liberal Politics* (New York: Cambridge University Press, 2002); Nicholas Wolterstorff, *Understanding Liberal Democracy: Essays in Political Philosophy*, ed. Terence Cuneo (Oxford: Oxford University Press, 2012); Robert Audi and Nicholas Wolterstorff, *Religion in the Public Square*; Nicholas Wolterstorff, "Why We Should Reject What Liberalism Tells Us about Speaking and Acting in Public for Religious Reasons," in *Religion and Contemporary Liberalism* (Notre Dame, IN: University of Notre Dame Press, 1997), 162–81.

12. Rawls, *Political Liberalism*, 8.

13. See John Rawls, *A Theory of Justice*, Revised Edition (Cambridge, MA: The Belknap Press of Harvard University Press, 1999), 17; Rawls, *Political Liberalism*, 8.

14. Rawls, *Theory of Justice*, 46, 19, 17.

15. Ibid., 18–19.

16. Gerald Gaus, *Justificatory Liberalism: An Essay on Epistemology and Political Theory* (Oxford: Oxford University Press, 1996).

17. Eberle, *Religious Conviction*, 339 n34.

18. Rawls' own JL is often interpreted as being a hybrid of "consensus" and "convergence" approaches. The former requires that all can support laws for similar public reasons. The latter requires only that all support laws for some or another reason, though these reasons will differ and even if some of the reasons are religious or otherwise sectarian. But I believe this hybrid interpretation of Rawls is mistaken. For Rawls, public reasons clearly are the type of reasons that all persons can share in common no matter their particular religious or comprehensive views. While comprehensive views differ, the set of public reasons that constitute the appropriate framework for public deliberation is one and the same set for all citizens.

19. Kevin Vallier and Fred D'Agostino, "Public Justification," ed. Edward N. Zalta, *Stanford Encyclopedia of Philosophy*, 2012, http://plato.stanford.edu/entries/justification-public/.

20. For Gaus' version of JL, see Gerald Gaus, *The Order of Public Reason: A Theory of Freedom and Morality in a Diverse and Bounded World* (New York: Cambridge University Press, 2011); Gaus and Vallier, "The Roles of Religious Conviction"; Gaus, *Justificatory Liberalism*.

21. Jonathan Quong, *Liberalism without Perfection* (New York: Oxford University Press, 2011), 266–73.

22. Another early and influential proponent of JL was Charles Larmore. I will be interacting with Rawls' texts, though, and not Larmore's. For Larmore see Charles Larmore, *Patterns of Moral Complexity* (New York: Cambridge University Press, 1987); Charles Larmore, *The Morals of Modernity* (New York: Cambridge University Press, 1996); Charles Larmore, "The Moral Basis of Political Liberalism," *Journal of Philosophy* 96 (December 1999): 599–625.

23. Thomas Nagel, "Moral Conflict and Political Legitimacy," *Philosophy and Public Affairs* 16, no. 3 (Summer 1987): 215–40; Andrew Lister, "Public Justification and the Limits of State Action," *Politics, Philosophy and Economics* 9, no. 2 (2010): 151–75; Andrew Lister, *Public Reason and Political Community* (New York: Bloomsbury, 2013); Jonathan Quong, *Liberalism without Perfection*; Stephen Macedo, "In Defense of Liberal Public Reason: Are Slavery and Abortion Hard Cases?," in *Natural Law and Public Reason*, ed. Robert P. George and Christopher Wolfe (Washington, D.C.: Georgetown University Press, 2000), 11–49; Corey Brettschneider, *When the State Speaks, What Should It Say? : How Democracies Can Protect Expression and Promote Equality* (Princeton, NJ: Princeton University Press, 2012). These are the texts by each of these authors on which I will mainly draw.

24. Cohen, "Democracy and Liberty."

25. Quong, *Liberalism without Perfection*, 12.

26. I believe I borrow the apt language of "unanimity condition" from Lister.

27. Like Lister, though unlike Scanlon, I think nothing of substance turns on whether JL is formulated in terms of unanimous acceptability or unanimous non-rejectability. See Lister, *Public Reason and Political Community*, 9; Scanlon, "Contractualism and Utilitarianism."

28. This quote is from *Political Liberalism*. A slightly later and slightly modified statement of the principle is found in "The Idea of Public Reason Revisited." Scrutiny of possible differences between the two is unnecessary at the moment, though, when our task is simply to bring the basic idea into view. See Rawls, *Political Liberalism*, 137; Rawls, "The Idea of Public Reason," 446–47.

29. Gutmann and Thompson, *Democracy and Disagreement*, 50 (emphasis mine).

30. Lister, "Public Justification and the Limits of State Action," 151.

31. Rawls, *Political Liberalism*, 391 n28. Here Rawls borrows a phrase from Jeremy Waldron.

32. For instance, to what uses of political power does JL apply? To constitutional essentials only, or to all laws? Cf. Ibid., 214; Quong, *Liberalism without Perfection*, 256–89. I do not consider this issue here.

33. Freeman, *Rawls*, 389.

34. Ibid., 479.

35. Ibid., 387.

36. Rawls, John, *Political Liberalism*, 224.

37. Eberle, *Religious Conviction*, 252–87.

38. Ibid.

39. William P. Alston, *Perceiving God* (Ithaca, NY: Cornell University Press, 1991); Eberle, *Religious Conviction*, 239–51.

40. In Nagel's words, what JLs want is a way of mediating political disputes wherein participants can "legitimately claim to be appealing not merely to their personal, subjective beliefs but to a common reason which is available to everyone and which can be invoked on behalf of everyone even though not everyone interprets its results in the same way." (Nagel, "Moral Conflict," 235.)

41. Eberle, *Religious Conviction*, 245.

42. Note that the concept of "public" reasons as discussed here is related to, though somewhat different from, the broader idea of "public reason." Although accounts of public reason differ in their construal of public reasons, they share a common aim: to elaborate the reasons and ways of reasoning that make for public justification, which, in turn, requires that legal coercion be justifiable to all. Rawls' is the best-known account of public reason. See Rawls, *Political Liberalism*; Rawls, "The Idea of Public Reason."

43. Martha C. Nussbaum, "Perfectionist Liberalism and Political Liberalism," *Philosophy and Public Affairs* 39, no. 1 (2011): 3–45.

44. Ibid., 24; Rawls, *Political Liberalism*, 54.

45. Nussbaum, "Perfectionist Liberalism and Political Liberalism," 25; Rawls, *Political Liberalism*, 59.

46. Bohman and Richardson, "Liberalism, Deliberative Democracy, and 'Reasons,'" 260–261, 267.

47. Rawls, *Political Liberalism*, 49 n1, 48-58.

48. Nussbaum, "Perfectionist Liberalism and Political Liberalism," 33.

49. See Simone Chambers, "Theories of Political Justification," *Philosophy Compass* 5, no. 11 (2010): 899; Rawls, "The Idea of Public Reason"; Simone Chambers, "Secularism Minus Exclusion: Developing a Religious-Friendly Idea of Public Reason," *The Good Society* 19, no. 2 (2010): 16–21; Gaus and Vallier, "The Roles of Religious Conviction"; Bohman and Richardson, "Liberalism, Deliberative Democracy, and 'Reasons.'"

50. Quong adds the third condition that reasonable citizens give "deliberative priority" to considerations of justice. That is, they prioritize justice-related considerations over other considerations stemming from their full-blown comprehensive views should they conflict. (Quong, *Liberalism without Perfection*, 233, 291.) Quong may be right to think this third condition a natural extension of the first two, but my three critiques of JL in chapters 3–5 are unaffected by characterizing reasonable persons in this somewhat different way. I proceed on the basis of Rawls' twofold description of such persons rather than Quong's threefold description.

51. Rawls, *Political Liberalism*, xxxv–xxxvi.

52. Ibid., 13–14; Lister, *Public Reason and Political Community*, 2–7.

53. Barry, *Justice as Impartiality*, 100, 99–111.

54. Quong, *Liberalism without Perfection*, 141–44.

55. For further description of a well-ordered society, see Part One of Rawls, *Political Liberalism*.

56. See Lister, *Public Reason and Political Community*, 15–23.

57. Ibid., 20–21.

58. Macedo, "In Defense of Liberal Public Reason," 12.

59. In personal correspondence Lister has suggested that in cases of disagreement over state inaction, JL is simply indeterminate—not libertarian. But even if that's true, I hardly see how that would be to Lister's advantage. For indeterminacy still falls short of positively justifying legal coercion. Hence, the threat of libertarianism remains and the difference between the "exclusion" and "inaction" defaults narrows.

60. Audi and Wolterstorff, *Religion in the Public Square*, 10.

61. Rawls, *Political Liberalism*, 3–4.

62. Freeman, *Rawls*, 383.

63. Cohen, "Democracy and Liberty," 185.

64. E.g., Brettschneider, *When the State Speaks, What Should It Say?*, 38–39.

65. John Rawls, *Justice as Fairness: A Restatement* (Cambridge, MA: The Belknap Press of Harvard University Press, 2001), 5; Freeman, *Rawls*, 332.

66. Audi and Wolterstorff, *Religion in the Public Square*, 134.

67. E.g., Brettschneider, *When the State Speaks, What Should It Say?*, 72, 89–90.

68. Rawls, *Justice as Fairness*, 21–33; Rawls, *Political Liberalism*, 32–34; Brettschneider, *When the State Speaks, What Should It Say?*, 35.

Chapter Three

A First Unacceptable Consequence of JL

The first test of any philosophical theory is internal consistency. The internal critique that will now occupy us for the rest of part I will take the form of pointing out three unacceptable consequences to which JL leads us. Pointing these out constitutes an internal critique since these are consequences which JL theorists themselves would repudiate. They conflict with legitimacy-related CCs JLs themselves hold. In the rest of the present chapter, I will explain the first unacceptable consequence to which JL leads—the de-legitimization of any and all uses of coercive political power.

This is the strong claim that I will defend, that JL would make all uses of legal coercion illegitimate. This implication would conflict with our CC that many real-world uses of legal coercion are indeed legitimate even amidst disagreement. We can assume that JLs share this CC. They are not anarchists. They ostensibly think that many real-world liberal democratic governments are legitimate, even if imperfect.[1] Yet JL would de-legitimize all such regimes, along with all legal coercion. Why do I make this strong claim? Why would JL lead to this conclusion when applied to the real world?

I begin with the heart of the argument, assisted by an objector inspired by Michael Bakunin. My argument is that the full breadth of political thought includes persons who, according to JL's own criteria of reasonable personhood, qualify as reasonable and yet who reject the very existence of a coercive state. I put forward a reconstructed Bakuninist as one such example. There is no use of legal coercion, therefore, that would pass JL's standard of legitimacy, involving as it does a unanimity condition. Having laid out the heart of the argument, I then unpack three factors that conspire to produce this result: first, JL's criteria for reasonable persons; second, the reasonable multi-interpretability of key political concepts; and third, JL's unanimity condition. I consider a couple of objections before concluding.

By way of introduction, it's worth noting anecdotally that in my experience the layperson's response to JL is often akin to this first unacceptable consequence. The unanimity condition of JL puzzles laypeople since their experience of real-world politics confirms the unlikelihood of achieving consensus on political issues. This common reaction of laypeople to JL's basic idea is a first, albeit very raw, piece of evidence weighing against the plausibility of a theory that ties legitimacy to unanimity.

Professional philosophers have raised similar concerns about JL.[2] My argument in this chapter is also similar to the objection that public reason is inconclusive,[3] though I hope my argument is stated with a fresh forcefulness and clarity. JLs themselves have already tinkered with their theory to avoid libertarian conclusions—in other words, to respond to what I call the "redistribution objection" to JL.[4] JLs have recognized that not only egalitarian redistribution but even something as basic as a joint system of national defense might be compromised by consistent application of JL's unanimity condition.[5]

JLs are right to be concerned. The redistribution objection portends problems for JL more severe than reducing government to the night watchman state. As I will now argue, given JL's characterization of "reasonable" persons, the reasonable multi-interpretability of key political concepts, and JL's unanimity condition, we should not expect even the night watchman state to pass muster.

THE HEART OF THE ARGUMENT

My claim in this chapter is that JL legitimizes no uses of legal coercion at all, a result clearly at odds with our convictions. My main reason for this claim is this: the real world furnishes us with examples of persons who meet JL's twofold criteria of reasonable persons and yet who would reasonably reject the very existence of coercive states. Given JL's unanimity condition, such persons' reasonable rejection of proposed uses of coercive political power would render all such uses impermissible.

In other words, for even the night watchman state to meet the unanimity condition, there would have to be no reasonable objections to the effect that a stateless society is preferable to a society governed by a minimal state. But aren't there such objections in the offing? Let us consider one such line of objection, reconstructed from Michael Bakunin's anarchist writings.[6]

According to Bakunin, recognizing the freedom and equality of all prohibits the existence of a centralized state and requires instead "a free federation of communes."[7] In the state, Bakunin saw a grave threat to freedom and equality since "social life could easily take on an authoritarian character through the concentration of power in a minority of specialists, scientists, officials, and administrators."[8] His solution was, "A vast network of free associations, federated at every level and preserving the maximum degree of local autonomy."[9] Bakunin dealt with the fact of reasonable pluralism, but by-passed a centralized state, arguing that "a free society must be a pluralistic society in which the infinite needs of Man will be reflected in an adequate variety of organizations."[10] He puts the point with a flourish, "Every command slaps liberty in the face."[11]

The crucial point is that the Bakuninist objector should qualify as reasonable according to JL's own twofold criteria of reasonable persons. As mentioned last chapter—and as I discuss further below—these two criteria are a readiness to cooperate fairly, recognizing others as free-and-equal, and a recognition of reasonable pluralism and of its having implications for social life. When these criteria are stated generally, the Bakuninist meets them both. He recognizes others as free-and-equal persons with whom he is willing to cooperate. His position also recognizes that society's members will hold diverse conceptions of the good.

The real difference between the Bakuninist, on the one hand, and the hypothetical contractors that JLs envisage, on the other, is not that the former is unreasonable according to JL's own criteria of reasonableness while the latter are reasonable. As I say, both possess the requisite qualifications. Rather the difference is that the Bakuninist simply holds conceptions of freedom, equality, and fairness that are strikingly different from what JL theorists think sensible. The Bakuninist and the JL theorist agree on the importance of these general concepts, but they disagree on the conditions for experiencing these values and the operative threats to them.

For instance, consider how the Bakuninist's conceptions of freedom and equality differ from those typical of JL. For the Bakuninist, freedom is "the absolute right of every adult man and woman to seek no other sanction for their acts than their own conscience and their own reason, being responsible first to themselves and then to the society which they have *voluntarily* accepted."[12] At first glance, this conception may appear palatable to JL. In some sense the JL and Bakuninist alike affirm the value of individual autonomy. But the differences between the Bakuninist's and JL's conception of autonomy are actually very significant. For one, the Bakuninist gives primacy to one's conscience in a way JLs seem not to. Freedom is primarily a response to one's conscience, living out the dictates of conscience unimpeded by others. By contrast, JL freedom is shaped by a social context. Given that one's life will be lived out in a social context governed by political coercion—a starting premise which the Bakuninist seems not to share—individual autonomy is adjusted to the demands one places on others and has placed on him by others. As such, JL's conception of freedom is a way of reconciling oneself to the political order under which one lives,[13] as opposed to the Bakuninist's more radical freedom which requires following one's conscience whether within society or not. So, for example, in a conflict between a religious community's conscientious beliefs and a social expectation of nondiscriminatory hiring practices, the Bakuninist much more than the JL would uphold the religious community's freedom of conscience and prescribe withdrawal from wider social and political structures if conscience requires.[14] Two, Bakuninist freedom can only be limited by social arrangements to which one actually and voluntarily consents in the real world. The JL simply does not see this as a practicable possibility. The JL assumes the existence of political coercion; the question becomes how to appropriately justify this coercion; and for that purpose counterfactual consent in idealized circumstances suffices. Three, *"freedom for all"*—which is the aim of the social revolution Bakunin envisages—requires "the radical dissolution of the centralized, aggressive, authoritarian State, including its military, bureaucratic, governmental, administrative, judicial, and legislative institutions."[15] By contrast, JLs see in a modern, centralized state no threat to their conception of individual autonomy. To put the difference still more starkly, the JL sees the state as enabling citizens to lead their own lives, by providing goods such as the "social bases of self-respect."[16] Conversely, the Bakuninist sees the state as threatening autonomy, given the way state power and social expectations can impede individuals from living according to their own conscience.

As for Bakuninist equality, "This is not the removal of natural individual differences, but *equality in the social rights of every individual from birth*; in particular, equal means of subsistence, support, education, and opportunity for every child, boy or girl, until maturity, and equal resources and facilities in adulthood to create his own well-being by his own labor."[17]

While again there is much here with which JLs would agree, there is also much that is controversial—and reasonably so. Bakunin's conception of equality requires a rich list of positive rights, and so would JL's. But Bakunin's conception of equality also regards these positive rights as oriented toward a particular goal, namely, each individual engaging in labor that is productive and dignifying—dignifying not in the sense of dignity-respecting, but dignity-bestowing. Bakunin shared Karl Marx's secular, materialist perspective in which humans' dignity consists in their capacity for free, productive, self-expressive labor. It is here the JL and Bakuninist part ways in their respective understandings of equality. For the JL views people as equal in having an equal right to lead their lives by their own lights, while the Bakuninist views them as equal in their right to the conditions for dignifying labour. Now is the Bakuninist unreasonable in holding this more particular view or in deploying it while negotiating social arrangements? I think not. For the Bakuninist's belief that cooperative labor lies at the basis of society and is the source of "dignity" and "rights"[18] strikes me as at least reasonable, even if not compelling. Moreover, the Bakuninist can hold and articulate this conception of equality while bracketing his wider and reasonably contestable atheistic, materialistic beliefs. Such bracketing is required by consensus versions of JL—though not by convergence versions—since reasons peculiar to one or another comprehensive views are not reasons that all can accept.

Similarly, there is no reason to think the Bakuninist fails to display what Rawls calls reciprocity, which is involved in the fair-mindedness that is JL's first criterion of reasonable persons. For Rawls, fair cooperation not only involves respecting others as free and equal, but reciprocity. This requires "that citizens believe in good faith that the fair terms of social cooperation that they propose and expect all to abide by are *reasonably acceptable to everyone* in their capacity as free and equal citizens, without their being dominated or manipulated, or under pressure because of an inferior social or political position."[19] It is true that the Bakuninist's anarchist objections would deprive the least well-off of social programs which, as JLs see it, make only the redistributive state "reasonably acceptable to everyone." However, for the Bakuninist it is not a lack of redistribution that poses the greatest threat to the least well-off. Rather, it is the state itself that poses the greatest threat, in light of the state's potential for centralizing power, resources, and expertise. Thus, given how he sees the operative threats to the sort of freedom he values, the Bakuninist can "in good faith" reject the state while displaying reciprocity.

Likewise, the Bakuninist offers a different interpretation of what reasonable pluralism means for social cooperation. Both the Bakuninist and JL accept it as a fact, but they disagree over what its implications are. According to JLs, pluralism implies that social cooperation ought be regulated by reasons that all can accept. Conversely, according to the Bakuninist, it simply means that society ought welcome diverse organizations that express the variety of comprehensive views present in society. To reiterate, "a free society must be a pluralistic society in which the infinite needs of Man will be reflected in *an adequate variety of organizations*" (emphasis mine). Rejecting a centralized state that tends to monopolize intellectual and material resources facilitates this diversification. For the JL, reasonable pluralism means that political power must be publicly justified. For the Bakuninist, it requires extensive devolution of this power.

Whether there are any actual Bakuninists in a given time or place is immaterial to the present point. Simply the fact that one could plausibly interpret freedom, equality, fairness, and the implications of reasonable pluralism in these diverse ways qualifies the Bakuninist as reasonable under JL's twofold criteria.

Of course, when these two general criteria are specified in more particular ways, the Bakuninist may fall beyond the pale of the reasonable. This may happen, for instance, if it is stipulated (rather than argued) that free-and-equal citizenship demands the provision of a social minimum, or if it is stipulated (rather than argued) that reasonable pluralism requires JL public justification.

But there are at least three strong arguments for why JLs cannot load the deck in such ways. As we go, keep in mind that JL understands "reasons all can accept"[20] in terms of reasons that all reasonable persons, suitably idealized, could accept as bases for legal coercion in a hypothetical procedure.

First, JLs cannot define reasonable personhood more narrowly because doing so would beg the question in favour of the substantive conclusions at which JLs hope to arrive. A hypothetical procedure simply involving persons who already hold JLs' preferred conclusions has no genuine heuristic, constructivist, or argumentative value.[21] Second, doing so would also render JL an inept tool for dealing with real-world diversity, which is certainly a primary JL aim. No longer would the hypothetical contractors approximate real-world diversity. Instead, it would represent only a narrower range of diversity, tailored to achieve unanimity only on the conclusions that JL theorists prefer.[22] Third, the more procedure-independent content with which JLs fix these concepts, the less can JL plausibly claim to represent a higher-order impartiality.[23] JL aspires to arbitrate between comprehensive views, not just express yet another such view. Presuming, then, that JL theorists neither want to beg the question nor fail to address real-world pluralism nor become just one comprehensive view among others, their criteria of reasonable persons will have to rest on general concepts of freedom, equality, fairness, and reasonable pluralism as opposed to specific conceptions thereof.

In short, it seems perfectly possible for a reasonable person to prefer a stateless society—as our reconstructed Bakuninist does. My judgment may differ. By my lights, anarchism may be wrongheaded. Yet do I fail to see any plausible grounds for rejecting the centralized state, and grounds that are perfectly expressible in public reasons? I do not, thanks in part to Bakunin, and the existence of such objections means that even the minimal state fails at the bar of JL's unanimity condition. Not all can accept it.

So the broader problem the redistribution objection portends for JL is the following. JL would not just make many legal measures illegitimate that our CCs tell us are legitimate. It would not simply de-legitimize redistribution while leaving other government functions intact. Taking into account the full range of views reasonable persons could hold, JL would make all legal measures illegitimate. JLs need to appreciate just how wide the range is that permitted by their own criteria of reasonableness.

FACTORS IN THE ARGUMENT

Let me now break down this argument into three of its elements. These are factors that conspire together to yield JL's unacceptable consequence of de-legitimizing all legal coercion. The first has already figured quite prominently in my presentation of the argument, but it is worth examining in greater detail as I believe it serves as a window into the internal logic of JL reasoning. Later the third element will do the same.

Who Counts as Reasonable?

To begin with, one must try and disambiguate who or what JLs mean to describe with the term "reasonable." The term is used in what I'm taking to be the canonical formulation of JL's principle of public justification: legitimate laws are those based on reasons every reasonable person can accept. Here it is persons who are reasonable or not. Sometimes it is an act that is deemed reasonable or unreasonable, as when JLs speak of reasons all can reasonably accept or reasons no one can reasonably reject. In a later statement of his liberal principle of legitimacy, Rawls doubly invokes the "reasonable." Legitimate laws are those justified on grounds that citizens can reasonably expect one another to reasonably accept. In this locution, not only is reasonableness predicated of the act of acceptance, but also of one's belief concerning the acceptability of a proposal to others.[24] Finally, in addition to citizens being (un)reasonable and acts of accepting, rejecting, and believing being (un)reasonable, JL also predicates (un)reasonableness of reasons. With reference to Eberle's analysis, we have already noted some of the many ways in which JLs try to capture the nature of public—or, in other words, reasonable—reasons. For instance, it might be said that reasonable grounds are intersubjective, replicable, or fallible in nature.[25]

This multiplicity of uses raises the question of the relationship between them. This is not an issue that JLs typically clarify. While they do not, I suggest that a certain order of priority must exist among their judgments of reasonableness, with its application to citizens being primary. I explain.

JLs aspire to justify liberal rights and institutions via a procedure that models democratic sovereignty, and given their proceduralist aspirations, JLs are committed to predicating reasonableness of citizens primarily and of reasons or policies only secondarily. If social arrangements are to be understood as self-legislated by free citizens, citizens themselves must determine what count as reasonable reasons and reasonable social agreements. Reasonableness is primarily predicated of citizens, and the reasonableness or unreasonableness of other phenomena downstream is determined by procedures in which qualified citizens participate.

Moreover, in addition to the logic of their constructivism, JLs should primarily predicate reasonableness of citizens insofar as they aim to meet the liberal demand that "the social order . . . be capable of explaining itself at the tribunal of each person's understanding."[26] In light of this quote, I've identified the animating spirit of JL as the desire to justify social arrangements to the citizens subject to them. Hence, this order of priority—predicating reasonableness primarily of persons rather than of reasons or agreements—best reflects the spirit of JL, and also preserves its proceduralist designs.

Similar considerations favor an ethical rather than epistemic interpretation of JL's conception of reasonable citizenship, to borrow again from Nussbaum. The ethical conception is more procedural, requiring only that a reasonable citizen meet Rawls' twofold criteria. The epistemic conception is more substantive, requiring that the comprehensive view held by a reasonable citizen exhibit certain characteristics constitutive of rationality. Rawls' twofold criteria may seem sparse, but it is their very sparseness that makes them suitable for a constructivist, proceduralist account. Moreover, in addition to the ethical conception's superior compatibility with proceduralism, it is worth remembering that the ethical conception is indeed Rawls' official stance,[27] despite the equivocations Nussbaum points out.

Who, then, counts as reasonable according to JL logic? Membership is not determined by particular reasons or social arrangements that must be accepted to qualify as reasonable. Rather, reasonable citizens are simply those who meet two basic ethical criteria. If JL is to stay true to its proceduralist aspirations, we should look to the views of these reasonable citizens for what reasons and acts are also reasonable.

Multi-Interpretable Concepts

JLs evidently believe that the idealizations of the hypothetical contracting situation will substantially decrease the extent of political disagreement when compared with the real world. I am arguing, however, that even with such idealizations—moral, epistemic, material—we still should not expect the range of disagreement to so narrow that unanimity could be reached on any political measure, including the very existence of a coercive state. Why shouldn't we expect this?

My presentation of the argument so far has implicitly depended upon and illustrated one reason why, but I will now draw out this reason and set it forth more clearly. We cannot expect unanimity because of the reasonable multi-interpretability of key justice-related concepts. Some such concepts are involved in JL's criteria of reasonable persons. As a result, the range of who qualifies as reasonable is broader than JLs typically suppose. So, too, is the range of reasonable grounds for rejecting coercion broader than is typically supposed.

For example, take the concept of freedom. What does it mean for citizens to be free? Does it mean that real-world governments legitimately rule only by the consent of the governed? So says America's Declaration of Independence. But does this conception of freedom mean actual consent or only tacit consent? And what might constitute tacit consent?[28] Perhaps freedom means negative liberties everyone ought enjoy. Or does it also mean a right to basic material goods?[29] Does our freedom consist in the political liberties, as the ancients thought? Or in civil liberties, as moderns are more inclined to think?[30] Are we free in some more abstract sense, such as Immanuel Kant's idea of persons as self-legislators of the ethical and political norms that govern them? Is freedom an essentially relational term, where free persons are those who stand in a relationship of nondomination to others?[31] Nor should we forget the Bakuninist's conception of freedom above which accords primacy to one's conscience.[32] Moreover, so far as I can see, all of these conceptions of freedom are compatible with the basic sense of freedom JL starts with, that individuals are free in having a capacity and right to lead their lives by their own lights. It is safe to assume there is some shared meaning between all these conceptions, some basic idea such as self-direction. But a vague concept like that is hardly sufficient for adjudicating any substantive political disputes.[33]

Now consider equality in this same light. At the beginning of his book, *Contemporary Political Philosophy: An Introduction*, Kymlicka says that political theorists of our time have come to occupy in common an "egalitarian plateau."[34] The book then goes on to discuss each of several schools of contemporary political philosophy, including utilitarianism, liberal equality, libertarianism, Marxism, communitarianism, and feminism. He suggests that each of these can be fruitfully understood as a different interpretation of the value of equality! (And so, too, can anarchism, the Bakuninist will hasten to add.) For example, "This more basic notion of equality is found in Robert Nozick's libertarianism as much as in Marx's communism. While leftists believe that equality of income or wealth is a precondition for treating people as equals, those on the right believe that equal rights over one's labour and property are a precondition for treating people as equals."[35] This means that even citizens who view one another as free-and-equal will have difficulty coming to unanimity on political decisions given their differing interpretations of what it means to "treat people as equals."

And just as there are diverse ways of interpreting equality and freedom, there are various reasonable interpretations of fairness. Does fairness require rendering to each according to desert, where desert is a function of one's virtue or vice? For much of Western history, justice and fairness were understood primarily in these terms. Does fairness demand "from each according to ability, to each according to need"? This was Marx's suggestion, and it still resonates. Does fairness render to each according to her actual contribution to the joint social product? The ethic of personal responsibility held by libertarians and laissez-faire capitalists would say it does. Sympathy for this dimension of fairness is also to be found in Rawls, who views people "as capable of taking responsibility for their ends,"[36] as well as in luck egalitarianism, which distinguishes between "disadvantage for which the sufferer cannot be held responsible" and that for which he can.[37] Or does fairness demand distribution according to natural rights held equally and inalienably by all?[38] Or perhaps it requires distribution according to some or another hypothetical procedure. JL is an example.

Reflect on this fact. Contemporary political philosophy is characterized by theorists who endorse views as diverse as utilitarianism, libertarianism, Marxism, communitarianism, and feminism, and as justice-as-fairness, justice-as-luck-egalitarian-equality, justice-as-rights, justice-as-entitlement, justice-as-desert, justice-as-impartiality, and so on. What makes possible their disagreement? In large part, their disagreement turns on the multi-interpretability of key concepts under discussion. They agree that people are free-and-equal and should be treated fairly. They just disagree on the meaning and implications of these general ideas.

Their disagreement reinforces my argument in this chapter. In light of the disagreement that exists among real-world political philosophers, is it reasonable to expect that hypothetical contractors—burdened by the same multi-interpretable concepts—will fare any better in reaching unanimity? I suggest not.

JL's Unanimity Condition

The reasonable multi-interpretability of key political concepts contributes to an explanation of why JL ends up de-legitimizing all legal coercion. The vagueness of these concepts, though, is something with which all political philosophers must reckon. So in the context of JL, what more directly explains why disagreement over these concepts leads to the consequence of de-legitimizing all legal coercion?

The culprit is JL's unanimity condition. JL requires that laws be based on reasons that all can accept, or that none can reasonably reject. However, given the wide range of views reasonable citizens could hold, no law can meet this requirement.

To address this concern, the unanimity condition cannot simply be removed from JL. It cannot since it is essential to JL given the problem to which JL is a response. In the previous chapter, I called this Rousseau's problem. The problem is how to vindicate the freedom and equality of democratic citizens who, on the basis of political views they do not share, are coerced against their will. How can a person be free who is coerced by his fellows, having had his vote outweighed by the majority? Notice this problem only arises if we believe that each and every citizen is free and equal. If every citizen is not, then it seems unproblematic that certain citizens be coerced by others or have their views dismissed by the majority. It would make sense that those who have less status or are less free should be subject to coercion by those who have more status or are more free. But that is obviously not the premise from which JL begins nor the situation JL addresses. JL assumes that everyone is free and equal, and Rousseau's conundrum remains so long as even a single person is coerced against her will. The larger moral framework presumed by JL is certainly individualistic and Kantian, not aggregative and utilitarian. To remove the unanimity condition from JL, therefore, would be to gut JL of one of its distinguishing features as well as render it only a partial solution to the problem it is meant to solve. Stripped of a unanimity condition, JL becomes something other than JL.

Let me explain and defend my account of JL's unanimity condition in yet one more way, by responding to the charge that I've misinterpreted JL. It may seem I've misinterpreted JL as follows. I have presented JL's unanimity condition as requiring that reasons for coercion be accepted by all reasonable persons. What it actually requires, though, is simply the acceptability to all of reasons for coercion. It requires only that reasons are such that they could be accepted, not that they necessarily are accepted. In other words, the purpose of JL isn't to resolve disagreements. Rather, it is simply to provide a framework for handling disagreements that is appropriate to free-and-equal citizens. It serves this purpose by the framework itself being acceptable to all, even if reasons within the framework for a given coercive measure aren't accepted by all. JLs such as Rawls and Quong clearly want to allow for the legitimacy of coercive legislation amidst disagreement. They require only that legislation be justified by reasons related to the shared values of freedom, equality, and fairness, and by reasons that are otherwise nonsectarian.

In light of this exegetically being the case, why do I characterize the unanimity condition as I typically do, as requiring that all find reasons for coercion acceptable and not merely as requiring that they be offered a certain type of reason? In other words, why interpret it as requiring reasons that all can accept as opposed to simply a framework that all can accept? And why do I insist that the unanimity condition, so characterized, is essential to JL? I interpret JL in this way given the plain meaning of JL's core principle. To reiterate, this principle is that legitimate coercion is based on reasons that all reasonable persons can accept. A theory like JL requires that "political principles, in order to be valid or legitimate, need to be justifiable to all those persons who will be bound by them."[39] "Political liberalism states that political principles are only legitimate if they could be endorsed by all reasonable persons."[40] The "basic project of political liberalism" is "to show how liberal rights and institutions can be reasonably justified to all citizens in spite of the fact of reasonable pluralism."[41] It is much more natural to interpret JL's core principle as requiring that reasons for coercive measures be unanimously acceptable than as requiring only that a framework for political discussion be unanimously acceptable.

Moreover, there is good reason to regard the unanimity condition so understood as essential to JL. I've already mentioned that one of JL's distinguishing characteristics is that it is individualistic rather than aggregative and we've seen that it addresses itself to Rousseau's problem. My construal of JL's unanimity condition, as applying to reasons rather than a framework for reasoning, is more consistent with these considerations. An additional point is similar. By requiring only a general framework, JLs fail at the essential task of justifying coercion to all affected persons. Persons who are merely offered a certain type of reason rather than reasons acceptable to them have hardly had social arrangements justified to them. Hence, given JL's essential task, its unanimity condition is best interpreted as requiring unanimity on reasons for coercion as opposed to simply unanimity on a framework for reasoning.

Later in this chapter I will revisit this last point, that JL fails to truly justify coercion to affected persons given the account's many qualifications and idealizations. Moving forward, my discussion proceeds on the understanding that JL applies to reasons for coercion and not simply to a framework for political deliberation.

In light of JL's unanimity condition, it is apparent that consent is an idea of central importance to JL. What unanimity secures is the consent of each individual. We are talking here of hypothetical, not actual, consent. Still, the idea of consent is centrally important to JL insofar as legitimate laws, for JL, can be represented as based on individuals' unanimous consent in idealized circumstances. In the present chapter, I speak in terms of JL's unanimity condition. Later (in chapter 8), when explaining how neo-Calvinist legitimacy avoids the first unacceptable consequence of JL, I will interact with the idea of consent. As I say, consent is implicated in JL's unanimity condition.

Now the JL theorist might grant that JL cannot be gutted of its unanimity condition and that my characterization of the condition is appropriate. But, he will insist, JLs are not proposing to give every real-world person a veto. They are simply giving every person a veto insofar as their cognitive, economic, and moral deficiencies are corrected for. And then he may put to me the question: among that idealized group of people, don't I think there would be many laws that no one would veto?

To reiterate, I do not. Certainly there are reasons offered in the real world that would not be offered by persons construed in this way. For instance, no person would object to climate change legislation on the basis of disreputable environmental science. Our contractors also would not have the kind of lapses in moral judgment that sometimes afflict otherwise egalitarian real-world citizens. Nor would anyone be found leveraging their wealth for political advantage. So the cognitive, moral, and economic idealizations would, I expect, have the effect of narrowing the range of reasons that are offered for or against proposed measures.

However, I also expect that these idealizations would not expand the range of laws that satisfy JL's requirement of unanimity. That is because there are still several ways in which reasonable citizens, operating within the space of public reasons, may conscientiously disagree with one another. To name three sources of such disagreement: they may disagree on the interpretation of general concepts, as I've emphasized. As well, they may disagree on how various public reasons and values ought to be weighted.[42] They may also disagree on the correct analysis of empirical data, in the way, for example, people disagree over the environmental impact of the oil sands in Alberta, Canada.[43]

Even if JL's idealizations narrow the range of reasons offered, many reasonable objections, expressible in public terms, remain. Climate change legislation may not be rejected on the basis of bad science, but on the moral grounds that another state priority is of greater moral urgency; or on the philosophical grounds that we cannot have obligations to future generations; or on the technological grounds that imminent advancements will address the environmental challenges of the future.[44] Group-differentiated legislation may not be motivated by irrational prejudice, but may be defended in the name of rectifying historic or systemically entrenched injustices. Egalitarian property rights may be reasonably rejected on efficiency grounds; or in the name of perfectionistic pursuits that require concentrations of wealth in particular sectors of society; or in the name of individuals having an inalienable right to their labor and the fruits of their labor.[45]

In short, although JL places certain reasons out of bounds, there are still no laws we should expect all reasonable persons to support. Thus, JL's unanimity condition de-legitimizes all legal coercion even in JL's idealized circumstances. JLs have given us no good reason to expect otherwise.

OBJECTIONS AND REPLIES

Objection: JL can avoid libertarian (or anarchist) implications by appealing to the notion of higher-order unanimity. There may be extensive reasonable disagreement concerning specific lower-order policies, as my argument so far has pointed out. But there is no room for reasonable disagreement concerning general higher-order purposes of the state, and JL is meant to apply at this higher level.

Reply: As Lister helps us see, this response doesn't work because there is reasonable disagreement over how to characterize these higher-order purposes as well as reasonable disagreement over the noncoercive baseline against which putative uses of legal coercion are evaluated. Lister refers to these two problems as the "aggregation problem" and the "measurement problem." I agree that these pose formidable challenges to the present objection, and I largely follow Lister in this reply.

Here is an example of how the "argument from higher-order unanimity"[46] in defense of JL is supposed to work. There are reasonable grounds both for accepting and rejecting nuclear armament. However, at a higher-order level of generality, there are no reasonable grounds for rejecting a common policy of collective defense. Since, according to the argument from higher-order unanimity, JL's unanimity condition applies to the latter issue rather than the former, a state may legitimately enforce a policy of collective defense so long as it resolves reasonably contestable issues—such as nuclear armament—democratically.[47]

However, Lister identifies two problems that I judge fatal to this strategy.[48] The first of these—the aggregation problem—arises from the fact that, for any pair of options both of which are reasonably rejectable, there are varying ways of characterizing the noncoercive baseline to which we default should neither of the options be enacted. Consequently, the higher-order unanimity strategy may have undesirable results depending on how this noncoercive baseline is characterized. For instance, as Lister says, "If the inactive or noncoercive baseline is no state at all, then some fairly strong forms of perfectionism would be legitimate, if chosen democratically."[49] Assuming, then, that perfectionist states are illegitimate—even if democratically chosen—the higher-order unanimity strategy cannot salvage JL.[50]

The second challenge faced by the higher-order unanimity argument is the measurement problem. This is the problem of measuring the coerciveness of the baseline set of laws that is supposed to be unanimously preferable to having no laws at all. Mightn't people reasonably disagree over how the coerciveness of the baseline itself is measured, and over the coerciveness of the baseline laws in comparison to the coerciveness of having no laws at all? Is a society "with no traffic lights and no freedom of conscience" less coercive than a society "with freedom of conscience and heavily regulated traffic"?[51] Is a state of nature less coercive than a night-watchman state or welfare state? As Lister rightly notes, answering these questions requires us "to assess the value of the liberties or opportunities that laws deny people, or create."[52] Put another way, measuring the coerciveness of any of these societies requires qualitative, not just quantitative, judgments about the freedoms that matter. But those judgments are sure to be the object of reasonable disagreement. Since the higher-order unanimity argument, then, aims to satisfy the unanimity condition by identifying a baseline that all will agree is minimally coercive, it falls short of its target.

In sum, appealing to the notion of higher-order unanimity cannot keep JL from having libertarian (or anarchist) implications. Given the aggregation problem, such an appeal could avoid libertarian implications but only at the risk of permitting perfectionist states. Given the measurement problem, such an appeal could avoid libertarian implications only if there were a way of making qualitative judgments about morally significant freedoms that was beyond reasonable rejection. Thus, the argument from higher-order unanimity does not disprove my contention that JL would de-legitimize all uses of legal coercion.

Objection: JL can avoid libertarian (or anarchist) implications by applying JL only within a "reasons frame." There is a difference between applying JL's unanimity condition to decisions and applying it to reasons-for-decisions. JLs only intend to apply it to reasons-for-decisions, not decisions. Consequently, libertarian (or anarchist) implications are avoidable given that reasons for noncoercion may be just as reasonably rejectable as reasons for coercion.

Reply: Lister believes JL is invulnerable to the charge of having libertarian implications. Rather than defending JL via higher-order unanimity, however, Lister pursues the "reframing strategy."[53]

The reframing strategy distinguishes two ways JL can be framed. First, it can be framed as applying to decisions. Within this frame, the default is presumed to be inaction. Should no decision be universally acceptable, the state is barred from acting. Second, JL can be framed as applying to reasons. Framed this way, even a reasonably rejectable final decision may satisfy the unanimity condition so long as the reasons on which it is based are of a suitably public sort. When applied to reasons, Lister says, the default is not state inaction but simply exclusion of inadmissible reasons.

How is this strategy supposed to save JL from libertarian implications? It supposedly does so by regarding reasons for state inaction as controversial as reasons for state action. Since reasons for state inaction are consequently excluded, JL rightly framed is not prejudiced toward libertarian results.

But does the reframing strategy really save JL from libertarian implications? It seems not. This reply doesn't work because rejecting reasons-for-decisions is tantamount to rejecting the decisions themselves. Lister may not say that the default of the reasons frame is state inaction, but for all intents and purposes it is. For if there are no reasons that meet with unanimous reasonable acceptability, then how can any state action be justified? None can be.

If it is thought the reframing strategy can save JL, it should also be noted that the means by which it forestalls libertarian implications simultaneously strips JL of its most distinctive characteristic, namely, the liberal-cum-JL aspiration of justifying coercive social arrangements to those who are subject to them. As we have already learned from Rawls and Jeremy Waldron, JL builds from the characteristic liberal aspiration to justify social arrangements "at the tribunal of each person's understanding." However, by tolerating a high degree of reasonable disagreement over matters such as the correct interpretation, empirical assessment, and weighting of reasons, JL within the reasons frame cannot sincerely claim to uphold this liberal ideal. It seems clear that reframed JL would be willing to legitimize various social arrangements even while these arrangements remained unjustified at the tribunal of many people's understanding. Consequently, the reframing strategy would have the ironic consequence of preventing libertarian implications but at the expense of JL itself. It threatens rather than saves JL.

CONCLUSION

In conclusion, according to JL, laws are legitimate only when based on reasons that no one can reasonably reject. Laws are legitimate only if they satisfy JL's unanimity condition. If no law meets the unanimity condition, no law is legitimate. Given the diversity of persons who meet JL's twofold criteria of reasonableness—a diversity that encompasses the Bakuninist—no law would be supported by all reasonable persons, even in idealized circumstances. Therefore, JL would prohibit any and all uses of legal coercion.

We considered a few ways that JLs might respond. They might try to dispense with the unanimity condition, but this response is unavailable to them since JL could not then respond to Rousseau's problem. The fact that JLs such as Rawls and Quong require unanimity only on a framework for deliberation rather than on coercive measures might be thought an effective response. But such a response involves a convoluted reading of JL's core principle, and jeopardizes JL's essential task of justifying coercion to affected persons besides. JLs might also retort that their theory does not purport to give every real-world person a veto, but only hypothetical persons who are freed of relevant cognitive, economic, and moral defects. However, I argued that while this might narrow the range of reasons for rejecting proposed laws, it still would not open up a range of laws that no one could reasonably reject.

I began this argument by noting that the layperson's initial reaction to JL is often incredulity at JL's unanimity condition. Pre-philosophical opinions are not infrequently demolished by philosophical scrutiny. In this case, though, the layperson's incredulity toward JL has been vindicated. This unacceptable consequence of JL gives us a first reason for rejecting JL as a framework for theorizing legitimacy.

NOTES

1. E.g., "Rawls thinks the capitalist welfare state is unjust, but it is still politically legitimate since it provides an adequate social minimum." (Freeman, *Rawls*, 398.)
2. See Wolterstorff's misgivings atRobert Audi and Nicholas Wolterstorff, *Religion in the Public Square*, 154, 99.
3. For discussion and a defence of public reason, see Micah Schwartzman, "The Completeness of Public Reason," *Politics, Philosophy and Economics* 3, no. 2 (2004): 191–220.
4. Lister, "Public Justification and the Limits of State Action," 154–55; Gaus, *Justificatory Liberalism*; Jonathan Quong, "Disagreement, Asymmetry, and Liberal Legitimacy," *Politics,*

Philosophy and Economics 4, no. 3 (2005): 301–30; Schwartzman, "The Completeness of Public Reason"; Nagel, "Moral Conflict."

5. Nagel, "Moral Conflict," 233–34.

6. Neither is this the only line of objection that compromises even the night watchman state. For another example, I suspect that a reasonable case for anarchism, expressible in public terms, might also be reconstructed out of Henry David Thoreau's work. See Henry David Thoreau, *Civil Disobedience and Other Essays* (Mineola, NY: Dover Publications, Inc., 1993). I also wonder whether the ideal of the self-sufficient, pioneering individual present in American political culture would be an example.

7. Michael Bakunin, *Bakunin on Anarchy*, ed. and trans. Sam Dolgoff (New York: Random House, Inc., 1971), xx.

8. Ibid., 8.

9. Ibid., 7.

10. Ibid., 20.

11. Ibid., 3.

12. Ibid., 76.

13. Rawls, *Political Liberalism*, 222; Macedo, "In Defense of Liberal Public Reason," 17.

14. I believe both Ronald Dworkin and Cécile Laborde have used similar examples, and that these have inspired my example in-text.

15. Bakunin, *Bakunin on Anarchy*, 96.

16. The most important of Rawls' primary goods, goods which serve as the currency for Rawlsian distributive justice.

17. Bakunin, *Bakunin on Anarchy*, 97.

18. Ibid., 92. The Bakuninist may also go further than this to claim, as Bakunin himself does, that labor is the "glory of mankind" but he need not. My point is that the Bakuninist has resources for articulating a distinctive conception of equality that is reasonable and expressible in terms of "public" reasons, even if his broader comprehensive view offers further reasons for this conception.

19. Freeman, *Rawls*, 375.

20. Cf. Bohman and Richardson, "Liberalism, Deliberative Democracy, and 'Reasons.'"

21. For the suggestion that the procedure is only useful as a heuristic, see Philip Pettit, *The Common Mind: An Essay on Psychology, Society and Politics* (New York: Oxford University Press, 1993), 297–307.

22. "According to [Gerald] Gaus, many defences of liberal neutrality tailor their conception of public justification so as to justify contemporary 'liberal-like' states. 'The task of political philosophy is not to legitimize current political regimes, but to examine the conditions under which political coercion can be justified.'" (Lister, "Public Justification and the Limits of State Action," 154.)

23. The idea of "higher-order impartiality" is from Thomas Nagel, "Moral Conflict," as is the contention that liberalism instantiates it.

24. Rawls, "The Idea of Public Reason," 446–47.

25. See Samuel Freeman, *Rawls*, 296 for a comparable list of the many items of which Rawls predicates reasonableness.

26. Jeremy Waldron, "Theoretical Foundations of Liberalism," *Philosophical Quarterly* 37 (1987): 149.

27. Rawls, *Political Liberalism*, 54; Rawls, "The Idea of Public Reason," 488.

28. A. John Simmons, *Moral Principles and Political Obligations* (Princeton, NJ: Princeton University Press, 1979), 100, 57–100.

29. Rawls believes in such a right, since citizens ought enjoy fair equality of opportunity, and not merely formal equality. See Rawls, *Political Liberalism*, 6, 356–63.

30. Benjamin Constant, "The Liberty of the Ancients Compared with that of the Moderns," in *Benjamin Constant: Political Writings*, ed. and trans. Biancamaria Fontana (New York: Cambridge University Press, 1988), 307–28.

31. See Philip Pettit, *Republicanism: A Theory of Freedom and Government* (New York: Oxford University Press, 1999).

32. For a contemporary exponent of the view that freedom is primarily freedom of conscience, see Chandran Kukathas, *The Liberal Archipelago: A Theory of Diversity and Freedom* (New York: Oxford University Press, 2003).

33. This last point is similar to the objection that public reason is inconclusive.

34. Will Kymlicka, *Contemporary Political Philosophy: An Introduction*, 2nd ed. (New York: Oxford University Press, 1990), 4–5.

35. Ibid., 4.

36. Rawls, *Political Liberalism*, 33–34.

37. G. A. Cohen, "On the Currency of Egalitarian Justice," *Ethics* 99 (July 1989): 906–44.

38. Think John Locke here.

39. Jonathan Quong, *Liberalism without Perfection* (New York: Oxford University Press, 2011), 17.

40. Ibid., 234.

41. Ibid., 316.

42. For instance:

> given that a laundry list of the platitudes implicated in the abortion issue requires supplementation by some ranking of those values, given that each of the premises of a putative public justification must be acceptable to rational and reasonable citizens, and given, more particularly, that the premise that *ranks* the values implicated in the abortion issue must be acceptable to rational and reasonable citizens, it's clear that Rawls can't articulate a public justification for the claim that the state ought to grant each woman a right to have an abortion in the first trimester. Any supplementary ranking of the implicated political values that gets the desired result will be anything but platitudinous: claims about platitudes are not *typically* platitudes themselves, and claims that rank the platitudes implicated in the abortion issue will *invariably* be controverted by fully rational and reasonable citizens. Nearly any ranking of the platitudes implicated in the abortion controversy, including Rawls's claim that 'at this early stage of pregnancy the political value of the equality of women is overriding' will be contested by reasonable citizens. (Eberle, *Religious Conviction*, 218–19)

43. I believe it's the work of Lister that brought to my attention these sources of disagreement that persist even in the space of public reasons.

44. I thank Jan Narveson for this last point.

45. Robert Nozick, *Anarchy, State, and Utopia* (New York: Basic Books, Inc., 1974).

46. It is Joseph Chan who coined this term, and Gaus has thoroughly developed the argument. See Joseph Chan, "Legitimacy, Unanimity, and Perfectionism," *Philosophy and Public Affairs* 1 (2000): 5–42; Gaus, *Justificatory Liberalism*; Gerald Gaus, *Contemporary Theories of Liberalism: Public Reason as a Post-Enlightenment Project* (Thousand Oaks, CA: Sage, 2003).

47. The example is taken from Lister, who in turn borrows it from Nagel. (Lister, "Public Justification and the Limits of State Action," 154–55; Nagel, "Moral Conflict," 233.)

48. Lister himself doesn't quite conclude that the higher-order unanimity argument is irredeemable, but he does pursue an alternative strategy for saving JL from libertarian implications. I will shortly call his alternative the "reframing strategy." See Lister, "Public Justification and the Limits of State Action," 161.

49. Ibid., 157.

50. Note that Gaus has responded to this objection of Lister's. Gaus' response seeks to disaggregate issues with reference to the idea of "justificatory dependency." See Gerald Gaus, "On Two Critics of Justificatory Liberalism: A Response to Wall and Lister," *Politics, Philosophy and Economics* 9, no. 2 (May 2010): 197–200, 200; Lister, *Public Reason and Political Community*.

51. Lister, "Public Justification and the Limits of State Action," 160.

52. Ibid.

53. Lister, *Public Reason and Political Community*.

Chapter Four

A Second Unacceptable Consequence of JL

We come now to a second internal critique of JL.

The CC on which I focus in this chapter is our belief that real-world legitimacy is conditional upon protecting certain basic rights. That is, we believe there are certain rights, such as those to bodily integrity and freedom of religion, that are necessary for legitimacy. Although I am not concerned with exactly which rights these are, I do take it that we all regard certain, specific basic rights as especially important. So the conviction here isn't simply that rights exist in the abstract. Nor is it even that people possess certain specific rights. Rather, it is that people possess basic rights and that protection of certain rights is necessary for legitimacy. This is a CC JLs share, as part of the motivation for JL is to justify liberal rights.

However, in this chapter I will argue that, far from making such rights more secure, JL actually undermines them. I will argue that JL undercuts legitimacy-conditional, basic rights[1] by conflicting with three characteristics we experience such rights as having. I explain three asymmetries between the rights JL makes possible and real-world basic rights. One is between JL's representation of rights as procedure-dependent and the fact that real-world rights obtain independent of procedures. A second asymmetry is between JL's contentless proceduralism and contentful real-world rights. A third asymmetry is between JL's representation of rights as resulting from group consensus and basic rights' apparent objectivity. Objective rights are rights that apply whether or not political actors recognize them. In short, we experience legitimacy-conditional rights as procedure-independent, contentful, and objective. But the rights JL affords are essentially procedure-dependent, contentless, and the product of group consensus.

I claim that JL undercuts basic rights. I use the term "undercut" semi-technically. To clarify my argument in this chapter, I borrow the distinction from epistemology between rebutting defeaters and undercutting defeaters.[2] The former constitute reasons for affirming not-x. The latter are not so strong. The latter merely undermine grounds for positively affirming x. I run the second sort of argument in this chapter. The asymmetries I highlight do not prove that, given JL, basic rights do not exist. But they imply that, given JL, we have no good reason for affirming basic rights as we experience them in the real world.

Let me be clear. I proceed on the assumption that we experience legitimacy-conditional rights as (1) obtaining independent of procedures, and as (2) having definite content, and as (3) being objective. Rather than being mere stipulations, though, these characteristics of basic rights simply result from observation, from observing how we—including JLs—talk about and apply basic rights in contemporary political discourse and practice. I will elaborate this point as we go.

The most important of these asymmetries is the first, as JL's proceduralism ultimately causes the other two asymmetries as well. I begin by exploring the distinction between procedural and substantive accounts of legitimacy, which gives another window into the internal logic of JL. I then move on to examine the three tensions that exist between JL and the characteristics of real-world rights.

THE DISTINCTION BETWEEN SUBSTANCE AND PROCEDURE

Remember the connection between JL's principle of public justification and JL's hypothetical proceduralism. The principle ties legitimacy to reasons that all reasonable persons can accept, and JLs elaborate this principle in terms of a hypothetical procedure in which persons exchange reasons and that culminates in a unanimous agreement. Who are the reasonable persons to whom the principle refers? The idealized parties to the hypothetical procedure. What are the reasons reasonable persons can accept? The reasons that would be acceptable to the idealized parties. What are legitimate forms of legal coercion? Those based on such reasons. Given their presumption that free-and-equal persons ought view themselves as authors of the norms that govern them, JLs are driven to constructivism and the proceduralism it involves.

The proceduralism to which JLs are committed can be better understood if we contrast procedure with substance. So let us clarify the distinction. Doing so will also pay dividends later on when examining the three asymmetries between JL and basic rights.

"Substance" in this discussion refers to determinate items that legitimacy or justice demands. Lists of rights, goods, or opportunities that each person is owed represent such items. For instance, the Universal Declaration of Human Rights is a list of substantive rights. So, too, are the Canadian Charter of Rights and Freedoms, the American Bill of Rights, and other bills of rights. The determinate items typically included on these lists are familiar: rights to security of the person, equal standing under the law, freedom of religion, freedom of speech, and others. In developing her capabilities approach to justice, Nussbaum provides substance in terms of ten specific capabilities that each person should enjoy: life; bodily health; bodily integrity; sense, imagination, and thought; emotions; practical reason; affiliation; other species; play, and; control over one's environment, both political and material control.[3] The Ten Commandments of the Hebrew Bible are also substantive: "You shall not murder. You shall not commit adultery. You shall not steal. You shall not bear false witness against your neighbor," and so on.[4] The point here is not that substance must always take the form of the list. Rather, it is simply that substantive accounts will always be specific in recognizing certain determinate items as demanded by legitimacy or justice.

Whereas substantive views identify specific goods or rights, procedural views emphasize processes instead. From Kant up to the present, the procedures are conceived of hypothetically.[5] Procedural theories may draw certain substantive conclusions—such as the basic liberties protected by Rawls' first principle of justice—but procedural theories justify such conclusions merely by inferring the expected outcome of a hypothetical procedure. It is procedures that are more foundational than specific goods or rights.

Reflective proceduralists admit that constructing a fair hypothetical procedures requires at least a thin conception of the good, but their aim is to avoid the substance involved in conceptions of the good. The very point of proceduralism is to justify social rules by the procedure itself, rather than by referring to substantive criteria that are independent of the procedure. It is because this is proceduralism's point that Fabienne Peter faults Estlund for using his list of primary bads as criteria for evaluating the outcomes of democratic procedures,[6] and it is because of this that Jürgen Habermas accuses Rawls of being insufficiently procedural in *Political Liberalism*.[7]

Why proceduralist logic demands the exclusion of substantive criteria is nicely captured by what Peter calls the "political egalitarian's dilemma."[8] On the one hand, the more the substantive requirements constraining a fair procedure, the fewer the matters to be settled by the procedure. On the other, the fewer the substantive requirements constraining a fair procedure, the greater the likelihood that a substantively unjust or illegitimate outcome will result. Such is the general dilemma that proceduralists face: guarantee justice at the expense of a thoroughgoing proceduralism, or uphold a thoroughgoing proceduralism at the risk of substantive injustice. Of course, since the procedures in question are hypothetical, one may think this risk unproblematic. But still Peter's "political egalitarian's dilemma" illuminates why the internal logic of proceduralism demands the exclusion of substantive criteria, namely, lest matters be settled apart from the decisions of the procedure's participants. We might add two more reasons why proceduralism must exclude substance, drawn the previous chapter's explanation of why JL cannot narrow its definition of reasonable personhood.[9] Proceduralism must avoid procedure-independent substance to avoid begging the question—substance is to be the output of the procedure rather than input—and must do so if it is to represent a higher-order impartiality for adjudicating competing claims.[10]

There can be mixing between the two. We have not only a simple opposition between procedural and substantive approaches. We also have, for instance, "perfect procedural"[11] approaches or "rational procedural"[12] approaches that attempt to combine them. Estlund's is an example.[13]

However, legitimacy accounts typically emphasize either one or the other and there is an important difference between the two. Moving forward, it will be helpful to keep the distinction between substance and procedure in mind as we evaluate the species of proceduralism that is JL.

JL AND THREE CHARACTERISTICS OF LEGITIMACY-CONDITIONAL RIGHTS

It is clear that JL is, in large part, designed to justify the basic rights we cherish. As Macedo writes, "The demand for public reasonableness is especially important where fundamental rights and liberties are at stake."[14] This special concern for "fundamental rights and liberties" is evidence that JLs share the CC that legitimacy is conditional on protecting certain basic rights.

However, despite their intention to secure basic rights, JLs' justificatory strategy actually undercuts them in light of the following three asymmetries.

Asymmetry #1: Procedure-Independence vs. Procedure-Dependence

First, an asymmetry exists between JL's representation of rights as procedure-dependent and real-world basic rights which are procedure-independent. I elaborate.

Being constructivists, Rawls and other JLs represent basic rights as resulting from a particular procedure. So, on JL, basic rights are procedure-dependent, as are any other agreed upon social arrangements. Granted, the envisaged procedure is hypothetical, not actual. Nonetheless, the principles of justice, including rights, are determined by a procedure of the suitably idealized sort. If we possess rights, it is because of this procedure.

However, real-world basic rights are checks on, rather than outcomes of, procedures. Respecting certain rights is a prerequisite of, rather than product of, acceptable political procedures. Whereas JLs attempt to eschew procedure-independent substantive conditions, the real-world trend has long been to strengthen and expand constitutionally protected rights. We evidently feel that fundamental rights should be invulnerable to procedures. Moreover, it seems we would feel this way even when dealing with persons who meet JL's twofold criteria of reasonable persons. I take it that JLs do think many real-world citizens satisfy these criteria, but I doubt that JL theorists would be willing to subject their basic rights to the judgment of that group, even if we ensured that the group only contained the real world's reasonable citizens and none of the real world's many unreasonable citizens.

We have already seen Macedo assert that JL "is especially important where fundamental rights and liberties are at stake," but this statement is misguided. It intimates that the more important the issue, the more willing we should be to let the group decide. The more important the putative right in question, the more willing we should be to let the right depend upon everyone's acceptance of it. However, this is precisely the opposite of how we actually operate. We constitutionally entrench certain rights because they are so important that we are unwilling to make them vulnerable to legislative procedures, and because they ought be protected even amidst political disagreements with others. Similarly, Rawls hardly makes a modest claim when he says of his theory that "only the substantive principles specifying content of political right and justice are constructed."[15] For this statement, too, flies in the face of actual experience, in which we feel basic rights are among the demands of justice least in need of a constructivist, procedural justification and most in need of protection from procedures. Basic rights are not mere social constructions, but they serve as criteria against which socially constructed institutions and laws are evaluated. *Pace* Macedo and Rawls, the more important the issue, the less important we take anything like JL's principle of public justification to be. Their statements have an air of plausibility only because the procedures they have in mind are hypothetical. But the hypothetical proceduralist argumentation of Macedo, Rawls, and other JLs under-appreciates the decidedly anti-procedural role played by real-world basic rights.

This conviction in the procedure-independent character of basic rights is mirrored in what JLs themselves say about their methodology. They admit to holding certain moral and political convictions prior to their proceduralist philosophizing. Rawls, for instance, explicitly says that he starts with certain "settled convictions," such as "the belief in religious toleration and the rejection of slavery,"[16] and then adjusts the "parameters" of his theory to bring it "in line with our intuitive judgments."[17] I take JLs' methodology so described as further evidence that they share the CC that legitimacy is conditional upon protecting certain basic rights.[18]

In sum, real-world basic rights exist in spite of procedures, not because of procedures. But the way in which JL characterizes basic rights exactly reverses this relationship. JL also thereby misconceives that relationship between basic rights and legitimacy. If certain basic rights really are necessary for legitimacy, then legitimacy is not simply a procedural matter. Thus, JL is at odds with real-world basic rights and undercuts them.

Asymmetry #2: Contentful Rights vs. Contentless Proceduralism

Now consider a second tension that arises from JL's proceduralism. On the one hand, real-world basic rights have determinate content—for instance, rights to bodily integrity, material subsistence, and equal standing under law. They possess these rights given the sort of beings we are with the interests and value that we have. On the other hand, JL lacks content in two key ways. It is contentless in that, in principle, the content of basic rights, if they exist, is left up to the contractors to decide. It is also contentless in that JL, and, in general, JLs themselves, do not specifically tell us what the contractors would decide. I now expand on each of these ways in turn.

It is not by accident that JLs leave the content of rights up to the contractors. This feature of JL logically follows from JL's proceduralist aspirations. JL aspires to understand legitimacy in proceduralist terms, and so the content of any rights that exist can only come from participants in the procedure. It mustn't come from fixed criteria independent of the procedure. The internal logic of their framework means that, in principle, the contractors can fix the content of rights however they wish and they must be let alone.

Put another way, this first sense in which JL is contentless is a structural feature of the view. As such, it persists even when a JL theorist endorses certain specific reasons or principles, as we shall see Rawls do in a moment. JL is structurally contentless in that even when JL theorists endorse specific reasons or principles, this content is the fruit, not the foundation, of deeper premises in a JL framework. At a more fundamental level, concepts such as those of reasonable persons and of fair procedures underpin any specific conclusions. And then the question is: should we understand these more fundamental concepts as contentful or contentless? The answer must be they are contentless, if JL is to be plausibly proceduralist. As mentioned in the previous paragraph, substance must come from the procedure itself, not from fixed criteria outside it.

JL is also contentless in the sense that neither it nor, in general, JLs themselves tell us which specific agreements are reasonable and which are not. Nor are we told which specific reasons would be accepted and which rejected. The framework beckons us to justify laws in terms of their being reasonable from every qualified vantage point. Yet it does not illuminate why a given law is reasonable. It gives no account of the human interests that are served, or of the human dignity that is respected, in virtue of which a specific reason or law is reasonable. JL leaves us in the lurch. It tells us to accept reasonable social arrangements, without telling us which arrangements are reasonable. It passes the buck to the hypothetical contractors, but does not tell us which claims of the contractors are reasonable. I call this feature of JL the "vacuity of the reasonable." Note that this is one context where "reasonable" has a different meaning than elsewhere in our discussion. Here it stands for what reasons and agreements contractors have good reason to accept, which ones are well justified and sensible to accept. The vacuity of the reasonable is that JL and JLs do not tell us what these are.

It might seem that JLs do give specific content, and it is not that JLs say nothing about content. Again consider the example of Rawls. Take his account of public reason. He doesn't simply say, "Deliberate in public terms. Now have at it!" In addition to his general guidelines for public reasoning, Rawls explicitly discusses the "content of public reason."[19] This content is given by a liberal conception of justice, and includes both certain principles of justice—such as the liberty principle which specifies individuals' basic liberties and accords priority to them—and considerations appropriate for use as public reasons. Rawls calls these considerations the "political values of public reason."[20] Freeman gleans a plethora of these values from his survey of the Rawlsian corpus:

> equal political and civil liberty, equality of opportunity, social equality and economic reciprocity, the common good, the social bases of self-respect, and the necessary conditions for these values (*Political Liberalism*, 139) . . . reasonableness, fair-mindedness, and a readiness to honor the duty of civility (*PL*, 224) . . . a more perfect union, justice, domestic tranquility, the common defense, the general welfare, and the blessings of liberty for ourselves and our posterity, all of which include more specific values under them, such as the fair distribution of income and wealth (*Collected Papers*, 584). Efficiency and effectiveness are political values, which would include economic productivity and maintaining free and efficient markets, and controlling economic, environmental, and other kinds of social loss or waste (*CP*, 584) . . . preserving the natural order to further the good of ourselves and future generations; promoting biological and medical knowledge by fostering species of animals and plants; and protecting the beauties of nature for purposes of public recreation and the 'pleasures of a deeper understanding of the world' (*PL*, 245) . . . appropriate respect for human life, the full equality of women, the reproduction of liberal society over time, and respect for requirements of public reason itself in political discussion of controversial issues, such as abortion (*Justice as Fairness*, 117) . . . the freedom and equality of women, the equality of children as future citizens, the freedom of religion, and the value of the family in securing the orderly production and reproduction of society and its culture from one generation to the next. (*CP*, 601)[21]

Nor is this list exhaustive.[22]

Despite all these points, JLs still do not, in general, give content to the reasonable. It remains vacuous. For while Rawls may provide us with a bevy of considerations suitable for use as public reasons, his account largely does not specify what uses of these reasons are and are not reasonable. Some specific conclusions are reached, such as the liberty principle. But these are few relative to the many political disagreements such reasons are meant to help adjudicate. In other words, such "content" gives us a rich vocabulary with which we can express our acceptance or rejection of a proposal, but it does not tell us which proposals it is reasonable to accept or reject.

So how does all that's been said here about JL—the internal logic of JL that structurally excludes content and the vacuity of the reasonable—comport with real-world legitimacy-conditional rights?

Put simply, it doesn't. To reiterate, our basic rights are contentful. They have determinate content. They entitle rights-holders to certain freedoms, certain goods, and a certain legal standing, in light of the kind of beings humans are, having the interests and value that we do. JL's contentless proceduralism stands in tension with this determinate content. Hence, I argue that JL undercuts basic rights by conflicting with this second characteristic of real-world rights as well.

The vacuity of the reasonable is, I think, a particularly glaring weakness of JL. It leaves unanswered the gaping question: what counts as reasonable? Which agreements are reasonable and which are unreasonable? Moreover— and crucially—why is it reasonable to accept some and why is it unreasonable to accept others? What's more, when a theorist does infer outcomes of a JL procedure, he implicitly relies on some or another answer to the latter. Yet the answer he uses is not given by JL itself. The JL framework occludes from sight the contentful answers on which the theorist implicitly relies, presenting the justification of the social arrangement in question as though it were merely a function of agreement itself and not of the reasons for the agreement. The vacuity of the reasonable is deeply implicated in this philosophical obscurity. Though it doesn't provide content, JL requires content to be operationalized. As Estlund might say, the "flight from substance" must end in substance.[23] And so, requiring content from somewhere, operationalizing JL involves importing contentful premises from outside of JL that remain obscured behind JL's contractual framework. Historically, David Hume pressed a similar objection against social contract theories, accusing them of an unnecessary shuffle. If persons would agree to a contract because it promotes social utility, then isn't it social utility that truly justifies the terms of the contract?[24] In our day, both Philip Pettit and Kymlicka have reiterated this critique of contractarian approaches,[25] and I adapt it here as a critique of JL. JL gives us anything but a "clear and uncluttered view"[26] of what makes specific, contentful social arrangements reasonable or unreasonable.

Asymmetry #3: Objective Rights vs. Rights-by-Consensus

Now consider a third asymmetry between JL's rights and actual legitimacy-conditional rights. It also stems from JL's proceduralism.

We hold basic rights to be objective. Objective rights are rights that apply universally, whether or not real-world political actors recognize them. The correlative duties generated by such rights are binding on individuals and societies whether or not individuals and societies are willing to fulfill them.[27] The alternative to objective rights are rights that, at best, only apply to particular contexts and the content of which is determined by the prevailing norms of those contexts. To speak roughly—but not inaccurately, I think—the alternative to objective rights is popular opinion.

I have said throughout the chapter, and have repeated here, that we hold basic rights to be objective. Let me briefly review and further explain what entitles me to do so.

Philosophical disagreement about the objectivity of basic rights belies what we demonstrably believe about their objectivity as reflected in our actual political practice. The objectivity of rights is a necessary precondition for rational criticism of unjust regimes in varied contexts. Without it, we could not rationally judge regimes of times and places not our own to be illegitimate on account of their failure to protect individuals' basic rights.[28] So our practice of doing so reveals our belief in objective basic rights. Further evidence is that we manifestly do not take popular opinion as a reliable indicator of what is just or legitimate. Nor do JLs.[29] That popular laws aren't necessarily legitimate is confirmed by numerous historical examples. Slavery wasn't just, even when many thought so, nor was religious intolerance. European imperialism is reprehensible in hindsight. The list could go on. The likes of William Wilberforce, Martin Luther King, Jr., and Nelson Mandela have iconically stood in the face of systemic injustice, and their examples put pay to the notion that legitimacy is a function of popular opinion. The list could go on. We do hold basic rights to be objective.

But do JL theorists say that legitimacy depends merely on popular opinion? No, at least not explicitly. So where exactly does this third asymmetry lie?

It lies in JL's representation of rights as depending upon group consensus. As we've seen, the procedure envisaged by JL culminates in an agreement that is acceptable to all parties. So while we are sure that legal coercion isn't legitimate simply because it enjoys popular support, JL presents us with an exception to this rule. For according to JL there is, in fact, one group on whose popular support determines the legitimacy of legal coercion, namely, the group involved in JL's hypothetical procedure.

Moreover, on reflection, perhaps it isn't so obvious that JL rejects popular opinion as the basis for rights. After all, in his critique of *Political Liberalism*

Raz levels essentially just this charge against Rawls, that *Political Liberalism* makes justice subject to nothing more than contingent, popular opinion.[30] Rawls' concept of an "overlapping consensus"[31] can, indeed, give this impression, as can his requirement that we build up from ideas already "implicit" in extant liberal democratic institutions.[32] Raz sees in such aspects of *Political Liberalism* an appeal to crude populism, and in effect argues that something isn't right just because it is popular.[33] The mere facts that extant liberal democratic citizens do hold certain values and that these values are, at or least might be, embedded in extant institutions does not establish that citizens ought to hold them or ought embed them in their institutions. Simply because an overlapping consensus might exist on a given conception of justice, that hardly justifies the conception in question. What does justify a conception, if it is justified, is not the mere fact of consensus but the reasons which exist in its favor.[34]

Although I do not think Raz's exegesis of *Political Liberalism* is entirely fair, in raising this objection Raz has indeed put his finger on something amiss in Rawls' approach. *Political Liberalism* stands in an awkward relationship to our conviction that something isn't right just because it is popular. So too does JL generally, given that it represents rights as issuing from the popular opinion of its hypothetical contractors. Consequently, JL undercuts legitimacy-conditional rights, by conflicting with their characteristic objectivity, and should be rejected.

OBJECTION AND REPLY

Objection: Far from undermining basic rights, JL's hypothetical scenario actually expresses their great importance. JL reinforces rather than undermines them. JLs hold legitimacy to be conditional on the protection of certain basic rights, but there is no tension between this conviction and the proceduralist justifications of these rights offered by JLs. Isn't a large part of JLs' motivation to justify basic rights? Then why think there is any tension between this CC and JL's proceduralism?

Reply: My response to this objection as follows. Even if the JL theorist's intention is to support basic rights, this is no guarantee that his explanatory strategy actually does so. In the case of JL, the proceduralist method that aims to justify basic rights actually conflicts with this aim. How? By representing rights as having characteristics that sharply differ from those of actual basic rights. It represents them as being procedure-dependent, contentless, and the product of group consensus, misaligning with real-world rights which are procedure-independent, contentful, and objective.

A comparison here between JL and rule-utilitarianism is instructive. Rule-utilitarians might also aim to protect rights, but key features of their utilitarian framework are out of step with rights themselves. Rule-utilitarians seek to underwrite individual rights, but they justify them in the name of aggregate utility. They seek to capture the strong deontic constraints rights represent, yet one wonders why a rule-utilitarian would be unwilling to permit rights' violations if such violations could maximize utility while going unnoticed by the public. J. J. C. Smart rightly objected that rule-utilitarianism reduces to inexplicable "rule worship" in such cases.[35] The tensions that exist between rule-utilitarianism and rights are different from those that exist between JL and rights. However, the comparison is illustrative in showing how there may be features inherent to an explanatory framework that run contrary to the character of rights' normativity. In the case of rule-utilitarianism, it is a utility-maximizing framework; in the case of JL, a proceduralist framework. Moreover, these are features that cannot be undone simply by the sort of modifications that rule-utilitarians and JLs respectively propose. In the case of the former, the utilitarian framework is modified as rule-utilitarianism. In the case of the latter, a proceduralist framework can be modified by, for example, stipulating who participates in the procedure or what reasons are exchanged in the procedure.

Although there is no logical contradiction between JL and basic rights, there is nonetheless a different sort of conflict between them, as the JL framework is ill-fit for explaining them. My argument is not that JL entails the non-existence of basic rights, but that JL rights do not explain basic rights as they exist in the real world. Since real-world basic rights are procedure-independent, contentful, and objective, surely their more natural explanation is one that trades in substance rather than procedure.

CONCLUSION

JL portrays basic rights as if they are a procedural matter. This is unacceptable. What we actually believe is that certain basic rights obtain independent of procedures, that legitimacy requires their protection, and that they cannot be overridden by procedures of any sort. JL undercuts such rights in virtue of the three asymmetries covered in this chapter. Thus, the JL framework fails to make good sense of basic rights. What is legitimacy generally about? Proceduralism proves not an apt category for answering this question, for theorizing the issue of legitimacy.

NOTES

1. Throughout this chapter, "basic rights" and "legitimacy-conditional rights" tend to have the same meaning.
2. See Thomas Kelly, "Evidence," ed. Edward N. Zalta, *Stanford Encyclopedia of Philosophy*, 2006, http://plato.stanford.edu/entries/evidence/.

3. Martha C. Nussbaum, *Creating Capabilities: The Human Development Approach* (Cambridge, MA: The Belknap Press of Harvard University Press, 2011), 33–34.

4. See Exodus 20:13–16 at *The Holy Bible: English Standard Version* (Crossway, 2005), 61.

5. See Howard Williams, "Kant on the Social Contract," in *The Social Contract from Hobbes to Rawls*, ed. David Boucher and Paul Kelly (New York: Routledge, 1994), 132–46.

6. Fabienne Peter, *Democratic Legitimacy* (New York: Routledge, 2009), 132ff.

7. Jürgen Habermas, "Reconciliation Through the Public Use of Reason: Remarks on John Rawls's Political Liberalism," *The Journal of Philosophy* 92, no. 3 (March 1995): 116.

8. See chapter 5, "Political Equality," in Fabienne Peter, *Democratic Legitimacy*.

9. See "The Heart of the Argument."

10. Again, that higher-order impartiality is a JL aim is from Nagel, "Moral Conflict."

11. Rawls refers to procedural approaches that reliably produce outcomes that are correct according to an independent standard as "perfect" procedural approaches. Those that cannot be assessed according to an independent standard are "pure" procedural approaches. For explanation, see Freeman, *Rawls*, 480.

12. See chapter 1 in Peter, *Democratic Legitimacy*.

13. See chapter 7 in Ibid.

14. Macedo, "In Defense of Liberal Public Reason," 12.

15. Rawls, *Political Liberalism*, 104.

16. Ibid., 8.

17. Rawls, *A Theory of Justice*, 262.

18. For yet more evidence that JLs have pre-philosophical substantive commitments, consider the lists of liberal commitments given by Eberle and Dworkin. Given that JL is, in large part, ostensibly designed to justify such items, JLs presumably view legitimacy as conditional upon their protection. See Eberle, *Religious Conviction*, 11; Ronald Dworkin, "Liberalism," in *A Matter of Principle* (Cambridge, MA: Harvard University Press, 1985), 187.

19. Rawls, *Political Liberalism*, 223–27.

20. In similar fashion, on Quong's account content is given by "the fundamental idea of society as a fair system of cooperation between free and equal citizens," and Brettschneider is clear that the idea of free and equal citizenship from which public reasons are drawn represent "substantive" values. See Quong, *Liberalism without Perfection*, 162; Brettschneider, *When the State Speaks, What Should It Say?*, 115.

21. Freeman, *Rawls*, 388–89.

22. Ibid., 478.

23. See chapter 5, "The Flight from Substance," in David M. Estlund, *Democratic Authority: A Philosophical Framework* (Princeton, NJ: Princeton University Press, 2008), 85–97.

24. David Hume, "Of the Original Contract," in *David Hume: Political Writings*, ed. S. D. Warner, and D. W. Livingston, (Indianapolis: Hackett, 1994), 164–81.

25. Pettit, *The Common Mind*, 297–302; Kymlicka, *Contemporary Political Philosophy*, 67–70.

26. Rawls describes theorists' goal as gaining such a view of their subject matter (Rawls, *Justice as Fairness*, 176).

27. While defining objectivity in this way, I believe I can sidestep meta-ethical questions about moral realism, anti-realism, and so on, given my narrow purposes which are simply to illuminate the presuppositions necessary to make sense of our legitimacy-related purposes. The general conception of objectivity I start with here can be understood as simply serving these narrow purposes, being one such presupposition.

28. See Wilfrid J. Waluchow, *The Dimensions of Ethics: An Introduction to Ethical Theory* (Peterborough, ON: Broadview Press, Ltd., 2003), 72–74.

29. Nagel, "Moral Conflict," 221.

30. Joseph Raz, "Facing Diversity: The Case of Epistemic Abstinence," *Philosophy and Public Affairs* 19, no. 1 (Winter 1990): 3–46.

31. See Lecture IV, "The Idea of an Overlapping Consensus," Rawls, *Political Liberalism*, 133–72.

32. Ibid., 13–14.

33. Raz, "Facing Diversity," 18.
34. Ibid., 20.
35. See J. J. C. Smart and Bernard Williams, *Utilitarianism for and against* (New York: Cambridge University Press, 1973).

Chapter Five

A Third Worry about JL

We now come to a third worry about JL, a third unacceptable consequence to which it might lead. The worry is that JL justifies coercion in paternalistic terms. I am more cautious, though, in advancing this argument than in my previous two critiques of JL. For one, the worry rests on a distinction which, while intuitively compelling, I find difficult to make clear philosophical sense of. And two, even if JL does involve the sort of paternalism that I allege, it may seem a benign and normatively insignificant sort. For the paternalism I focus on does not, in the first instance, occur between real-world persons (though, as I shall explain, real-world persons stand ultimately to be affected). In this respect it is different from Wolterstorff's paternalism concern with JL.[1] My concern is instead with the very conceptual structure of JL. Nonetheless, given our CC that it is illegitimate to coerce others on paternalistic grounds—a CC certainly shared by JLs themselves—I think my concern worth pursuing.

Given the more tentative nature of my present suggestion, I do not intend for it to bear much weight in my overall argument. I intend my first two critiques to bear more weight, along with the two corresponding arguments of chapters 8 and 9. Consequently, here I will only sketch this third worry about JL.

How might JL involve paternalism? It does so by restricting real-world persons' freedom based on what idealized persons think is good for them. The crux of the problem is JL's directive to consult hypothetical persons rather than their real-world counterparts. Moreover, constraining liberty for people's good is different from constraining liberty for the sake of justice. My suggestion requires an examination of how claims about people's interests figure into JL justifications. I will argue that appealing to people's interests isn't necessarily problematic, but that doing so in the particular way that

JL does is problematic. As I say, this paternalism is a structural element of the JL framework. It is not implicated only in the application of JL (though the application of JL involves paternalism, too, as Wolterstorff points out).

My sketch in this chapter is broken down into two parts. First I discuss what constitutes paternalism, then I explain how JL instantiates it. I will consider both how JL involves a question of self-interest and how it idealizes the persons asked. Both elements contribute to JL's paternalism.

THE MEANING OF PATERNALISM

Let us begin by considering what paternalism is. Doing so will set a standard against which we can assess the possible paternalism JL involves.

In general, "paternalism involves constraints on liberty intended to benefit the person whose liberty is constrained."[2] There are three elements of paternalism we should consider. Paternalism involves a restriction on liberty. It also involves a particular kind of justification for the restriction, namely, one that appeals to the interests of the individuals whose liberty is being restricted. A third element—implicit though not explicit in the statement just quoted—is a substitution of judgment. Although affected parties are coerced for their good, it is not the affected parties themselves who judge what this good is. Quong thinks the very essence of paternalism is a negative judgment of others' ability to lead their own lives well.[3] I will briefly comment on these elements in order.

The first is that paternalism involves restrictions on liberty, and we must begin by appreciating that restrictions of liberty are, indeed, at stake when theorizing legitimacy. They are at stake both in evaluating the legitimacy of particular social arrangements as well as in articulating general frameworks for conceptualizing legitimacy. Both JL and my neo-Calvinist account are ultimately concerned with the legitimacy of laws, and laws restrict liberty. That all laws restrict liberty, to one degree or another,[4] I take to be intuitive and commonsensical, though admittedly some philosophers would disagree.[5]

Why is it important to recognize that liberty restrictions are at stake in theorizing legitimacy, even at the relatively abstract level in which I'm interested? It is because every liberty restriction is a possible site of paternalism. Since all measures deemed legitimate—whether by JL or neo-Calvinist lights—restrict liberty, they always run the risk of being paternalistic if inappropriately justified.

Before moving on, let me reiterate that real-world coercion is at stake in JL. Despite its appeal to hypothetical persons and procedures, it is real-world persons who stand to be coerced.

Rawls, for instance, says that the precise point of public reason is that we may "come freely to accept . . . the ideals, principles, and standards that specify our basic rights and liberties, and effectively guide and moderate the political power *to which we are subject*."[6] Furthermore, many of the examples JLs consider, such as abortion or same-sex marriage or tax-funded social programs, reflect their interest in actual laws.[7] Consequently, we do need to recognize the coercion of which JL speaks as a possible site of paternalism, for it is countenancing actual coercion.

The second element of paternalism is the particular kind of justification it involves. Paternalistic restrictions appeal to the interests of those whose liberty is being restricted. As Gutmann and Thompson write, "The paternalist claim is not that the conduct is morally wrong but that it is harmful to the citizen herself. . . . Legal paternalism is the restriction by law of an individual's liberty for his or her own good."[8] This difference between claiming that conduct is "morally wrong" and claiming that it is "harmful to the citizen herself," is crucial. Or as I will say, there is a crucial difference between liberty restrictions for the sake of justice and restrictions for people's good. Paternalistic justifications resemble the latter.

A third element is bound up with paternalism's interest-based, rather than justice-based, justification. Who is to represent affected parties' interests? Who is to decide what is good for them? The presence or absence of paternalism turns on this question. For paternalism doesn't merely consist in restricting someone's liberty for their good. After all, if affected parties, representing their own interests, endorse laws as being in their own interests, those laws hardly seem paternalistic. Rather, paternalism occurs when laws are justified in the name of affected parties' interests and it is someone other than the affected parties themselves who judge their interests. Paternalism involves a substitution of judgments. As such, it runs counter to an influential Millian line of thought that presumes that individuals are the most effective advocates of their own interests.[9]

So far I have simply set the context. I have not yet argued that JL does, in fact, involve paternalism. I have established that JL is a possible site of paternalism, and I hope the question of whether or not JL involves paternalism now seems intelligible and pertinent.

Having already seen that liberty restrictions are at stake in JL, whether or not JL is, in fact, guilty of paternalism will depend on the last two factors just covered. Are JL's justifications of coercion based on people's self-interest? And who represents affected parties' interests? Given JL's hypothetical proceduralism, the answer to the latter should already be relatively clear, so I will make only a couple further points regarding the relationship between JL's hypothetical persons and the actual persons they represent. But first I consider the former question at greater length, for it is less obvious whether JL's justification is, in fact, one of self-interest.

JL AND PATERNALISM

The Questions JLs Ask

What I first want to consider is the type of justification JL offers for coercion. If I am right that JL involves paternalism, I need to show that JL restricts liberty for people's good, that the self-interest of affected parties is fundamental to JL's justification.

What does the JL thought experiment require of us? It requires us to consider a proposal from citizens' diverse vantage points. We are to ask whether or not, from the perspective of each, a proposal is acceptable. More specifically, we are to evaluate a proposal from each perspective primarily in regard to the effect that the proposal will have on someone's reasonable self-interest. Consider first Rawls, and then Scanlon. Scanlon's contractualism is relevantly similar to JL for the sake of the following analysis. Scanlon's core idea is this: "An act is wrong if its performance under the circumstances would be disallowed by any set of principles for the general regulation of behavior that no one could reasonably reject as a basis for informed, unforced, general agreement."[10] To be fair to Rawls, we should bear in mind that, as noted earlier, he requires unanimity only on a framework for deliberation rather than on reasons for coercion, but I think the following argument is nonetheless unaffected.

Rawls identifies his contractors as having two fundamental powers.[11] While one is a sense of justice, the other is the capacity for forming, revising, and pursuing a conception of the good. Wanting to pursue their respective conceptions of the good, citizens desire as large a bundle of social primary goods as they can. Rawls describes primary goods as goods that it is only rational for every person, no matter their comprehensive view, to want for themselves.[12]

When these contractors go to choose a conception of justice and principle of legitimacy to govern society,[13] note carefully the question Rawls puts to them. Essentially they are to ask themselves this: what social arrangements are most prudent for me to choose as I seek to protect and further my interests? The contractors' sense of justice is built into the conditions under which the agreement is made, in features of the original position such as the veil of ignorance and the veto given to each individual. It is operative, too, in their willingness to comply once the agreement is made and the veil lifted. In the negotiation of the agreement, though, it is their sense of self-interest that is primary. It is with reference to self-benefit that they evaluate proposals.[14]

What Rawls' contractors are not called to do is seek others' well-being or equality of condition. Asking them to do so would, on Rawls' view, be asking for too much altruism. As a Christian, Timothy Jackson objects to Rawlsian justice on the grounds that it does not direct people toward agape love.[15] But we cannot reasonably require self-sacrificial love of others, Rawls would say, even if it is virtuous. G. A. Cohen criticizes Rawls for his narrow focus on institutions, and believes an egalitarian ethos ought to regulate our individual choices and not just society's basic structure.[16] But Rawls thinks that the justness of the basic structure—society's major political and economic institutions—is all that a political conception of justice can ask. Such a conception is intentionally thin, as required in contexts of reasonable pluralism.

In Scanlon's hypothetical scenario, the question put to the parties is somewhat different from that put to Rawls' contractors. As Estlund summarizes it, Scanlon's participants ask themselves the question, "'Do I find this proposal acceptable in light of my interests (reasonably weighted) and in light of my aim of coming to agreement with others similarly motivated?'"[17] There is not a maximization injunction here, as there is for Rawls' contractors.

But what their questions importantly share is a focus on contractors' self-interest. Scanlon's hypothetical contractors are, as Estlund puts it, "*reasonably self-serving*."[18] It isn't that Scanlon's contractors don't care whether others are fairly treated. But, as on Rawls' account, their concern is channeled into the construction of the procedure itself. For instance, "perfect information, communication, and motivation"[19] are imputed to each contractor, idealizations designed to mitigate possible unfairness. Chiefly, fairness is ensured by giving every participant a veto and in requiring unanimity. Given these conditions, the question put to Scanlon's contractors then becomes a basically straightforward question of self-interest. "Do I find this proposal acceptable in light of my interests . . . ?" In fact, Scanlon's participants are expressly instructed not to consider whether a proposal places undue burdens on others. They are "motivated only by what [Scanlon] calls 'personal reasons,'" and "[t]hey reject proposals only if they themselves have personal reasons against them."[20]

Scanlon's participants are not asked the "*primary question*" of what they owe to one another.[21] Rather they are asked what Estlund calls the "*subsidiary question*," which, for Scanlon, is the aforementioned question of whether a proposal is acceptable in light of participants' self-interest. This distinction between a theory's primary question and subsidiary question is important. The primary question is the topic ultimately at issue, while the subsidiary question helps guide us to philosophical considerations relevant to explaining the topic. The subsidiary must differ from the primary. Otherwise it fallaciously begs the question. The procedure cannot simply assume what it is meant to explain. Consequently, the hypothetical contractors cannot "employ a concept of, specifically, right or justice or whichever primary question the contractualist account is addressing."[22] The subsidiary question also shapes the way in which answers to the primary question are justified. Given Scanlon's subsidiary question, then, his account involves interest-based justifications.

We can generalize these points to all JLs. All JL accounts put to their hypothetical contractors an essentially self-interested question, not one of human interests generally, nor of justice, morality, or the common good. Does a proposal maximize an individual's bundle of primary goods? Is it acceptable given an individual's interests? Is it rejectable given these interests? Put generally, does it serve an individual's reasonable self-interest? These are the questions JLs ask.

At this juncture, let me try to preempt a couple of ways I can imagine readers might misinterpret my argument. It might seem that my concern is with Rawls' characterization of persons as having a fundamental interest in forming, revising, and pursuing a conception of the good. It is not. Similarly, it might seem that I am charging JL with paternalism of the following sort. JL is paternalistic, so the charge would go, by covertly imposing on others a comprehensive view based on individual autonomy. But many people do not so valorize the power to form and revise a conception of the good, perhaps believing this power should be subordinated to religious orthodoxy or for some other reason. So prioritizing this power preferences one comprehensive view over others, and, as such, is paternalistic. However, neither is this my objection.

Rather, my concern is that, in virtue of the question JLs put to their hypothetical contractors, JLs end up restricting liberty for people's good and not for the sake of justice. The operative contrast is not between a comprehensive view that prioritizes individual autonomy and ones that do not. Instead, borrowing the aforementioned distinction from Gutmann and Thompson, it is the contrast between restricting an individual's liberty "for his or her own good" and doing so because it "is morally wrong." In other words, the operative distinction is between coercion for people's good and coercion for the sake of justice. I take it there is a real and important difference between the two. I suggest that JL falls on the wrong side of this divide, and does so by putting to its contractors a question of self-interest.

Admittedly, distinguishing how human interests factor into an interest-based justification from how they factor into a justice-based one is tricky. Later in this chapter, though, in replying to an objection, I offer at least a provisional way of understanding the difference.

Who Answers JLs' Questions?

Given that liberty restrictions are at stake and that JL justifies these restrictions on the basis of affected parties' interests, JL's possible paternalism depends upon who represents these interests. If it is the affected parties themselves, paternalism is not an issue. But if it is someone else, paternalism results. So who answers JLs questions and thereby represents these interests? Alas, the answer is clear: it is not actual persons, not the persons who stand to be coerced. Rather, it is their hypothetical counterparts, in the idealized procedure, who answer the questions.

While this paternalism is unusual in that affected parties' views are replaced by those of hypothetical persons, and not by those of other real persons, we mustn't lose sight of this plain fact: JL does not allow real-world persons to speak for themselves. They are structurally barred from representing their own interests, yet they stand to be coerced in the name of their own interests. If not paternalistic, how else to describe coercion so justified? Even if JLs have good reason to desist from asking actual persons, concerned that real-world persons not infrequently accept unjust social arrangements, that in no wise diminishes the fact that the JL framework does prevent real-world persons from representing their own interests.

I acknowledge that JLs intend to respect citizens' right to represent their own interests. For instance, theorizing legitimacy in terms of multi-perspectival acceptability, as JL does, is meant to reflect real-world diversity.[23] The metaphor of contract would be otiose if the contractors weren't meant to represent diversity, nor would each contractor need a veto. In fact, JL requires this intention since real and hypothetical persons must be meaningfully linked if the latter are to plausibly provide a way in which the former can see themselves as the authors of the norms that govern them.

However, JLs' intention to represent real-world diversity is thwarted by the various ways in which they idealize the hypothetical contractors. To review, they are idealized cognitively (having information and reasoning skills many or all real persons lack), materially (having resources and political voice many real persons lack), and morally (having character real persons lack). As a result of these idealizations, a further difference arises: hypothetical contractors hold a narrower range of views on issues such as redistribution and abortion[24] than do their real-world counterparts. Earlier I noted this disparity in chapter 3 when presenting the example of the Bakuninist.

Also, note carefully that, as far as paternalism is concerned, it doesn't matter that the judgments of idealized persons would presumably be far superior to those of flesh-and-blood persons. For citizens' right to speak for themselves politically is one they retain even when they exercise it imperfectly. I take it that such a right—an autonomy right that survives errors in judgment—is bedrock to liberalism. Indeed, not only JLs, but also neo-Calvinists, understand individuals' right to lead their own lives as a right that survives all sorts of mistakes, no matter whether these judgments are due to epistemic, moral, economic, or other factors. But it is just such a right that JL denies to real-world persons.

In concluding this subsection, let me stress that paternalism is a structural problem within the JL framework. It does not merely arise in practically applying JL. As biased, fallible, imperfect persons, there are, to be sure, epistemic problems we face in applying JL. Can I as a flesh-and-blood philosopher applying JL really do an adequate job of representing what others think who occupy viewpoints not my own? But the paternalism I'm exposing is implicated in the framework itself. The very categories in terms of which JL understands legitimacy necessitate that laws be justified on paternalistic grounds: a question of self-interest, and a substitution of hypothetical persons' judgment for that of real persons, while the latter stand to have their liberty restricted. Putting the point another way, even if all the epistemic challenges that attend applying JL were overcome—that is, even if we as flesh-and-blood philosophers could perfectly predict the outcome of JL's hypothetical procedure—JL would still engender paternalism by framing legitimate coercion in terms of these categories.

OBJECTIONS AND REPLIES

Since I only mean to sketch this third worry, I will do little more here than identify some of the more important objections my charge of paternalism likely provokes.

Objection: My argument rests on a misrepresentation of JL. While I emphasize the role of self-interest in JL's procedure, the results of the procedure may be legally enforced only because they are principles of justice. Rawls would not say that a law is legitimate because it advances persons' self-interest, but because it advances justice as fairness. It would be paternalistic for Rawls to say, "Law x is legitimate since your hypothetical counterparts see x as being in your reasonable self-interest." But what he instead would say is, "Though it may not be in your self-interest, law x is legitimate because it is a requirement of treating others fairly and justly."[25]

Reply: Although this is what JLs would say and would want to say, it is not what their reasoning amounts to. To the contrary, given its structure, their reasoning reduces to the very sort of interest-based justifications they would disavow. They want to say that x is a legitimate law because x is a requirement of justice. But why is x a requirement of justice? Precisely because x serves everyone's reasonable self-interest, so goes the JL answer. Granted, the qualifying adjective "reasonable" is important here, as it represents fairness-related limits on how individuals may permissibly pursue their self-interest. Nevertheless, while it qualifies the appeal to self-interest at the heart of JL, it does not eradicate it. JL reasoning may force us to prune our self-interested claims, yet it also appeals to self-interest to explicate what justice requires.

Objection: Far from being paternalistic, JL operates with a very thin theory of the good, as thin a theory as possible, and certainly thinner than those of its rivals in political theory.

Reply: As I said above, my concern is not that JLs are imposing a conception of the good on the rest of us. Rather, it is that JL structurally deprives real-world persons of the right to represent their own interests when legitimacy is, *ex hypothesi*, said to be a function of what is in real-world persons' reasonable self-interest. My concern is not that JLs smuggle in an autonomy-emphasizing comprehensive view. It is that they explicitly substitute hypothetical contractors' views for those of real-world persons.

Objection: While JL's hypothetical contractors may be asked a question of self-interest, they are denied access to their conceptions of the good as a way of answering it. If paternalism involves imposing one's conception of the good on others, then how can an agreement made under such constraints possibly have paternalistic implications?

Reply: It is true that Rawlsian JLs deny contractors access to their comprehensive views (though other JLs, like Gaus, do not). However, there are different forms of paternalism. For instance, religious intolerance and seatbelt laws, while both paternalistic, surely represent distinct forms of paternalism. Nor should we assume there are only two forms. Thus, while JL might prevent one kind, it nonetheless involves another. On the one hand, it prevents legal establishment of an official religion or ideology. On the other hand, for those laws it does allow—even if they restrict liberty far less than religious intolerance—it nevertheless justifies them on paternalistic grounds given the very terms in which it conceptualizes legitimacy. Paternalism occurs just so long as real-world persons are kept from speaking for themselves, even if the hypothetical persons who speak for them do not rely on a particular conception of the good in doing so.

Objection: JL may involve a certain amount of paternalism, but any theory of legitimacy will be paternalistic to some degree. To its credit, JL is minimally paternalistic.

Reply: Since talk of human interests will play a role in any account of basic rights—a point I grant and discuss in later chapters, drawing on Charles Taylor—it may appear that any theory of legitimacy will be paternalistic. But this appearance is misleading, for it conceals the different ways that human interests factor into interest-based as opposed to justice-based justifications of laws. The difference seems to be as follows. In a justice-based justification, human interests are viewed in a universal and objective sense. Conversely, in an interest-based justification they are viewed severally and subjectively, as JL views them given its backdrop assumption of reasonable pluralism. But it is just this sort of difference which the present objection conceals.[26]

Throughout, I have assumed that there is an intuitive and significant difference between coercion for people's good and coercion for the sake of justice. My suggestion that JL involves paternalism turns on this distinction. It may be, then, that JL should only be considered guilty of paternalism insofar as we can make principled, philosophical sense of the distinction between interest-based and justice-based justifications. This is a difficult task I admittedly leave incomplete, even after speaking further to this issue in chapter 10. But so long as there is a significant difference between interest-based and justice-based justifications—however we spell this difference out—JL seems to fall on the wrong side of this divide.

CONCLUSION AND TRANSITION

I now draw both the present chapter and part I to a close.

I began part I by setting up the particular question related to political legitimacy in which I am interested. The question is: what is the right framework for thinking about political legitimacy? In other words, what are the most apt categories for philosophically conceptualizing and evaluating the legitimacy of legal coercion? I seek to understand legitimacy as a context-transcendent normative standard, should such an understanding be available. In chapter 2, I argued that while JL often advertises itself as merely an account of democratic legitimacy, it cannot help but apply beyond democratic contexts given its characterization of persons as free-and-equal. Thus, JL represents one candidate answer to my guiding question, as a general framework for theorizing legitimacy *qua* context-transcendent standard. Chapter 2 also explained JL's core principle and its hypothetical proceduralism. According to JL's principle of public justification, legitimate legal coercion is based on reasons that all reasonable persons can accept. Its proceduralism helps explicate this principle.

Then in each of chapters 3 to 5, I have focused on a different CC we hold concerning real-world legitimacy. In chapter 3, it was our CC that much real-world legal coercion is legitimate, even amidst disagreement. In chapter 4, it was our CC that real-world legitimacy depends upon protecting certain basic rights. In chapter 5, it has been our CC that paternalism is illegitimate. These are CCs that JLs themselves hold, and, as such, my arguments have leveraged them for an internal critique of JL. JL leads to consequences that are unacceptable as they conflict with these CCs.

My critique here in chapter 5 has been that paternalism is structurally involved in JL, in virtue of the very conceptual categories JL uses to frame legitimacy. One is reasonable self-interest, and while appealing to human interests, per se, isn't problematic, the particular way in which JL does so—severally and subjectively—is. Another of JL's categories is idealized persons, and still another is self-legislation, which motivates JL's proceduralism and constructivism. Although I did not focus on the concept of self-legislation here, I will do so in chapter 10 when explaining how neo-Calvinist legitimacy avoids the paternalism JL engenders.

My goal in this project is to provide a better philosophical framework for understanding the conditions that make for political legitimacy, and I am taking as desideratum for such a framework the ability to make sense of our real-world CCs concerning legitimacy. In part I, I have tried to show that JL runs afoul of three of these CCs. Not only do my arguments undermine JL by exposing tensions internal to the theory. They also mean JL struggles to meet our desideratum for a philosophical account of legitimacy. Consequently, we have good reason to turn away from JL in search of an alternative. My suggestion is that we look to the neo-Calvinist tradition of social thought. So to neo-Calvinist thought I now turn.

NOTES

1. Wolterstorff envisions us, in applying JL, confronted by someone who disagrees with us. JL would then have us "make the patronizing judgment that the cause of your disagreement is that you are suffering from some epistemic impairment or deficiency and that, if you were freed from that impairment or deficiency, you would agree with [us] that [our] reason is a good and decisive reason for the proposal." This, too, is a valid concern. It is just not my concern, at least not at present. See Wolterstorff, *Understanding Liberal Democracy*, 90–91.
2. Lister, "Public Justification and the Limits of State Action," 156.
3. See chapter 3 in Quong, *Liberalism without Perfection*.
4. Taylor explains that laws vary in their moral significance. See Charles Taylor, "What's Wrong with Negative Liberty," in *Philosophy and the Human Sciences: Philosophical Papers 2*, by Charles Taylor (New York: Cambridge University Press, 1985), 211–29.
5. Pettit, for instance, on his neo-republican, nondomination account of freedom, might say that some laws enable freedom rather than restrict it. See Pettit, *Republicanism*.
6. Also Macedo cites this passage from Rawls approvingly. (Rawls, *Political Liberalism*, 222 [emphasis mine]; Macedo, "In Defense of Liberal Public Reason," 16–17.)
7. E.g., Lister, "Public Justification and the Limits of State Action"; Lister, *Public Reason and Political Community*.
8. Gutmann and Thompson, 261.
9. John Stuart Mill, "Considerations on Representative Government," in *On Liberty and Other Essays*, ed. John Gray, Oxford World's Classics (New York: Oxford University Press, 1991), 244–45.
10. T. M. Scanlon, *What We Owe to Each Other* (Cambridge, MA: Harvard University Press, 1998), 153.
11. Rawls, *Political Liberalism*, 48–54.
12. These goods include such things as income and wealth; rights, powers, and opportunities; and the social bases of self-respect. (Ibid., 178–87; Freeman, *Rawls*, 152, 478.)
13. Rawls, *Justice as Fairness*, 94–97.
14. Estlund summarizes the question put to Rawlsian contractors as, "Which of the proposals before me will maximize my bundle of primary goods?" (Estlund, *Democratic Authority*, 246.)
15. Timothy P. Jackson, "To Bedlam and Part Way Back: John Rawls and Christian Justice," *Faith and Philosophy* 8, no. 4 (October 1991): 423–47.

16. G. A. Cohen, *Rescuing Justice and Equality* (Cambridge, MA: Harvard University Press, 2008), 68–80.

17. David M. Estlund, *Democratic Authority*, 246. I closely follow Estlund throughout this discussion of Scanlon.

18. Ibid., 245.

19. Ibid., 250.

20. Ibid., 248.

21. Ibid., 246.

22. Estlund lucidly explains this point as follows:

> There is a good reason for having the parties address a subsidiary question rather than the primary question. If they were to address the primary question, then the whole theoretical apparatus would fail to have any heuristic value in explicating the nature of justice or right. The primary question would remain for the contractors themselves to fathom, and their own choices would be philosophically moot. Thus, it is an important feature of contractualism that the parties in the initial situation address a subsidiary question and not the primary question of justice or morality.
>
> The conclusion to draw is that the contractors we posit cannot themselves be applying the standard of right or justice at all, contractualist or noncontractualist." (Ibid., 247–48.)

23. Lister characterizes JL in terms of "multi-perspectival acceptability." (Lister, *Public Reason and Political Community*, 9.)

24. Eberle, *Religious Conviction in Liberal Politics*, 218–19.

25. I thank Will Kymlicka especially for interaction on this points.

26. Similarly, it might objected, as one reviewer thought, that the paternalism I allege is "simply a feature of theorizing itself." However, since the kind of paternalism I've highlighted results from certain identifiable features of the JL framework, I believe it is avoidable if we approach legitimacy differently. The neo-Calvinist theory I develop is meant as such an alternative. Again, the problem isn't simply talk of human interests, but the way in which human interests are incorporated into JL. Neo-Calvinist theory will incorporate them differently.

Part II

The Neo-Calvinist Alternative

Chapter Six

An Outline of Neo-Calvinist Thought

Having examined three unacceptable consequences of JL, I now turn to neo-Calvinism for a hopefully superior approach to legitimacy. The present chapter will not yet lay out exactly what this alternative neo-Calvinist account is. That more specific task is taken up chapter 7. Rather, the present chapter is meant simply to introduce neo-Calvinism as a distinct, intellectually and historically significant tradition of social thought. This chapter especially targets secular readers who may be unfamiliar with the theorists and ideas of neo-Calvinism, though I suspect there will be many Christian readers who are unfamiliar with neo-Calvinism also.

To this end, I begin with some preliminary remarks. I explain who constitutes the tradition and what broadly distinguishes Reformed social thought, of which neo-Calvinism is a variant, from other schools of Christian social thought. The bulk of the chapter then introduces neo-Calvinism in terms of nine tenets that frame neo-Calvinist thought in general. These are convictions that would frame a neo-Calvinist analysis of any issue within political philosophy. This includes a neo-Calvinist approach to legitimacy, such as my own, as will become evident in chapter 7.

I suspect that the following tenets will prompt many questions from secular readers straightaway. Not least among these may be broad questions such as those of God's existence or the divine inspiration of Christian scripture. Questions specific to particular tenets will also presumably arise. For instance, can the *Imago Dei* discussed under tenet 1, or the theological framework of creation/fall/redemption discussed under tenet 2, be reconciled with contemporary evolutionary theory?

In this discussion, I will be setting aside many questions, both broad and narrow. My purpose in this chapter is not to deal with all objections that might be brought against neo-Calvinism and the tenets that frame it. There certainly is not room to do so, nor is doing so my focus.

Instead, in what follows, neo-Calvinism will largely be presented in its own terms. The reader hitherto unfamiliar with the tradition will be presented with an array of conceptual resources that can, at a later stage, be brought to bear on the issue of political legitimacy. My present goal is simply to lay out a conceptual repertoire altogether different from that on which JL draws, in the hope of developing an approach to legitimacy that will succeed where JL fails. The neo-Calvinist conceptual repertoire is presented in this chapter, while its reconstruction into a theory of legitimacy awaits us in the next chapter.

For starters, it is helpful to understand that neo-Calvinism is a species of a larger Reformed tradition that is different historically from other schools of Christian social thought. Reformed Christians were but one group that broke away from the Roman Catholic Church during the Protestant Reformation, Lutherans and Anabaptists being the others.[1] Among the ways these three groups differed from one another, as well as from Roman Catholics, was in their political theologies. In particular, they differed in their views on the proper relationship between church and state.

Broadly speaking, Reformed social thought diverges from the others as follows.[2] There is a historic strand of Catholic[3] political theology that makes the state subject to the church. While historically not all Catholic thinkers have affirmed this position, and while Vatican II represents an official departure from it, many influential Catholic figures have indeed affirmed it. Among them are Pope Boniface VIII (ca. 1235–1303), papal apologists such as Honorius Augustodunensis (ca. 1080/90-ca. 1156), Giles of Rome (ca. 1243–1316), and James of Viterbo (d. 1308), as well as the influential founder of the Salamanca School, Francisco de Vitoria (ca. 1483–1546).[4] This view of church-state relations was brazenly asserted by Pope Gregory VII (ca. 1030–1085) in his power struggles with King Philip I of France and King Henry IV of Germany,[5] and it claims for the church a "plenitude of power" over matters both spiritual and temporal. Furthermore, although Vatican II represents an official departure from this view and its earlier historical formulations, the principle of subsidiarity now endorsed by the Catholic church arguably retains the view in modified form. As neo-Calvinist authors have pointed out, subsidiarity still understands society as a hierarchy with the church positioned above the state and other "mediating structures."[6]

Conversely, Lutheran political theology has tended to make the church subject to the state. Where the head of state subscribed to orthodox Lutheran theology, Martin Luther allowed the head of state to simultaneously serve as head of the church. Over time, Luther increasingly turned "to the civil magistrate to reform and oversee external church order."[7] This was Luther's "Erastian turn."[8]

The Anabaptist tradition takes a third approach to political theology: the church withdrawn from the state. According to the early Anabaptist leader Peter Ridemann, "no Christian is a ruler and no ruler is a Christian."[9] On the Anabaptist view, Christians ought withdraw from political office, political affairs, and civil society at large. The Anabaptists of the Reformation are the forerunners of modern-day Mennonite, Amish, and Hutterite communities. In sum, their political theology consisted in the twin convictions of "separation and apolitical pacifism."[10]

Over and against its Catholic, Lutheran, and Anabaptist counterparts, according to a the Reformed view church and state are both rightful authorities within their respective domains. Unlike Anabaptists, Reformed thinkers viewed civil government positively, regarding it as an institution divinely ordained for certain tasks. It does not lie outside God's perfect grace, but is an expression of it. And unlike Catholics and Lutherans, Reformed thinkers subordinated neither church nor state to the authority of the other. On balance, "Unlike Luther and the Anabaptists"—or Catholics, we might add—"the Reformed leaders sought a greater balance and cooperation between church and government."[11] Now simply saying that church and state are rightful authorities within their respective domains leaves unanswered the crucial question of what these respective domains are. Neo-Calvinism's answer to this question will soon become clear. For now, though, it is vital to note that enforcement of particular religious beliefs, Christian or otherwise, is not among the tasks for which God has ordained the state.

So as a first way of understanding neo-Calvinism, it should be understood as a representation of the Reformed view that recognizes church and state both as rightful authorities within their respective domains. As such, it is far removed from the Catholic, Lutheran, and Anabaptist alternatives listed above. It is only one version of Reformed social thought, though, its distinctiveness revealed not so much in this general Reformed view as in the nine tenets that follow shortly.

Who composes the neo-Calvinist tradition?

The first figure I consider is John Calvin (1509–1564). While it may seem anachronistic to include him in the tradition, his inclusion is appropriate because later thinkers now known as neo-Calvinists consciously build upon many of Calvin's ideas. His social thought is most clearly on display in Book 4, chapter 20 of his *Institutes of the Christian Religion*.[12] In drawing on Calvin, I focus primarily on this chapter. To be sure, neo-Calvinists do not endorse all of Calvin's ideas or political practice (including his support of the notorious decision by Geneva city council to execute Servetus for heresy). Nonetheless, he is foundational to the tradition.

The next historical figure on whom I focus is Abraham Kuyper (1837–1920), who I expect will be less familiar to readers. Indeed, I focus on Kuyper more than any other single figure in the tradition. Calvin is an essential forerunner to neo-Calvinism, but it is Kuyper who first formulates many of neo-Calvinism's distinctive ideas and who stands at its headwaters. This Dutch polymath was a major religious, political, and intellectual figure in the Netherlands around the turn of the twentieth century. Among other achievements, Kuyper founded the Free University of Amsterdam in 1880, where he worked as a theology professor, and served as Prime Minister of the Netherlands from 1901 to 1905.[13] In 1898 he gave an important series of lectures at Princeton University on the relationship between Christianity and, among other things, politics. These lectures sound many of neo-Calvinism's distinctive themes. When discussing Kuyper's ideas, I draw mainly from this series of lectures.[14]

Herman Dooyeweerd (1894–1977) is the next historical figure I engage who made significant contributions to neo-Calvinist thought, though I do not engage him as extensively as some readers might expect. So let me explain. Dooyeweerd served as a long-time law professor at the Free University founded by Kuyper, and his work represents the most influential, sophisticated, and extensive development of Kuyper's seminal neo-Calvinist ideas. I draw on Dooyeweerd's texts, *The Christian Idea of the State* and *A Christian Theory of Social Institutions*,[15] as well as on secondary Dooyeweerdian scholarship[16] and "critical retrievals" of Dooyeweerd's ideas.[17]

But to help explain why I don't engage Dooyeweerd more than I do, let me distinguish neo-Calvinism from its close cousin, Reformational philosophy. Doing so will also help sharpen our focus on neo-Calvinism. Despite the affinities between the two, I take them to differ in that neo-Calvinism is primarily a social theory—as reflected in the preoccupations of its founder, Kuyper—while Reformational philosophy, though not indifferent to social issues, represents a broader, systematic philosophy. Also, Kuyper, with his notion of sphere sovereignty as a fundamental principle of social organization, is undoubtedly the founding father of neo-Calvinism. By contrast, it is Dooyeweerd and Dirk H. T. Vollenhoven,[18] who both elaborated basic Kuyperian ideas into sophisticated, technical philosophies, who are more accurately the founders of Reformational philosophy. Due to differences such as these, then, I identify Dooyeweerd, in the first instance, with Reformational philosophy rather than with neo-Calvinism. So I draw on Dooyeweerd, because he has exerted considerable influence on generations of neo-Calvinists and contributed significantly to neo-Calvinist thought. Yet I don't draw on him as much as I would were my interest, in fact, Reformational philosophy as opposed to the social theory of neo-Calvinism.

A relatively unbroken chain of contributors to neo-Calvinist thought runs from Kuyper down to the present. Kuyper and Dooyeweerd represent the tradition's founding generation, and have been followed by, in order: H. Evan Runner (1916–2002), pivotal in transplanting neo-Calvinist thought to North America; then Calvin Seerveld (b. 1930), Bernard Zylstra

(1934–1986), and Hendrik Hart (b. 1935)[19]; and, at present, Lambert Zuidervaart, Jonathan Chaplin, Bob Goudzwaard, David T. Koyzis, and James Skillen. Note that some of these figures, such as Hart and Zuidervaart, have ontological and philosophical concerns that go well beyond social theory. Thus, they are more accurately identified with Reformational philosophy than neo-Calvinism, but have a very close affinity with the latter.

I also periodically draw on the political philosophy of Wolterstorff,[20] though he is not a typical neo-Calvinist, if one at all. He shares with neo-Calvinists Reformed background and influences, and on occasion he expressly endorses certain neo-Calvinist ideas or exhibits sympathy for them.[21] He is much more influenced by analytic political philosophy than other neo-Calvinists, though, engaging at length the likes of Rawls, Dworkin, Raz, and Richard Rorty.[22] It is for this very reason that Wolterstorff is a uniquely fruitful interlocutor for me—as my project also seeks to bring secular and Christian social thought into dialogue—even while he fails to typify the specific neo-Calvinist version of Christian social thought on which I focus.

These, then, will serve as my chief sources for neo-Calvinist thought: Calvin, Kuyper, and Dooyeweerd, as well as Chaplin, Goudzwaard, Koyzis, Skillen, and, as appropriate, Wolterstorff.[23] It may be objected there are other theorists worth considering. Undoubtedly there are,[24] and I will periodically draw on others. But those I've listed here suffice to provide an outline of the tradition, a tradition is that unique and rich. I now turn to the tenets that constitute this outline.

TENET 1: ALL PEOPLE ARE EQUAL, NATURALLY FREE, AND ULTIMATELY ACCOUNTABLE ONLY TO GOD.

Foundational to neo-Calvinist thought is the conviction that all people are equal. This is a commonplace of political discourse today. Yet neo-Calvinism's grounding of this equality, and its understanding of the meaning and implications of this equality, are noteworthy.

Neo-Calvinists share the conviction that every human being is made in the image of God. This is the doctrine of the *Imago Dei*.

> So God created man in his own image,
> in the image of God he created him;
> male and female he created them.[25]

All are made in God's image, regardless of gender or any other social marker, no matter a person's stage of development or decline, or level of ability or disability. At the same time, the scope of the *Imago Dei* does not extend to non-human animals[26] (though this hardly means that nonhuman animals are undeserving of respect).

Neo-Calvinists will largely find themselves in agreement with other Christians on these general points. But beyond these general points, neo-Calvinism starts to take on a distinctive character in its particular understanding of the meaning and implications of this universal divine image.

To begin, neo-Calvinists view the *Imago Dei* as directly having not just theological and moral, but political, implications. It is the foundation of humans' political equality. Kuyper's worldview involves "the recognition in each person of human worth, which is his by virtue of his creation after the divine likeness, and therefore of the equality of all men before God *and his magistrate*."[27]

Political equality in what sense, though? Even if we narrow the focus from moral and theological equality to political equality, the specific meaning of political equality remains contested, as evidenced by the earlier discussion in chapter 3 of the multi-interpretability of political concepts.

One meaning of neo-Calvinist equality is that no one has a natural right to politically rule over others. "No man has the right to rule over another man," Kuyper writes. "As man I stand free and bold, over against the most powerful of my fellowmen."[28] That no one rules by natural right is a point neo-Calvinists share with Locke. *Pace* Aristotle, there are no natural slaves. *Pace* Sir Robert Filmer's "divine right of kings" view, none has a right to kingship based on patriarchal lineage. *Pace* Plato and Mill, none is entitled to more political power than others based on intelligence or aptitude. As Kuyper again says, all persons "stand as equals before God, and consequently equal as man to man," and whether citizens are "men or women, rich or poor, weak or strong, dull or talented" is politically irrelevant.[29]

Another meaning is to be found in contemporary neo-Calvinists' tendency to talk of the sovereignty of individuals alongside the sovereignty of institutions. As we shall see in tenets to come, one of the most valuable and distinctive contributions of neo-Calvinist social thought is its emphasis on institutions as opposed to individuals. As articulated by Kuyper, the idea of sphere sovereignty concentrates on the institutions operative in society's various spheres of activity. Yet neo-Calvinists after Kuyper, including present-day neo-Calvinists, routinely speak of sphere sovereignty as applying to individuals as well as institutions. The state must uphold the sovereignty of both "other societal structures and of individual persons."[30]

What this application of sphere sovereignty to individuals indicates is that, for neo-Calvinists, political equality means there are matters over which individuals have a right to exercise autonomous control, and that the scope of these matters is equal for all individuals. This individual sovereignty is understood by Koyzis in terms of authority. While individual freedom and authority are commonly conceived as being in tension with one another, Koyzis conceives of individual freedom as itself a form of authority. Freedom consists in the authority to make certain decisions regarding oneself.

Political equality, so conceived, is equality of authority to make such decisions.

And in what does Koyzis ground this individual authority? The *Imago Dei*. "We shall begin by arguing that *authority is resident in an office given by God to humanity at the creation, viz., the image of God.*"[31] Moreover, this "grant of authority" entailed by the divine image "is what makes for the uniqueness of human beings in God's world."[32] Human beings have been granted this authority, this freedom, but not nonhuman animals. In sum, the *Imago Dei* grounds a uniquely human political equality that consists in individuals possessing an equal authority to exercise sovereignty over themselves. The state must not only ensure that others respect an individual's sphere of sovereignty, but also must itself respect it.

In addition to what it is, it is important to understand what this freedom is not. Individuals' freedom is not self-generated, neither is their dignity nor their freedom even inherent in the sense of being entirely nondependent on external factors. For their dignity results from the imprint of the divine image, and their sovereignty over themselves is, as Koyzis says above, a "grant" from God. Viewing God as ultimately sovereign, neo-Calvinists repudiate the Kantian ideal of the self-legislating agent, a point to which I return later. Neo-Calvinist freedom is not a freedom from God, but a freedom under God. It is not a freedom from divine norms, but under divine norms.

The correlate of this conception of individual freedom is that individuals do not only possess political freedom and equality at the behest of the state. Neo-Calvinists here can be seen as building upon Calvin's principle of the immediacy of the believer's relationship to God. The state does not mediate between individuals and God, and neither does the church. It is for states to recognize and protect the authority granted individuals by the divine image, but it does not grant the authority itself. The directness of God's rule over our lives is a prominent neo-Calvinist theme.[33] It not only has implications for social spheres and for institutions—God exercises "direct rule over all of life"[34]—but for individuals in their equality and freedom. From this angle, neo-Calvinist political equality consists in all individuals standing directly before God, equally accountable for their stewardship of the authority granted them.

One might ask whether the *Imago Dei* corresponds to any particular part of human beings. But neo-Calvinism tends not to identify the divine image with any particular capacity, such as rationality or spirituality, nor is it much concerned with debates over whether the divine image entails substance dualism or with the ontological categories such debates presuppose.[35] Instead, neo-Calvinists are more likely to affirm that "God's image encompasses the total person and the entirety of humanity."[36] It encompasses both mind and body, and affects all aspects of humans' lives. This includes the political, where it grounds political equality and freedom and, in turn, all that these values imply for social life.

TENET 2: ALL ARE COMMISSIONED TO SOCIOCULTURAL DEVELOPMENT, RENEWAL, AND TRANSFORMATION.

Even more distinctive of neo-Calvinists than their understanding of the *Imago Dei* is their understanding of the meaning and importance of the verse that immediately follows it in Genesis 1: "So God created man in his own image.... And God blessed them. And God said to them, 'Be fruitful and multiple and fill the earth and subdue it, and have dominion over the fish of the sea and over the birds of the heavens and over every living thing that moves on the earth.'"[37] Neo-Calvinists call this the "cultural mandate," and, as suggested by the name, they view it as a perennial call to human beings to develop culture as God intended it, and to reform or transform it where it has gone awry.[38]

The first thing to note is that the mandate is given to all people. People of all times and places in human history are called to develop culture and societies. Of course, relatively few people throughout history have had access to the Hebrew Bible, and even of those who have relatively few have interpreted Genesis 1 in quite this way. (I leave aside, though, an exegetical discussion of neo-Calvinism's idiosyncratic interpretation.) Nonetheless, natural human proclivities toward, and the ubiquity of, culture-making and social organization are evidence that the mandate applies to all. Humans are intuitively aware of the mandate, even if not consciously aware of it or, worse, ignore it.

Similarly, all are called to steward the natural world, whether explicitly commanded to do so or not, and are held responsible for doing so. Environmentalism is part of the cultural mandate and a growing emphasis in recent neo-Calvinist thought. Environmental stewardship for neo-Calvinists, though, is not simply a case of leaving nature untouched, as one strain of environmentalism would have it. Rather, as stewards, humans are to be actively involved in caring for and directing the natural world. On reflection, it is apparent that environmental quietism is misguided. Being in the world, and a part of the world interdependent with other parts, all we humans do inevitably affects the natural world. This includes even our pretensions to withdraw from it. Neo-Calvinist Paul Marshall, with Lela Gilbert, discusses the example of Yellowstone National Park, where officials had to choose whether to reduce an elk population that was overeating the park's vegetation. They comment, "We don't have the option to make no choices, to leave 'nature' alone. We have only the option to make wise choices."[39] So the call to steward the natural world goes out to all of us, as does the cultural mandate of which it is a part.

What is it that the mandate calls us to? For it is not a matter of imperialistically populating and dominating the planet.

Rather, it is a call to develop cultures and societies and thereby open up the rich, variegated possibilities inherent in creation. We are to "govern and develop God's creation," doing so with "justice and loving care."[40] God has endowed humans with an array of capabilities, which, "properly developed," are "part of our calling"[41] and enable us to realize our creative potential. Part of the mandate is certainly to form families and raise children. But the cultural mandate is immeasurably broader. It encompasses agriculture, architecture, commerce, politics, law, philosophy, religion, music, the visual arts, the dramatic arts, athletics, education, science, technology, and more. Any positive contribution to culture and society, any constructive use of skill, and any opening up of creation's manifold possibilities for beauty, truth, and goodness, is, as neo-Calvinists see it, a response to the cultural mandate.

The positive call to sociocultural development is the primary meaning of this second tenet. Why also mention "renewal" and "transformation"?

In short, it is because of the fall. The cultural mandate must be understood in terms of the creation/fall/redemption paradigm that serves as the theological backdrop for neo-Calvinist social thought. In broad strokes, according to this paradigm the entire cosmos was originally good; but humanity rebelled against God in the fall, which produced brokenness in both the human and nonhuman world; yet God has retained something of creation's original goodness, and now, through Jesus as well as his people, God is working to redeem his originally good creation en route to its full restoration in the eschaton. Rebellion against God is the essence of what theologically, is called "sin." The brokenness caused by sin first severs humans' relationship with God, but its effects extend to humans' relationships with one another, to human institutions, even to the nonhuman world. Humans develop culture, but they also deform culture. They implement unjust laws and repeal just laws. Intolerant and oppressive ideologies take hold. Businesses pollute indiscriminately, while individual consumers don't care. In such circumstances, the call to develop culture takes the form of renewing or transforming broken cultural and social practices.[42]

Renewal is what's called for in most cases of broken cultural and social practices, or what neo-Calvinist Al Wolters labels "reformation." Neo-Calvinists' emphasis on renewal results from their deep belief that creation retains something of its original goodness despite the fall. Reformation "recognizes that no given societal order is *absolutely* corrupt; thus, no societal order need ever be totally condemned."[43] Renewal redeems in a literal sense: it retains the good that's been preserved, corrects the bad, and recovers the good that's been lost while also opening up new goods not yet realized. Neo-

Calvinists distinguish between structure and direction. Structure refers to something's ontological "constitution," what makes [something] the thing or entity that it is, its "nature."[44] Conversely, believing everything to be fundamentally in service to God or in opposition to God, direction refers to this fundamental spiritual-normative orientation. Even misdirected institutions, though, retain their structure. In such cases renewal consists in reorienting cultural and social practices, and in realigning institutions with the norms appropriate to their distinctive structures.

But neo-Calvinism also calls for transformation when needed. "Transformation" is what Zuidervaart calls for in cases of "societal evil," which he characterizes as the "institutions" and "patterns that seem most oppressive and trends that seem most destructive to interconnected flourishing."[45] He relates these grave evils to "systemic deformation[s]," "large-scale historical structure[s] and process[es] that permeate[] a society, equally affect[ing] conflicting groups within that society, and fundamentally violat[ing] human life before the face of God."[46] Even where the cultural mandate calls for transformation, though, the goal remains essentially the same: to develop culture and society, realizing the potential of the skills we've been given, and unfolding the world's manifold possibilities for good. To this we are all, and always, called.

TENET 3: THERE IS SOMETHING UNNATURAL ABOUT COERCIVE POLITICAL POWER. IT IS ONLY NECESSARY "BY REASON OF SIN."

The creation/fall/redemption paradigm raises this question: was civil government part of the original design plan? Many institutions clearly were, such as marriage and family. Others clearly were not, such as chattel slavery or prostitution. What about government? Does government, with the coercive force it involves, represent development or deformation? This is a disputed issue in neo-Calvinist thought.[47] Yet I will pick up one clear line of thought from Kuyper, and will take it as representative of the tradition as a whole. This issue shouldn't be thought interesting only as a theological, or in-house, dispute for neo-Calvinists, because our answer to this question will inform our understanding of the purpose of government, which in turn will inform our understanding of the limits of legitimate law. And the historicity or non-historicity of the fall aside, imagining what a world without human wrongdoing would look like is an exercise in which any theorist can engage, and it is instructive to do so.

Would government exist in a world without sin? Kuyper answers, "For, indeed, without sin there would have been neither magistrate nor state-order. . . . Neither bar of justice nor police nor army nor navy is conceivable in a world without sin; and thus every rule and ordinance and law would drop away, even as all control and assertion of the power of the magistrate would disappear, were life to develop itself, normally and without hindrance, from its own organic impulse."[48] In doing so he adopts a longstanding strand of Augustinian thought. Augustine had written centuries earlier, "The first cause of servitude, therefore, is sin, by which man was placed under man in a condition of bondage . . . servitude itself is ordained as a punishment by that law which enjoins the preservation of the order of nature, and forbids its disruption. For if nothing had been done in violation of that law, there would have been no need for the discipline of servitude as a punishment."[49] Skillen comments, "Augustine believed that God created humans to rule over other creatures, not over one another. He saw ruling and subjection to rulers as a consequence of sin."[50] In short, Kuyper memorably says that God has instituted government "by reason of sin."[51]

The historical roots may be Augustinian and the phrase Kuyperian, but this sentiment is found elsewhere in the neo-Calvinist tradition as well. For example, Dooyeweerd writes, "This typical founding-function of the state reveals immediately that it is a divine institution for the sake of sin."[52] Similarly, through "temporal societal structures," Dooyeweerd says, "God's general or common grace arrests the dry-rot caused by sin."[53] Wolterstorff also seemingly shares this sentiment, as he is "struck by the fact" that St. Paul teaches that "the God-given task of government is deterring, punishing, and protecting against wrongdoing."[54] It is human wrongdoing that occasions the coercive state. Wolterstorff himself holds much the same view.[55]

On this Kuyperian line of thought, humans are naturally social, just not naturally political. Various forms of social organization would exist in a world without sin, but would do so without need of a coercive state to oversee them. In this regard Skillen and Rockne McCarthy contrast Kuyper with the thinking of Thomas Aquinas. "The state is not 'natural' in an inherent teleological way as it is for Thomists."[56] Since, for Thomists as for Aristotelians, humans by nature only flourish in politically integrated societies, political institutions would exist with or without sin. But it is a mistake to think that "the power of the sword is . . . not an essential part of the structure of the state," as Dooyeweerd says.[57] This Kuyperian line of thought "stands radically opposed" to the "individualist conceptions of human nature," and holds that "Human beings are social creatures."[58] So there is nothing unnatural about social organization, only something unnatural about coercive political power.

I said above that the question of prelapsarian government is disputed, and contemporary neo-Calvinists do seem to take a rather different view of things. One difference is that they are more likely to highlight roles played by government other than its retributive role. For instance, throughout *We Answer to Another*, Koyzis is very sensitive to government's coordinating function. Governments not only fight crime, but issue currency, establish central banks, maintain public infrastructure, redistribute taxes, negotiate international treaties, and so on. Even when Koyzis critically discusses views in which coordination is central, I read his critical comments as an acknowledgment of truth in these views.[59] Chaplin diverges from the Kuyperian line of thought when he says Dooyeweerd is wrong to view the state as essentially coercive. "The problem" is that "if the state as such is necessary on account of sin, then all its activities must be explicable essentially as ways of dealing, juridically, with the consequences of sin. However, by no means all these activities, as he at some length describes them, can be explained in this way. This is especially the case with those that fall within the requirements of the 'public interest' (such as transport infrastructure, financial coordination, etc.)."[60] The essential structure of the state should not be thought of as the "'territorial monopoly of coercive power,'" Chaplin suggests, *pace* Dooyeweerd.[61] Skillen diverges in yet another way, with his ebullient call to civic engagement. He seems to call for much more than the negative task of punishing wrongdoing.[62] Positively, the cultural mandate involves the "building of political communities."[63]

However, these may not reflect real points of disagreement between Kuyper and recent neo-Calvinists as much as simply different points of emphasis. For these contemporary neo-Calvinists can still grant that much legal coercion is necessary only "by reason of sin," even if not all. Criminal law, policing, the judicial system, the prison system, the military—all these are plausibly due only to sin. So perhaps coercive political power isn't unnatural through and through, but there is something unnatural about it. Moreover, it is something commonly thought to lie at, or near, the heart of government, namely, protecting citizens from suffering wrongdoing at the hands of others. Put another way, neo-Calvinists can agree that legal coercion is necessary "by reason of sin," just not only "by reason of sin." Finally, even if there is disagreement over the question of prelapsarian government, there is no denying the necessity of government to combat sin in the postlapsarian world in which we live. In present circumstances, government largely, though not exclusively, exists to redress injustice caused by sin and to thereby promote human comity and well-being.

We are all aware of the need for cultural renewal and transformation, even if we disagree over what practices and institutions need renovation, and, in part, this will involve building better political communities. But what guidelines are we to follow in renovating society? More fundamentally, what makes possible the renovation of society? The next tenet explains.

TENET 4: SOCIOCULTURAL RENEWAL OUGHT BE PURSUED ALONG THE LINES OF DIVINE CREATION ORDER.

Traditionally, divine order is a *sine qua non* of neo-Calvinist thought. This motif is inherited from Calvin, as is neo-Calvinists' understanding of this order in terms of divine ordinances rather than natural law. This notion of order is much broader than that which figures into the teleological argument of natural theology, an argument which infers an intelligent designer from order apparent in aspects of the nonhuman world. The neo-Calvinist notion is closer to that of divine sovereignty, God's providential control over both the human and nonhuman world. More idiosyncratically, the neo-Calvinist notion also goes beyond God's design of human beings—that is, his design of their physiology and his making them in the divine image—to include the social practices and institutions that humans implement over time.[64] The divine order includes a blueprint, as it were, of social institutions as God intends them to be. So when we undertake sociocultural renewal, it is this underlying order that both represents the guidelines we ought follow and makes possible institutions' renewal.

After Kuyper and Dooyeweerd, though, subsequent neo-Calvinists have gradually moved away from an understanding of divine order as invariant structural principles for social institutions. Zuidervaart cites ontological, epistemological, and theological reasons for doing so.[65] For instance, Chaplin relocates structure from institutions to individuals, suggesting that "the normative design of social structures emerges out of a *normative conception of the human person*."[66] In general, recent neo-Calvinists talk less of "creational ordinances" than of norms, the latter being more flexible and contextual. Zuidervaart characterizes them as "dynamic and historically unfolding guidelines," and Goudzwaard, rather modestly, as "pointers."[67]

Nonetheless, the injunction to renew culture along creation order lines still represents the tradition taken as a whole. For one, the tradition's founders, Kuyper as well as Dooyeweerd and Vollenhoven, very much thought in terms of an enduring creation order that remains the basis for present social institutions. Two, while certain neo-Calvinists, such as Zuidervaart, have shifted considerably from the earlier view of creation order, others, such as Koyzis, more or less retain the earlier view. And three, even those who have shifted still agree with certain salient aspects of the earlier view. For instance, they would affirm institutional pluralism as a positive opening up of God-given possibilities, distinct norms as relevant to society's varied institutions, and shaping institutions according to these norms as a response to a divine calling.

While neo-Calvinists read Genesis 1 as teaching that God creates both the natural world and humans' social world, God creates them in different ways. In the former he does so immediately, but mediately in the latter, through historical human actors. "[God] put the planets in their orbits, makes the seasons come and go at the proper time, makes seeds grow and animals reproduce, but entrusts to mankind the tasks of making tools, doing justice, producing art, and pursuing scholarship. In other words, God's rule of law is immediate in the nonhuman realm but mediate in culture and society."[68] The claim that God creates humans' social institutions might seem inscrutable, and a denial of the obvious empirical fact that humans have established and maintain their social practices. So, again, in what sense does God create human culture? He does so in the same way we say a "human sovereign" creates when he "gives orders to his subordinates" and his subordinates carry them out.[69] For example, it is not incorrect to say that Nebuchadnezzar II built the hanging gardens of Babylon,[70] or that Eisenhower built America's interstate highway system. Of course, these are colloquial expressions, and God's relationship to his creation is much more intimate than Nebuchadnezzar's or Eisenhower's relationship to theirs. But the analogy at least approximates neo-Calvinists' idea.

What this means is that although God creates humans' social world, neo-Calvinists still can, and do, recognize a vital role for human agency in the development of social institutions. Neo-Calvinists follow Dooyeweerd in characterizing this role as "positivization." Positivization is the process whereby humans give determinate shape to a general, creation order principle, in particular socio-historical circumstances. It is the "'giving of form'" to a norm, requiring "'the normative power of human judgment.'"[71] The legal code of a particular society is an example.[72] "The stone obeys necessarily, the eagle responds instinctively, but a person must exercise personal responsibility: we are called to positivize the norm, to apply it to specific situations in our lives."[73] Humans, then, do create norms and institutions in a real, though not exclusive, sense.

What God has done in creation vis-à-vis the social world is imbue the world with possibilities, but possibilities that remain "latent" until realized by human agents. This potential must be "unlocked and actualized in human history and civilization."[74] Koyzis describes "governments, political parties and legal systems" as "real creational possibilities,"[75] and neo-Calvinists would certainly say the same of other paradigmatic social institutions such as families, churches, universities, and labor unions. Put another way, there are "creational underpinnings"[76] to all cultural and social practices, but God only provides the underpinnings and it is up to us to realize their potential.

The notion of responsibility Wolters mentioned above is important: while God creates both the natural and social worlds, the nonhuman world invariably follows natural laws whereas humans exercise choice in following the divine norms for culture and society. It is up to humans whether they choose to follow or flaunt these norms. We ought follow divine creation order in the design and renewal of our social institutions, though we may wrongly do otherwise. To mark the difference between the physical and nonphysical aspects of human life—i.e., the biological and physiological, as opposed to the moral, spiritual, social, aesthetic, rational, etc.—Dooyeweerd differentiates between "laws" and "norms." The creation principles governing our physical aspects are laws, and cannot be ignored, unlike the norms that govern our nonphysical aspects.

Related to positivization, neo-Calvinists emphasize the historical nature of the process whereby humans implement, refine, and transform social norms. Positivization occurs through a process of historical unfolding. Given the role of human agency in this process, cultures and institutions are different in different times and places. In the same way humans can be said to positivize norms—shaping them while not originating them—humans also unfold creational possibilities. The world's good possibilities wouldn't be realized unless humans took an active and dynamic role in realizing them in the course of history.

One aspect of the historical unfolding process is of particular interest to us, namely, societal differentiation. Another term coined by Dooyeweerd, differentiation refers to the process whereby unitary societies internally disperse social functions across multiple institutions.[77] The Roman *familia* of antiquity and the guilds of medieval societies represent relatively undifferentiated communities,[78] in contrast to modern Western societies and their separation of church and state, independent press, academic freedom in universities, free market economy, bills of rights, and so on. This process, too, is an unfolding of creational possibilities for society. It is not haphazard, nor mere historical accident, but rooted in creation order.

In sum, this order provides both the conditions that make social institutions possible and the norms we ought follow as we fashion, operate, and reform them.

Now holding that society ought be renewed along creation order lines raises this question: can only believers access this creation order? What about nonbelievers? The answer: the cultural mandate is for all, and so, too, is the creation order. It is accessible to all, as explained in the next tenet.

TENET 5: THE NORMATIVE CREATION PRINCIPLES FOR CULTURE AND SOCIETY ARE ACCESSIBLE TO ALL (NOT ONLY BELIEVERS).

Since the creation order is divine, it might be thought accessible only to believers. Not so.

To understand why neo-Calvinists think this, we need first to recognize that creational principles are inescapable. Recalling the earlier distinction between structure and direction, the idea is that structure remains even when misdirected. For any thing to exist as a thing is to exhibit, in some or another way, the characteristics that, according to creation order, make a thing the kind of thing that it is. Similarly, vestiges of the relevant institutional norms can be found even in corrupt institutions. For instance, "The state's task of doing justice, even when it is perverted in some fashion, tends inevitably to reassert itself."[79] The creation/fall/redemption paradigm helps make sense of this point. God does not save the world by starting over from scratch. Rather, salvation is a reclamation and extension of creation's original goodness. Redemption presumes that the object of redemption survives its bondage. It is creation's structure that survives, and redemption consists in its re-direction.

The key idea here is common grace. "Common grace means simply that God in his mercy preserves his creation against the full consequences of sin even amidst the unbelief of mankind."[80] God does not utterly reject creation after the fall, but preserves its structure, allowing humans freedom to choose its direction. He does this by common grace. Following in the Reformed tradition, neo-Calvinists distinguish this from "special" grace. Whereas the latter is that uniquely enjoyed by believers, resulting in their eternal salvation, the former is enjoyed by all people, believers and nonbelievers alike, in their day-to-day lives. It is manifest in mundane matters such as God's causing the sun to rise and crops to grow.[81] Kuyper describes what lies outside special grace as "the wide and free domain of 'common grace.'"[82]

Common grace is key because it links the persistence of the creation order and the accessibility of this order to all. Both are gifts of common grace. Both are accessible to believers and nonbelievers alike. Thus, believers and nonbelievers alike can discern, at least in broad strokes, the creation norms to follow in renovating culture and society.

An example of unbelievers discerning creational norms is the moral law of which all are aware in their conscience. This example is drawn not so much from neo-Calvinism as from Reformed thought more broadly, in which it figures prominently. The classic scriptural text is Romans 2:14–15: "For when Gentiles, who do not have the law, by nature do what the law requires, they are a law to themselves, even though they do not have the law. They show that the work of the law is written on their hearts, while their conscience also bears witness, and their conflicting thoughts accuse or even excuse them."[83] This idea is incorporated into the Westminster Confession of Faith (WCF) article 2.1, which says that God created humans "having the law of God written in their hearts."[84] The Westminster Shorter Catechism characterizes the moral law as the Golden Rule—to do as you would be done by—some version of which is purportedly present in all religions.[85] Calvin characterizes the moral law simply as the demands of "equity," which refers generally to conduct in accord with fairness and probity.[86] Being general in nature, the moral law is accessible to all. Or to put it in neo-Calvinist parlance, the moral law is part of the creation order.

Neo-Calvinists indicate multiple ways in which both believers and nonbelievers access creation norms. Intuiting them is perhaps the primary way. As we will see shortly, according to creation order society's various institutions are distinct and irreducible. Accordingly, in our "pretheoretical experience," Koyzis says, "we have no difficulty distinguishing between a country club and a marriage, a family and a telephone company, a university and a political party, even if we might not be able to account immediately for these differences theoretically."[87] "[E]veryone intuitively understands the difference between marriage and family and the role of husband and father respectively in each."[88] Similarly, Wolters observes that, "Educators . . . develop an intuitive sense for the distinctive structure of a school; if school board members try to run it like a business, they recognize that violence is being done to the nature of an educational institution. They are attuned"—naturally, intuitively—"to its normative structure, to the law that holds for it."[89] The cases given by Koyzis and Wolters are but examples. We can expect to intuit the structures and norms of other institutions in a similar manner.

Creation order is also accessible through historical reflection. This methodological point is emphasized by Dooyeweerd. Social philosophy must take seriously the relevant sociological data, including the history of institutions and their variable forms. "On the basis of thoughtful observation of a number of cultures over a long period of time, it is possible, in some manner, to discern the norms underlying their specific usages."[90] That is, from specific social practices and institutions in history, we can glean enduring general norms and institutional structural principles. One implication of this call to careful historical analysis is that, unlike intuition, this means of accessing creation order is not easily practiced by all. While equally available to believers and nonbelievers, it requires systematic and informed study. Dooyeweerd would say such study is a part of the social theorist's task. The present point, though, is simply that, by historical reflection, creation order can be accessed by anyone regardless of their religious persuasion.

Neo-Calvinists urge their co-religionists to learn from nonbelievers. From the perspective of believers, this might be viewed as a third way—in addition to intuition and historical reflection—of accessing creation order. Their urgings are also another reflection of the belief that creation order is accessible to both believers and nonbelievers. Neo-Calvinists Richard J. Mouw and Sander Griffioen stress this point. They write, "The recognition of directional plurality"—i.e., religious pluralism—"can help us to see the ways in which we can gain new insights from our involvement in a broad-ranging interaction with diverse points of view, even when we consider that diversity to be grounded in idolatrous intellectual projects."[91] Zuidervaart contends that philosophical anthropologists, secular as well as religious, ought "respect . . .

the findings of contemporary science,"[92] and he critiques Dooyeweerd's epistemology for implying, against Dooyeweerd's own intentions, that only believers have genuine knowledge.[93] All this, too, is a result of common grace.[94] Learning from nonbelievers would not be possible were the creation order only accessible to believers.

But what about disagreement? Doesn't it indicate that creation order isn't universally accessible after all? As the fact of reasonable pluralism points out, disagreement is endemic in free societies, especially regarding morality and religion, and this observation might be thought to falsify this tenet of neo-Calvinism.

If I may answer on neo-Calvinists' behalf, no, the sheer fact of disagreement doesn't show that creation order is inaccessible, or accessible only to some. Rather, it shows simply that some aspects of this order can be difficult to discern, due to both internal and external obstacles humans face. Internally, the basic neo-Calvinist explanation, at least of much disagreement regarding religion and morality, is sin. Since humanity has rebelled against God, our reason is impaired, our apprehension of creation order is clouded, and we often lack the resolve to do what we know we ought do. Externally, economic exigencies, societal prejudices, and political competition are among the factors that can powerfully shape misperceptions of creation order, especially in regards to institutional norms. Correlatively, they are obstacles to overcome if we are to rightly grasp creation order.

Furthermore, it is crucial to note that neo-Calvinists think it illegitimate to use scripture or creed to decide disputes in the public square. It is true Calvin says that scripture "removes the obscurity of the law of nature,"[95] and Kuyper does speak of the "*necessitas S. Scripturae*" that results from the fall.[96] But while scripture is appropriate and required in the church, it is inappropriate in the state, where its use would clearly place the state outside the state's sphere of legitimate authority. Tenet 7 further discusses neo-Calvinism's reasons for church-state separation.

So the creation order is to guide our labors of sociocultural renewal and it is accessible to believers and nonbelievers alike. The next tenet highlights a part of this design that is of particular interest: social pluralism.

TENET 6: SOCIETY IS COMPOSED OF DIFFERENT SPHERES, AND EACH OUGHT BE FREE WITHIN ITS RESPECTIVE DOMAIN.

Divine order, as we have seen, is an all-encompassing idea, covering both the natural and social world. It covers every aspect of life, including our private lives—our friendships, our family relationships, our self-care and self-regarding behaviors, and so on. But of particular interest is what it says about social organization. This brings us to perhaps the single best-known and most important idea of neo-Calvinist thought: sphere sovereignty.

The basic idea of sphere sovereignty is that society is divided into various "spheres," each of which is "sovereign" within its own domain. These spheres cannot be ranked hierarchically, but have equal right to sovereignty within their respective domains. And all this is by divine design, God having designed each to make a unique contribution to human flourishing, each in its own way. Kuyper is more responsible than anyone for this vision. He claims, "In a Calvinistic sense we understand hereby, that the family, the business, science, art, and so forth are all social spheres, which do not owe their existence to the state, and which do not derive the law of their life from the superiority of the state, but obey a high authority within their own bosom."[97] Or as Gordon Spykman summarizes it, "'Each sphere has its own identity, its own unique task, its own God-given prerogatives. On each God has conferred its own peculiar right of existence and reason for existence.'"[98]

Readers might immediately wonder about sphere sovereignty's relationship to the Catholic idea of subsidiarity or to the recent literature on civil society, as there is an obvious affinity between sphere sovereignty and these two. I will not now take the time to explore the differences, however. I refer readers elsewhere[99] and instead remain focused on giving an outline of neo-Calvinism.

The idea goes by various names. Koyzis talks of "pluriformity," Mouw and Griffioen of "associational pluralism," Chaplin of "institutional pluralism," and the term "social pluralism" is also used.[100] But all these are essentially the same concept, that of a society rightly divided into separate spheres of activity, each with its own unique character and authority. In what follows, I will use "sphere sovereignty" most commonly, sometimes interchanging it with "institutional pluralism."

While articulated relatively recently as a theoretical concept, sphere sovereignty is a part and outcome of the historical unfolding of the world's creational possibilities, and of the process of societal differentiation in particular.[101] New social spheres and institutions have opened up as advances have been made in various fields—law and politics, religion, the arts, commerce, science, technology, etc. To ignore sphere sovereignty, then, is to close creational possibilities, stifle creativity, leave uncultivated human skill, and suppress human freedom. Moreover, as a dynamic historical process, there is no reason to think societal differentiation has come to an end. We ought remain open to its ongoing transformative effects.

The typical spheres and institutions neo-Calvinists have in mind are familiar ones. They include the family, business, science, and the arts, as mentioned above by Kuyper.[102] Typical others include the church, state, education, and marriage (as distinct from family). We saw earlier that increasingly neo-Calvinists have recognized individuals as spheres themselves.

Zuidervaart would also bring cultural communities,[103] and seemingly the environment, under the purview of sphere sovereignty as well. Traditionally it has focused on institutions, though, and it is its institutional focus that is distinctive. And it applies to institutions such as those listed in this paragraph.

So far I have presented the basic idea of sphere sovereignty, Kuyperian in shape, but let me briefly note Dooyeweerd's more sophisticated version. Zuidervaart identifies two key differences in their accounts. "First Dooyeweerd argues that sphere sovereignty is not merely a societal principle but a creation-wide principle."[104] Being interested in broader ontological issues, Dooyeweerd theorizes not so much sphere sovereignty as modal sovereignty, a view of the ontological structure of the entire created order. The view posits fundamental, irreducible ways, or modes, in which things can function. Dooyeweerd identifies fifteen such modes: numerical, spatial, kinematic, physical, biotic, psychic, logical, historical, lingual, social, economic, aesthetic, juridical, ethical, and faith.[105] While entities exist simultaneously in multiple modes, each entity has one primary mode, which Dooyeweerd calls its "leading function" and which helps make it the distinctive sort of thing that it is. This includes social institutions: the juridical mode is primary for the state, the economic mode for business, the faith mode for churches, etc. Second, while Dooyeweerd like Kuyper highlights the distinct structure and purposes of society's various institutions, he also emphasizes their interconnectedness. He argues for "'sphere universality' as a correlate to sphere sovereignty."[106] Among the ways they intersect are what Dooyeweerd calls "enkaptic interlacements."[107] He recognizes that, for example, political parties and the state are distinct, yet closely related, institutions, as are labor unions and business. His picture of society is less that of a pie divided into pieces, and more that of a web, with complex interconnections between social actors who function differently in different contexts and with respect to different social actors.

Nonetheless, Dooyeweerd's social philosophy is not fundamentally different from Kuyper's idea of sphere sovereignty. It elaborates it, but does not disagree with it. While his account includes the interconnections between institutions, each institution is still understood in terms of a distinguishing function. Institutions' unique functions ground a right to sovereignty over their own affairs, even as we recognize that institutions simultaneously operate in other modes in which they are not sovereign. For Dooyeweerd as for Kuyper, institutional pluralism is part of creation order, divinely designed. All this also means that for Dooyeweerd, as for Kuyper, no one institution is omni-competent, including the state. In short, Dooyeweerd, like Kuyper before him and neo-Calvinists after him, is an institutional pluralist. Moving forward I will focus on Kuyper's more general notion of sphere sovereignty.

But I don't think what I will say is fundamentally in disagreement with Dooyeweerd's more nuanced picture.

Consider now certain implications and features of sphere sovereignty.

First, as just mentioned, sphere sovereignty means that no single sphere is omni-competent. No sphere can claim to encompass or oversee all the others, and one sphere's sovereignty does not derive from another's. Throughout the Middle Ages, it was the church that claimed omni-competence and trespassed into other spheres. At the time of Kuyper's seminal formulation of the idea, throughout the twentieth century, and up until recently, the state has been thought the greatest threat to other spheres' sovereignty. But new threats are emerging in history, as neo-Calvinists have pointed out. The capitalist economy now poses perhaps the greatest threat. Elaine Storkey writes, "Effectively a new organizing principle has moved into place in the West that acts in the same totalitarian way as statism did in a previous era. . . . It is the principle of consumerism."[108] Goudzwaard has also warned of technology's dominance over other spheres, and I think we might worry about science in a similar vein. No matter the sphere, though, transgressing other spheres is illegitimate.

Second, in light of spheres' distinct functions and purposes, each is governed by distinct norms. Institutions are not free within their spheres to do just whatever they want, but they are sovereign insofar as they follow the distinctive norms relevant to the sphere in which they operate. Examples of such norms include "fidelity, justice, economic stewardship, social courtesy" and "logical consistency,"[109] and it seems these would correspond to the institutions of marriage, government, and business, and to the social and analytic modes, respectively. Zuidervaart suggests "solidarity" as the norm for civil society, and "resourcefulness" for the economy, in addition to also prescribing justice for the state.[110] These are but examples. There will both be norms for other spheres and institutions, and likely other norms for these spheres and institutions, too. The general point is that each sphere has something like its own inner logic.[111] Subsequent neo-Calvinists have not followed Kuyper in using organic language to characterize this inner logic.[112] But they instead think in terms of spheres' distinctive norms.

Fourth, we can also approach sphere sovereignty from the perspective of role differentiation in an individual's life. At one and the same time, individuals can be "spouses, parents, sons and daughters, church members, employees, students, teachers and café patrons."[113] And of course this list could go on. These roles are not reducible to one another, as neither are those institutions and spheres in which these roles are played out reducible to one another. "To be truly human in maturity," Skillen says, "is to be able to experience life as an integral whole even though the wholeness manifests differentiated complexity."[114] In a sense, each individual is a microcosm of society as a whole—integrated, yet differentiated.

Put simply, the upshot of tenet 6 seems to be this: institutions have rights, not just individuals. As mentioned, perhaps the most distinctive contribution of neo-Calvinism is its institutional focus, which counterbalances the fixation on individual rights characteristic of so much Western political theory. Moreover, the institutional rights of neo-Calvinism aren't simply instrumental or pragmatic. They are principled, having more a deontic than utilitarian basis. Sphere sovereignty can be formulated without talk of institutional "rights," but principled institutional rights are a natural way of understanding its normative implications. In a chapter that draws heavily on Kuyper, Wolterstorff affirms our "natural right to get together to establish such social entities as may serve our common purposes."[115] Skillen and McCarthy write, in summarizing Bernard Zylstra's views, "If government's task is to give to each its rightful due, then institutional and associational rights must not be ignored or reduced to individual rights."[116] They will be had by institutions such as "families, schools, trades unions, churches, charitable associations, [and] corporations."[117] In general, sphere sovereignty gives institutions a positive right of autonomy over their internal affairs, and a negative right to freedom from external interference. More specific rights will be spelled out in light of an institution's distinctive character, purpose, norms, and authority structures.

Lastly, we should note that sphere sovereignty is not only about church-state relations, but about social organization more broadly.[118] That said, church-state relations are of particular interest, as a historically and philosophically contested issue and given the religious orientation of neo-Calvinism. Consequently, the next tenet highlights perhaps the single most important implication of institutional pluralism.

TENET 7: THE STATE *OUGHT* BE SEPARATE FROM THE CHURCH (AND OTHER RELIGIOUS INSTITUTIONS).

It might be thought that a religiously-inspired political theory will inevitably collapse church and state. Donald Atwell Zoll, for one, seems to think so, and I assume this will be a worry of many secular readers. But a religious thinker such as Tom Driver shares this worry, too, saying that Christianity can only be reconciled to democracy by giving up its claim to exclusive truth.[119] Tenet 7 should correct this misperception of political theology and assuage these concerns. It explains why, in principle, church and state ought be separate according to neo-Calvinists.

Simply stated, the neo-Calvinist model of church-state relations is this: "The sovereignty of the state and the sovereignty of the church exist side by side, and they mutually limit each other."[120] Representing different spheres, neither church nor state can infringe on the other's sphere. They serve distinct purposes, are mutually irreducible, and their respective authorities are cooriginal. First, from the perspective of the state, the state ought not dominate the church. Civil authority is a limited authority. "[T]he state's authority is limited by the pluriform authorities even within its political jurisdiction, such as the family, the school, the business enterprise, and the labor union"[121]—and by the church as well. The state's unique character and purpose set internal limits to its legitimate authority. At the same time, external limits are set by the spheres of authority of individuals and of other institutions, including that of the church.

But second, it is also true that from the perspective of the church, the church ought not dominate the state. I take it this is the less intuitive claim, given a religious framework. So let me now consider this perspective at greater length. To begin with, for the religious believer, the simplest answer to the question of why separate church and state is just this: God designed them so. Read simplistically, this is the gist of neo-Calvinist sphere sovereignty. This answer might satisfy believers, but there is much more that can be said from a Christian perspective. In fact, several additional arguments for church-state separation can be drawn from neo-Calvinist writings.

Mouw and Griffioen base church-state separation on the hope of the eschaton. This is the culmination of history at which, according to Christian belief, Jesus will return, the truth vindicated, and all the world set right. According to this line of religious thought, Christians ought forswear a geopolitical Christendom now because God's kingdom will only be fully realized—and social institutions only fully subjected to him—in the eschaton. "[I]t is the eschatological vindication of the truth that makes it possible for us to accept pluralism in the here and now."[122]

Koyzis defends church-state separation on the basis of God's respect for human free choice. Explaining why Christians ought to uphold the religious freedom even of those they think religiously misdirected, he writes, "Our desire to protect such religious freedom issues not out of indifference or skepticism toward our own ultimate beliefs but out of recognition that in the present age, in [Lesslie] Newbigin's words, God wills to provide a space and time for people freely to give their allegiance to his kingdom."[123] God does not force people to believe in him, desiring instead that people come to him voluntarily. Who are we, a Christian might think, to give people any less freedom than God himself does?

A similar argument, but one focused more on ecclesiology, is given by Wolterstorff. Since the church is born of the Spirit, rather than of coercion which "is a work of the flesh," the church will insist upon religious freedom.[124] To be the "peculiar kind of community"[125] that it is, the church must insist on both the freedom to join the church's numbers and the freedom not to join. "For, to say it once again, the church is born not of the flesh but of the Spirit."[126]

Still another argument for church-state separation, also based on ecclesiology, distinguishes between the true church and the visible, institutional church. According to Catholicism, the church is a "visible, palpable, and tangible institution," says Kuyper.[127] But he argues this ecclesiology leads to political repression: "with Rome the system of persecution issued from the identification of the visible with the invisible church."[128] By contrast, Kuyper follows Calvin for whom the church is a "mystic organism."[129] Since no church institution is isomorphic with the true church, no church institution should coopt the state presuming to uniquely represent God. Distinguishing the true church from the institutional church is the "solution of the problem."[130]

In addition to these arguments, the long history of church-state separation in broader Reformed thought should also help mollify concerns about a church takeover. According to WCF 23.3, "The civil magistrate may not assume to himself the administration of the Word and sacraments, or the power of the keys of the kingdom of heaven." Heidelberg Catechism 83 explicates the "keys of the kingdom" as "the preaching of the holy gospel" and "Christian discipline toward repentance." The civil magistrate, then, is prohibited from these activities of preaching and church discipline. Effectively it is prohibited from establishing a particular religion. From the other direction, however, WCF 31.5 states, "Synods and councils are to handle, or conclude nothing, but that which is ecclesiastical: and are not to intermeddle with civil affairs which concern the commonwealth, unless by way of humble petition in cases extraordinary; or, by way of advice, for satisfaction of conscience, if they be thereunto required by the civil magistrate." In parallel fashion, the church official tempted to "intermeddle with civil affairs" is prohibited from doing so. Neo-Calvinists are heirs to this legacy and affirm it wholeheartedly.

Having considered their model of church-state relations, neo-Calvinists would also extend this model to the relationship between the state and all religious institutions. Wolterstorff gives a fairness argument for doing so: "What is relevant instead is the commitment of the church to justice. It would be unjust for the state to grant to the church the freedom I described while denying the counterpart freedom to others."[131] Neo-Calvinists certainly share this commitment to justice. Therefore, since Christians insist on freedom for the church, other religious institutions are also entitled to freedom. (That said, as "separation of church and state" is more familiar language, I will customarily speak of "church-state separation" as opposed to "religion-state separation." The former should always be read as meaning the latter, though.)

Before moving ahead, it is worth reiterating that neo-Calvinists see church-state separation as a matter of principle, not merely as a *modus vivendi*. We have seen various reasons why they do. Principally, though, it is because the distinctiveness of the institutions is neither a historical accident or social compromise, but a part of creation order. As a result, they are committed to church-state separation even in Christian majority societies.

Recognizing that church and state are distinctive, having distinct purposes and norms, raises this important question: what is the state's task? The next tenet addresses this question.

TENET 8: THE PURPOSE OF THE STATE IS PUBLIC JUSTICE.

What, then, is the state's purpose?

It is to do what Dooyeweerd calls "public justice." "The state," as Chaplin explains Dooyeweerd's idea, "is charged with establishing, through law, a just balance among numerous legitimate claims thrown up by complex, dynamic modern societies."[132] The state must follow the norm of public justice given its distinctive character as a "juridically qualified, impartial, public-interest" institution.[133] This idea and term have been widely adopted by subsequent neo-Calvinists. God has ordained the state "with a unique task in his world: to do justice to the diversity of individuals and communities in his world."[134] This task, public justice, is "intrinsic to [the state's] makeup."[135]

The mere term "public justice" doesn't say much. What is unique about public justice as a conception of justice, distinct from others?

On this conception, the state's task is essentially one of balancing, of balancing the potentially conflicting demands of different social actors. Public justice is a matter of "adjudicating the respective claims of the various, multiple spheres of society," such that society develops "in a balanced, proportionate fashion."[136] Koyzis describes a "healthy society" as one "in which the various spheres of human activity develop in balanced, proportionate fashion."[137] Accordingly, where the state fails to do public justice, "societies tend to develop in lopsided ways, with one or more of these spheres claiming more than they have a right to."[138] To do public justice, then, is to uphold sphere sovereignty, to ensure that no sphere outweighs others in the sense of trespassing into others' rightful domains.

The social actors whose interests and claims need be weighed, and whose sovereign spheres need protection, include both institutions and individuals. This, too, helps distinguish public justice as a conception of justice. We in the individualistic West are keenly aware of the threat institutions can pose to individuals, but the natural rights of institutions must also be protected from excessive individualism. Koyzis writes:

> Under the influence of various forms of liberalism, the individual may assume too large a place at the expense of other spheres. Communities, including such basic ones as marriage and family, increasingly break down as they are deemed to serve no longer the wants of the aggregating individuals they com-

prise. The rights of individuals come to take priority over the rights of communities, even of institutional churches making unpopular lifestyle demands on their communicants as a condition for continued membership.[139]

In addition to institutions and individuals, we've seen that Zuidervaart includes cultural communities among those social actors whose interests public justice must take into account. Even the environment, too, he seems to suggest, must be included. Neo-Calvinist public justice moves us well beyond a myopic preoccupation with individualism.

Another crucial element of public justice is its concern for the common good. While it weighs and balances the rights claims of all society's varied actors, the boundaries of social actors' respective spheres are determined in light of the common good. Neo-Calvinists do not protect boundaries between spheres simply for boundaries' sake. Wolterstorff has criticized Dooyeweerd for doing so, arguing that it only makes sense to defend spheres' borders and sovereignty if defending them ultimately promotes human flourishing.[140] To respond to this concern, contemporary neo-Calvinists tend to view sphere sovereignty with more flexibility than did Kuyper and Dooyeweerd, and they also emphasize more the public good that sphere sovereignty is ultimately meant to serve. As Skillen says, the distinctive purpose of government isn't only to do public justice, but to *"uphold[] public justice for the common good of all."*[141] In holding that rights claims can only be determined in light of the common good, though, neo-Calvinist is not a form of consequentialism or utilitarianism. For the distinctive, internal integrity of various spheres still needs to be respected, and grounds certain autonomy rights and rights against external interference. But neo-Calvinists' emphasis on the common good is a recognition that claims can only be adjudicated in their social context, and that claims are part of a dynamic socio-historical process.

This conception of justice—balancing the claims of all society's actors in light of the public good—raises the question: how exactly is the state to do this? How is it to weigh these claims and interests? Neo-Calvinists have given specific answers regarding certain issues. Education is an example, with neo-Calvinists generally arguing for educational pluralism, that is, for more equitable support of public and private schools and for greater educational choice.[142] In general, though, neo-Calvinists do not provide very specific criteria for weighing competing rights claims. Public justice "is not so easily summed up in a pithy epigram," but is a matter of "weighing these claims carefully."[143] Neo-Calvinists do not tell us what judgments we should make when doing public justice, but identify the general considerations we should bear in mind when making such judgments. These considerations include: the unique character of a sphere or institution, with its distinctive purpose, norms, and authority structures; the interconnectedness of social actors, and the common good; also social and historical context, given the unfolding nature of norms and the gradual differentiation of society. Public justice can be done by carefully attending to such factors.

Note two last points regarding public justice.

One is that neo-Calvinists are not anti-government intervention. They might give the impression they are by emphasizing the limits of state action and by restricting state action to public justice, but the impression is misleading. We can go as far back as Kuyper, who identified three situations where the state should intervene in other spheres. The first is when different spheres conflict with one another. The second is when vulnerable individuals need protection within a given sphere. The third is when intervention is required to maintain the overall unity of the state.[144] Contemporary neo-Calvinists would go further still, placing greater emphasis on the interconnectedness of spheres and on the common good, viewing boundaries between spheres more flexibly, and recognizing changing historical circumstances in which the state increasingly provides social services. Neo-Calvinism is not opposed to government programs, but simply emphasizes the need for a robust civil society alongside government programs. It is only against government interventions that come at the expense of civil society, not against interventions that complement and support it. No sphere should be passive in pursuing its distinctive purposes, including the state.

My focus has been the state, but public justice also applies to other political institutions, including transnational ones. As public justice is the primary norm for states to follow given their political nature, so, too, is it the primary norm to follow for any political institution. Chaplin explains, "What we call the 'nation-state' is, of course, still the primary example today, but the imperatives of public justice . . . apply also (and should apply more thoroughgoingly) to state-like transnational political authorities such as the United Nations, the European Union, the International Monetary Fund, the World Trade Organisation, as well as to subnational authorities like provincial governments, the Scottish Parliament, the city of Berlin or the town of Soweto."[145] And, in fact, it is not only political institutions that need follow the norm of public justice, though they are particularly responsible for doing so. Individuals, too, must do public justice insofar they play political roles and influence political institutions. Who is responsible for bringing about social change? "'All of us.'"[146]

There is one more tenet of neo-Calvinist social thought to consider. I have tried to present all of the preceding tenets in a logical flow. The final tenet somewhat breaks with this flow. Nonetheless, it seems a fitting place to end for it serves as an umbrella tenet that extends over all the others.

TENET 9: ALL REALITY IS ULTIMATELY ORDERED BY GOD AND ALL HUMAN AUTHORITY ULTIMATELY DELEGATED BY GOD.

The classic scriptural statement of this conviction is found in the opening verses of Romans 13. There, St. Paul writes, "Let every person be subject to the governing authorities. For there is no authority except from God, and those that exist have been instituted by God. Therefore whoever resists the authorities resists what God has appointed, and those who resist will incur judgment."[147] Suggesting that "the claims to *sovereignty* asserted by kings, states, nations, and democratic peoples represent a certain unwillingness to acknowledge the limits that God has placed on all authorities," Koyzis says that human political sovereignty is really only *"supreme political authority within a designated territory*. This is more compatible with a biblical understanding of created limits." He goes on, "Only God is sovereign in the full sense. All human authority derives from God's sovereignty, either immediately or mediately, or both."[148] It is God who ultimately lies behind human governments.

But in what sense?

Neo-Calvinists are obviously all aware of the various mechanisms by which real-world rulers have come to power in human history. For instance, some have come to power through military conquest, some through royal birthright, some through democratic elections. Kuyper himself founded a political party, was elected a member of parliament, and served as prime minister of the Netherlands from 1901 to 1905. And yet Kuyper also shares the conviction of Romans 13 that God ultimately establishes governments.[149] So whatever the claim is taken to mean, it is clearly not a denial of plain historical facts.

Rather, neo-Calvinists would read Romans 13 as teaching that the state "is grounded in the divine order of creation."[150] This is how Chaplin characterizes the state *qua* "creature," that is, as something created. We saw above (tenet 4) that God creates not only the nonhuman world, but also humans' social world, including culture and social institutions. He does so not immediately but mediately, through human agents endowed with skills and capabilities. The state is among the institutions God creates in this way.

The claim that God establishes governments is more about political office than about the particular individuals who occupy this office in various times and places. This is important. I assume most neo-Calvinists would also say that God sovereignly oversees the installation and removal of particular individuals, even wicked and oppressive ones, in some broader theological sense. But that is not the focus of Romans 13, nor the meaning of this ninth tenet. This is important because, at least provisionally, it undercuts the accusation that a good God would not install tyrants of history such as Hitler or Stalin. Romans 13 doesn't teach that he did. It only teaches he established the office they abused. It is also important lest we read Romans 13 as teaching servile acquiescence in the face of whatever cruel or unjust edicts governments might issue. It does not. Instead, it teaches that God has ordained political office to perform a particular task, such that we are obligated to obey governments only insofar as they perform their God-given task. The authority of political office holders who perform this task is legitimate, and that of officials who fail to is illegitimate. This is a neo-Calvinist reading of Romans 13, and how tenet 9 should be understood.

CONCLUSION

In concluding, note that the foregoing tenets merely represent a general outline, and any theory built up out of them will need to take up more specific positions on various issues. As such, particular neo-Calvinist accounts will differ from one another. They will do so even while agreeing on all or most of the foregoing tenets. Just as there are varieties of JL, so will there be varieties of neo-Calvinism.

Specific neo-Calvinist accounts may address one of any number of topics in political philosophy, including legitimacy. In the chapters to follow, that will be my task: to address the issue of legitimacy with conceptual resources drawn from the neo-Calvinist tradition. In particular, I will respond to my guiding question by using these resources to develop a framework for understanding what legitimacy is even about. Remember my question: what is the right framework for thinking about legitimacy, for theorizing and evaluating specific legitimacy-related claims? By developing such a framework in chapter 7, I hope to partially vindicate the suggestion that political theorists turn to neo-Calvinism for an alternative to JL. I will then complete my case for neo-Calvinist legitimacy in part III, where I will argue that neo-Calvinist legitimacy can succeed at precisely those points where JL leads to the unacceptable consequences canvassed in part I. In sum, I have outlined here a tradition that I believe can help us toward a better understanding of legitimacy.

NOTES

1. See Alister McGrath's account in "Chapter 3. The Reformation and Post-Reformation Periods, *c.*1500-*c.*1700." Also, compare James Skillen's account, both for his identification of these three breakaway groups and for his account of the differences between them that is similar to my own. Alister McGrath, *Christian Theology: An Introduction* (Cambridge, MA: Blackwell Publishing Ltd., 1994), 55–74; James W. Skillen, *The Good of Politics: A Biblical, Historical, and Contemporary Introduction* (Grand Rapids, MI: Baker Academic, 2014), 81–100.

2. Readers interested in more rigorous examinations of the history of Christian political thought should consult the works of Oliver O'Donovan and Joan Lockwood O'Donovan, of

Quentin Skinner, and of Brian Tierney. David VanDrunen provides a detailed, though somewhat controversial, history of Reformed political thought in particular. (I thank Mike Wagenman for informing me of the controverted status of VanDrunen's account.) See Oliver O'Donovan and Joan Lockwood O'Donovan, eds., *From Irenaeus to Grotius: A Sourcebook in Christian Political Thought* (Grand Rapids, MI: William B. Eerdmans Publishing Co., 1999); Quentin Skinner, *The Foundations of Modern Political Thought: The Age of Reformation*, vol. 2 (Cambridge: Cambridge University Press, 1978); Brian Tierney, *The Idea of Natural Rights: Studies on Natural Rights, Natural Law and Church Law 1150-1625* (Atlanta, GA: Scholars Press, 1997); David VanDrunen, *Natural Law and the Two Kingdoms* (Grand Rapids, MI: William B. Eerdmans Publishing Co., 2010). The goal of my project is not primarily a detailed history of ideas, but understanding a significant issue of normative political theory, namely, political legitimacy. So while my historical comments here are accurate as generalizations, they admittedly gloss over much detail which I simply leave to others.

3. Throughout, all references to "Catholics" or "Catholic" thought are references to Roman Catholicism as opposed to other varieties of Catholicism.

4. O'Donovan and O'Donovan, *From Irenaeus to Grotius*.

5. Ibid., 240–43.

6. E.g., David T.,Koyzis, *Political Visions and Illusions: A Survey and Christian Critique of Contemporary Ideologies* (Downers Grove, IL: InterVarsity Press, 2003), 218–23. In referencing neo-Calvinists, here, I don't mean they impute to their Catholic contemporaries so crude and simplistic a view as that the church should control the state. I only mean that neo-Calvinist critiques of subsidiarity are one reason for thinking that Catholic thought has yet to completely divest itself of state-subject-to-church thinking. In any case, even if Catholics have now successfully distanced themselves from the view that makes the state subject to the church, this is only a recent historical development. "Union of church and state had been the common pattern since the era of Constantine, and all pontifical declarations of the 19th century rejected separation of church and state as pernicious." Until, and as recent as, Vatican II, "This position was steadfastly maintained despite the fact that the union of church and state had been accepted by the Protestant countries of Europe" ("Roman Catholicism," *Britannica*, accessed June 22, 2013, http://www.britannica.com/EBchecked/topic/507284/Roman-Catholicism).

7. O'Donovan and O'Donovan, *From Irenaeus to Grotius*, 555.

8. Ibid. "Erastianism" is the name historically given to the view that church authority is subject to the state. The name derives from Thomas Erastus (1524–1583), a professor at the University of Heidelberg who, in the midst of Reformation debates over church-state relations, argued that the church did not have the right to excommunicate members.

9. Quoted in John Calvin, *Institutes of the Christian Religion*, ed. John T. McNeill, trans. Ford Lewis Battles (London: S. C. M. Press, 1961), 1487.

10. O'Donovan, and O'Donovan, *From Irenaeus to Grotius*, 632.

11. Skillen, *The Good of Politics*, 92.

12. Calvin, *Institutes*.

13. For a leading current biography of Kuyper, see James D. Bratt, *Abraham Kuyper: Modern Calvinist, Christian Democrat* (Grand Rapids, MI: William B. Eerdmans Publishing Co., 2013).

14. Abraham Kuyper, *Lectures on Calvinism* (Peabody, MA: Hendrickson Publishers, 2008). These lectures were originally delivered as the Stone Foundation Lectures at Princeton University.

15. Herman Dooyeweerd, *The Christian Idea of the State*, trans. John Kraay (Nutley, NJ: The Craig Press, 1968); Herman Dooyeweerd, *A Christian Theory of Social Institutions*, ed. John Witte, Jr., trans. Magnus Verbrugge (La Jolla, CA: The Herman Dooyeweerd Foundation, 1986).

16. E.g., Jonathan Chaplin, *Herman Dooyeweerd: Christian Philosopher of State and Civil Society* (Notre Dame, IN: University of Notre Dame Press, 2011).

17. "Critical retrieval" is how a leading contemporary follower of Dooyeweerd, Lambert Zuidervaart, refers to an approach that builds on Dooyeweerd by appropriating his insights while critically addressing his weaknesses (Lambert Zuidervaart, *Religion, Truth, and Social*

Transformation: Essays in Reformational Philosophy [Montreal and Kingston: McGill-Queen's University Press, 2016], 48–53).

18. For Vollenhoven, see Dirk H. T. Vollenhoven, *Introduction to Philosophy*, ed. John H. Kok and Anthony Tol (Sioux Center, IA: Dordt College Press, 2005).

19. Cf. Lambert Zuidervaart, *Religion, Truth, and Social Transformation*, 20–22.

20. E.g., Nicholas Wolterstorff, *Justice: Rights and Wrongs* (Princeton, NJ: Princeton University Press, 2008); Nicholas Wolterstorff, *Justice in Love* (Grand Rapids, MI: William B. Eerdmans Publishing Co., 2011); Nicholas Wolterstorff, *Understanding Liberal Democracy: Essays in Political Philosophy*, ed. Terence Cuneo (New York: Oxford University Press, 2012).

21. E.g., chapter 14, "Institutional rights as limits on the authority of the state," in Nicholas Wolterstorff, *The Mighty and the Almighty: An Essay in Political Theology* (New York: Cambridge University Press, 2012), 157–71.

22. For these engagements see, respectively, Wolterstorff, *Understanding Liberal Democracy*; Wolterstorff, *Justice*; Wolterstorff, *Understanding Liberal Democracy*, 211–13; ibid., 41–52.

23. Among the main works by these authors on which I rely, and have not already mentioned, are Goudzwaard, *Globalization and the Kingdom of God*; Koyzis, *Political Visions and Illusions*; David T. Koyzis, *We Answer to Another: Authority, Office, and the Image of God* (Eugene, OR: Pickwick Publications, 2014); Skillen, *The Good of Politics*.

24. Johannes Althusius (1563–1638) would be prominent on this list.

25. Genesis 1:27 (*The Holy Bible: English Standard Version* [Crossway Bibles, 2005], 1.).

26. A characteristic of human rights is that "the entire package of human rights is not shared with any nonhuman animal. The entire package is uniquely human" (Wolterstorff, *Understanding Liberal Democracy*, 181.).

27. Kuyper, *Lectures on Calvinism*, 22 (emphasis mine).

28. Ibid., 69.

29. Ibid., 17–18.

30. James W. Skillen, "The Pluralist Philosophy of Herman Dooyeweerd," in *Christianity and Civil Society: Catholic and Neo-Calvinist Perspectives*, ed. Jeanne Heffernan Schindler (Lanham, MD: Rowman and Littlefield Publishers, Inc., 2008), 111. Koyzis, *Political Visions and Illusions*, 233, 237; Jonathan Chaplin, *Faith in the State: The Peril and Promise of Christian Politics* (Toronto, ON: Institute for Christian Studies, 1999), 22; Skillen, *The Good of Politics*, 120, 124.

31. Koyzis, *We Answer to Another*, 21 (emphasis in original).

32. Ibid., 91.

33. Bob Goudzwaard, "Christian Politics in a Global Context," in *Political Order and the Plural Structure of Society*, ed. James W. Skillen and Rockne M. McCarthy, Emory University Studies in Law and Religion (Atlanta, GA: Scholars Press, 1991), 341–42; Al Wolters, *Creation Regained* (Grand Rapids, MI: William B. Eerdmans Publishing Co., 1985), 82–83; Bob Goudzwaard, "Globalization, Regionalization, and Sphere Sovereignty," in *Religion, Pluralism, and Public Life: Abraham Kuyper's Legacy for the Twenty-First Century*, ed. Luis E. Lugo (Grand Rapids, MI: William B. Eerdmans Publishing Co., 2000), 334–35; Skillen, *The Good of Politics*, 126.

34. This phrase is from the editors' introduction to Goudzwaard (Goudzwaard, "Political Order," 335).

35. A Christian philosopher, though not a neo-Calvinist, who has explicated and defended at length the *Imago Dei* against reductive metaphysical naturalism is J. P. Moreland. See J. P. Moreland, *The Recalcitrant Imago Dei: Human Persons and the Failure of Naturalism* (London, UK: SCM Press, 2009).

36. Koyzis, *We Answer to Another*, 136.

37. Genesis 1:27-28 (*The Holy Bible*, 1.).

38. E.g., Koyzis, *We Answer to Another*, 21.

39. Paul A. Marshall and Lela Gilbert, *Heaven Is Not My Home: Learning to Live in God's Creation* (Nashville, TN: Thomas Nelson, 1999), 128.

40. Skillen, *The Good of Politics*, 124.

41. Ibid., 177.

42. I borrow the language of "renewal" and "transformation" from Zuidervaart, who identifies "sociocultural renewal" and "societal transformation" as among the basic themes of Kuyper-inspired thought (Zuidervaart, *Religion, Truth, and Social Transformation*, 14.).

43. Wolters, *Creation Regained*, 77.

44. Ibid., 49, 49–52; Vollenhoven, *Introduction to Philosophy*, 56–62.

45. Zuidervaart, *Religion, Truth, and Social Transformation*, 18.

46. Ibid., 233.

47. E.g., "A central problem arising from [Dooyeweerd's] account . . . is whether the coercive element within [the state] is consistent with its supposed basis in the creation order" (Jonathan Chaplin, "Dooyeweerd's Notion of Societal Structural Principles," *Philosophia Reformata* 60 [1995]: 26).

48. Kuyper goes on to further describe coercive legal power as a "mechanical means of compelling order and of guaranteeing a safe course of life" and as "something against which the deeper aspirations of our nature rebel." (Kuyper, *Lectures on Calvinism*, 67–68.)

49. Augustine, *The City of God against the Pagans*, ed. R. W. Dyson (New York: Cambridge University Press, 1998), 943–44.

50. Skillen, *The Good of Politics*, 97.

51. Kuyper, *Lectures on Calvinism*, 68–69.

52. Dooyeweerd, *The Christian Idea*, 40.

53. Ibid., 4. See tenet 5 below for further discussion of the idea of common grace.

54. Wolterstorff, *The Mighty and the Almighty*, 99.

55. E.g., ibid., 113.

56. James W. Skillen and Rockne M. McCarthy, eds., *Political Order and the Plural Structure of Society*, Emory University Studies in Law and Religion (Atlanta, GA: Scholars Press, 1991), 400.

57. Dooyeweerd, *The Christian Idea*, 41.

58. Skillen and McCarthy, *Political Order*, 400.

59. One example is Koyzis' discussion of Yves René Simon's account. There are several others (Koyzis, *We Answer to Another*, 171–78.).

60. Chaplin, "Dooyeweerd's Notion," 27.

61. Ibid.

62. See chapter 10, "Citizenship as Vocation" (James W. Skillen, *The Good of Politics*, 143–53).

63. Ibid., 143.

64. "'creation' has a scope much broader than common usage gives it." (Wolters, *Creation Regained*, 21.)

65. Zuidervaart, *Religion, Truth, and Social Transformation*, 254.

66. Chaplin, *Herman Dooyeweerd*, 106 (emphasis in original).

67. Zuidervaart, *Religion, Truth, and Social Transformation*, 229. Goudzwaard is quoted by Zuidervaart.

68. Wolters, *Creation Regained*, 14.

69. Ibid.

70. "Hanging Gardens of Babylon," *Britannica*, accessed June 30, 2016, https://www.britannica.com/place/Hanging-Gardens-of-Babylon. Actually, it is historically uncertain whether Nebuchadnezzar II or another ruler oversaw construction of the hanging gardens, but this uncertainty is irrelevant to the philosophical point made in-text.

71. Skillen, "The Pluralist Philosophy of Herman Dooyeweerd," 102.

72. See the glossary at Dooyeweerd, *A Christian Theory of Social Institutions*, 113.

73. Wolters, *Creation Regained*, 15.

74. Ibid., 63.

75. Koyzis, *Political Visions and Illusions*, 186.

76. Ibid.

77. See, for example, Chaplin, *Herman Dooyeweerd*, 79–82.

78. See Lecture VIII, "An Analysis of Undifferentiated Social Organizations," in Herman Dooyeweerd, *A Christian Theory of Social Institutions*, 79–85.

79. Koyzis, *Political Visions and Illusions*, 9.

80. Ibid., 229.
81. Kuyper, *Lectures on Calvinism*, xii.
82. Ibid., 115. For an extended discussion of common grace, see Richard Mouw, *He Shines in All That's Fair: Culture and Common Grace* (Grand Rapids, MI: Eerdmans, 2001).
83. See *The Holy Bible*, 940; Calvin, *Institutes*, 848; VanDrunen, *Natural Law and the Two Kingdoms*, 133.
84. For similar statements from other historic Reformed documents, see the Westminster Larger Catechism 17, 92, and 93, and the Westminster Shorter Catechism 40.
85. WSC 42.
86. See Calvin, *Institutes*, 1504; O'Donovan and O'Donovan, *From Irenaeus to Grotius*, 684.
87. Koyzis, *Political Visions and Illusions*, 209.
88. Ibid., 210.
89. Wolters, *Creation Regained*, 23.
90. Koyzis, *Political Visions and Illusions*, 200.
91. This statement comes from a subsection entitled, "Learning from Idolatries" (Richard J. Mouw and Sander Griffioen, *Pluralisms and Horizons: An Essay in Christian Public Philosophy* [Grand Rapids, MI: William B. Eerdmans Publishing Co., 1993], 107).
92. Zuidervaart, *Religion, Truth, and Social Transformation*, 210.
93. Ibid., 74–75.
94. Koyzis, *Political Visions and Illusions*, 229.
95. VanDrunen, *Natural Law and the Two Kingdoms*, 106.
96. Kuyper, *Lectures on Calvinism*, 47.
97. Ibid., 77.
98. Spykman quoted in Richard Mouw, "Some Reflections on Sphere Sovereignty," in *Religion, Pluralism, and Public Life: Abraham Kuyper's Legacy for the Twenty-First Century*, ed. Luis E. Lugo (Grand Rapids, MI: William B. Eerdmans Publishing Co., 2000), 91.
99. For discussion of subsidiarity and comparison to sphere sovereignty, see Skillen and McCarthy, *Political Order*; Koyzis, *Political Visions and Illusions*, 229–34; Koyzis, *We Answer to Another*, 131–33; Jonathan Chaplin, "Subsidiarity as a Political Norm," in *Political Theory and Christian Vision: Essays in Memory of Bernard Zylstra* (Lanham, MD: University Press of America, Inc., 1994), 81–100. For civil society theory and neo-Calvinism, see Jonathan Chaplin, "Civil Society and The State: A Neo-Calvinist Perspective," in *Christianity and Civil Society: Catholic and Neo-Calvinist Perspectives* (Lanham, MD: Lexington/Rowman & Littlefield, 2008).
100. E.g., Koyzis, *We Answer to Another*, 132, 165; Mouw and Griffioen, *Pluralisms and Horizons*, 13–19; Chaplin, *Faith in the State*, 18.
101. For more on this process see Koyzis, *We Answer to Another*, 102–9.
102. Kuyper, *Lectures on Calvinism*, 77.
103. Zuidervaart, *Religion, Truth, and Social Transformation*, 241–42.
104. Ibid., 225.
105. Chaplin, *Herman Dooyeweerd*, 59.
106. Zuidervaart, *Religion, Truth, and Social Transformation*, 225.
107. Chaplin, *Herman Dooyeweerd*, 67–70.
108. Storkey, "Sphere Sovereignty and the Anglo-American Tradition," in *Religion, Pluralism, and Public Life: Abraham Kuyper's Legacy for the Twenty-First Century*, ed. Luis E. Lugo (Grand Rapids, MI: William B. Eerdmans Publishing Co., 2000), 201; Goudzwaard, *Globalization and the Kingdom of God*, 31.
109. Koyzis, *Political Visions and Illusions*, 198.
110. See chapter 13, "Macrostructures and Societal Principles: An Architechtonic Critique," in Lambert Zuidervaart, *Religion, Truth, and Social Transformation*, 252–76.
111. "For every societal relationship (family, state, church, etc.) God has posited its own law of life; He created in each of them an inner structure, in its own sphere sovereign" (Dooyeweerd, *The Christian Idea*, 24).
112. Kuyper, *Lectures on Calvinism*, 67–68, 81–82, 112.
113. Koyzis, *Political Visions and Illusions*, 210.

114. Skillen, *The Good of Politics*, 157.
115. Wolterstorff, *The Mighty and the Almighty*, 171. See chapter 14, "Institutional rights as limits on the authority of the state."
116. Skillen and McCarthy, *Political Order*, 410.
117. Chaplin, *Faith in the State*, 20.
118. Mouw, "Some Reflections on Sphere Sovereignty," 87–88, 91–92.
119. See the discussion of Zoll's and Driver's concerns at Mouw and Griffioen, *Pluralisms and Horizons*, 3–4.
120. Kuyper, *Lectures on Calvinism*, 92.
121. Koyzis, *We Answer to Another*, 149.
122. Mouw and Griffioen, *Pluralisms and Horizons*, 173.
123. Koyzis, *Political Visions and Illusions*, 204.
124. Wolterstorff, *The Mighty and the Almighty*, 122.
125. Ibid., 125.
126. See Ibid., 124–25.
127. Dooyeweerd says essentially the same. (Kuyper, *Lectures on Calvinism*, 12; Dooyeweerd, *The Christian Idea*, 12–13.)
128. Kuyper, *Lectures on Calvinism*, 89.
129. Ibid., 12.
130. Ibid., 89.
131. Wolterstorff, *The Mighty and the Almighty*, 127.
132. Chaplin, *Herman Dooyeweerd*, 36.
133. Skillen, "The Pluralist Philosophy of Herman Dooyeweerd," 109.
134. Koyzis, *Political Visions and Illusions*, 249.
135. Ibid.
136. Ibid., 265.
137. Ibid., 253.
138. Ibid.
139. Ibid.
140. Wolterstorff, *Until Justice and Peace Embrace* (Grand Rapids, MI: William B. Eerdmans Publishing Co., 1983).
141. Skillen, *The Good of Politics*, 170.
142. E.g., McCarthy, Skillen, and Harper, *Disestablishment a Second Time*.
143. Koyzis, *Political Visions and Illusions*, 265.
144. Kuyper, *Lectures on Calvinism*, 83.
145. Chaplin, *Faith in the State*, 17.
146. Zuidervaart, *Religion, Truth, and Social Transformation*, 379 n35.
147. Romans 13:1–2. (*The Holy Bible*, 948.)
148. Koyzis, *We Answer to Another*, 145.
149. Kuyper, *Lectures on Calvinism*, 68.
150. Chaplin, *Faith in the State*, 14.

Chapter Seven

A Neo-Calvinist Theory of Legitimacy

So what might a neo-Calvinist account of legitimacy look like?

As I say, there is no one answer to this question. A variety of legitimacy accounts may be reconstructed out of the tenets outlined in the previous chapter. The account I outline in the present chapter, then, is not intended to be the definitive account of neo-Calvinist legitimacy. But it is one which, I believe, represents some of the best insights of the tradition and helps us make sense of our convictions about real-world legitimacy. For simplicity's sake I will henceforth speak of my account as if it were the neo-Calvinist account, but remember it is only one possibility among others.

The core insight of neo-Calvinist legitimacy is that legitimacy is about preventing basic wrongs. As per tenet 3, legal coercion is necessary "by reason of sin." Whereas the core principle of JL is its principle of public justification, this is its neo-Calvinist counterpart.

In explicating this central insight, my neo-Calvinist theory of legitimacy advances three ideas. Of the three, the first two are especially important. First, legitimacy-conditional wrongs are violations of natural rights, whether natural rights of individuals or institutions. Second, legitimacy-conditional wrongs are tied to basic human flourishing. Third, these basic rights and wrongs represent an exogenous normative standard. Other neo-Calvinist theories of legitimacy may have different points of emphasis, but these three, and especially the first two, are key to my approach. In time, I hope to show that they lend themselves to a more "clear and uncluttered" understanding of what makes for legitimate legal coercion.

Putting them together, the approach I will reconstruct from neo-Calvinist premises may be summarized as follows. Legitimacy is a function of preventing basic wrongs: that is, preventing (a) violations of individual and institutional natural rights, that are (b) tied to basic human flourishing, and that (c) represent an exogenous normative standard.

What will I do in the chapter at hand? Largely three things. One task is to simply explain the account. A second is to show how this account of legitimacy can be built up out of the premises outlined in the previous chapter, that is, explain what makes this theory of legitimacy a neo-Calvinist theory of legitimacy. Third, I will provide some initial argumentation to help motivate the plausibility of the account. If I can at least provisionally show an account reconstructed from neo-Calvinism to be philosophically defensible, then I will have made some headway toward my secondary goal of advancing the tradition as a source of conceptual insights for political theorists. This argumentation is intended only to lend prima facie plausibility to my neo-Calvinist account. Ultimately, I will attempt to vindicate the account by arguing it succeeds precisely at those points where JL fails. Making that argument, however, is the mission of part III.

What do I not intend to do in this chapter? One thing I will not do is produce a checklist of legitimacy conditions that can be readily used to categorize real-world coercion as legitimate or illegitimate. This lack of checklist is in keeping with the higher level of abstraction at which my guiding question is pitched. My neo-Calvinist account will, I believe, shed much philosophical light on specific convictions we hold about legitimacy. But this hardly means it will readily settle all disputes about particular uses of coercion. That said, neither does JL. Both are pitched at a higher level of generality.

Now, then, how might the neo-Calvinist tradition illuminate the issue of political legitimacy? I will begin with the central neo-Calvinist insight, then discuss the three ideas that develop it.

THE CENTRAL INSIGHT

To appreciate the distinctiveness of my neo-Calvinist approach, let me begin with a little historical background. The history of Western political thought is replete with theories that either theorize legitimacy in ways we now patently reject or that fail even to distinguish legitimacy from justice. For instance, Aristotle infamously held that some people are born natural slaves. Freedmen who rule over them do so legitimately in virtue of the natural inferiority of slaves' rationality.[1] For much of Western history, legitimacy was viewed as a matter of royal birthright. On Filmer's notorious account, those who share in this royal bloodline enjoy a divine right to rule. Meanwhile a view such as utilitarianism seems not to distinguish between justice and legitimacy at all. Utilitarianism directs us to maximize utility. Doing so may require a coercive state, though not necessarily depending on the outcome of the hedonic calculus. If a state is required, there is no principled limit to the coercive measures that may be taken in the pursuit of utility maximization.[2] Tying legitimacy to actual consent was radically egalitarian for its time, but is roundly rejected by contemporary theorists given its impracticality. Various other approaches would have us explain legitimacy in terms of promoting one or another perfectionist state of affairs, whether Marxist, Thomist, or otherwise. However, we are now sure it is unjust and illegitimate to impose any one comprehensive view, secular or religious, on others. Neither do I know how, say, a Marxist or Thomist would account for the distinction between justice and legitimacy in any case.

JL has stepped into this foray as a possible framework for better understanding political legitimacy. However, as we saw in part I, the JL framework leads to various unacceptable consequences. I believe these unacceptable consequences reflect that JL, too, has failed to capture the underlying logic of our legitimacy-related CCs. So the concept of legitimacy remains poorly understood.

Where, then, are we to start?

A suggestion that emerges from neo-Calvinism is that we begin by appreciating the problem to which the coercive state is a response. The problem is this: in the absence of the state, people are free to harm one another with impunity in the most damaging and degrading ways. At the hands of their fellows, people may be physically assaulted or killed. They may be deprived of the material necessities of life. They may be forcibly enslaved, or forced to act against their deepest convictions. Both their dignity and interests are threatened in sundry ways. For the most part, those who are powerful—physically, economically, socially, intellectually—may be able to prevent themselves from being so harmed, and, if harmed, may be able to effectively press their case against their aggressor. But, absent the state, those who are weak are especially vulnerable, with no means of effective redress at their disposal. And as Thomas Hobbes well noted, even for those who are powerful, the difference between them and weaker persons is never so great that the stronger is invulnerable to the collective aggression of the weaker. Thus the state, in the first instance, is a way of preventing individuals from suffering these basic wrongs and of upholding their cause when they do suffer. Locke was right: absent the state, individuals cannot act as their own judges, juries, and executioners but in an unfair and ineffective way. So coercive public institutions exist to uphold laws that will protect the basic dignity and interests of all, both the relatively strong and the relatively weak. In other words, they exist to prevent basic wrongs.

This, in effect, is what tenet 3 of neo-Calvinism says. Coercive political power is only necessary "by reason of sin." After stating that God establishes governments, Romans 13 goes on to say that civil authorities "are not a terror to good conduct, but to bad."[3] They exist as "God's servant for your good," which they promote by "bear[ing] the sword" for the purposes of carrying out "wrath on the wrongdoer." We need not interpret this passage as saying it is illegitimate for the state to perform any functions other than preventing and prosecuting basic wrongdoing.[4] But what this passage confirms is that the first and most foundational function of the state is the prevention and prosecution of wrongs.

Again, while the state plays a variety of roles in modern societies, prevention of wrongdoing is especially relevant to the legitimacy of the state. This is in keeping with Kuyper's suggestion. The key to understanding why prevention of wrongdoing is essential to state legitimacy, in a way that the state's coordinating or other functions is not, lies, I think, in appreciating the brokenness of the present, actual world. Modern states serve important coordinating functions and resolve collective action problems. For instance, they build and maintain society's infrastructure systems, they regulate traffic, and they manage public goods such as water and the natural environment. They also promote individuals' good by administering various social programs, such as public education, healthcare, unemployment insurance, and pensions. Now in a world without sin, we should grant that the state's coordinating functions suffice to legitimize the coercive power of the state. Does this carry over into the real world, then? In the world as it is, do the state's coordinating functions alone suffice to legitimize its coercive force? I think not. They do not because preventing wrongdoing, especially violations of basic rights, is much more urgent than whatever interests are served by the state's coordinating functions, as real as those interests may be. The interests represented by basic rights, at which the state aims in preventing wrongdoing, are more important. In the world as it is, then, any state that performs various coordinating functions but fails at the more important task of protecting basic rights is illegitimate. No matter how effectively it may perform coordinating functions, no real-world state can plausibly claim legitimacy if it leaves basic rights unprotected. Put another way, protecting basic rights is both a necessary and sufficient condition of political legitimacy, while none of the state's coordinating functions is either necessary or sufficient.

We would do well, then, to take seriously the insight that government is only necessary "by reason of sin." It may be off-putting to view the state's essential function in negative terms, as preventing wrongdoing. But starting with human sinfulness proves helpful here in gaining a clearer picture of what legitimacy requires. As I said, I will explicate this central insight in terms of three further ideas: basic wrongs are violations of natural rights, that are tied to basic human flourishing, and that represent an exogenous normative standard. I now move to these ideas.

BASIC WRONGS AND NATURAL RIGHTS

In theorizing legitimacy as a function of preventing basic wrongs, the wrongs neo-Calvinist legitimacy has in view are violations of natural rights. These may be rights either of individuals or institutions. Let me highlight three features of such rights, whether individual or institutional. The third feature is especially important.

First, natural rights are, unsurprisingly, natural. This means that they belong to people simply in virtue of their being human. In this respect, they are akin to what Wolterstorff calls "human rights." For Wolterstorff, human rights are distinct from "human-person rights."[5] The former are truly human rights, in that all people equally possess them simply as members of the human species. The latter are possessed only by mature human adults, however, and not by infants, the severely mentally disabled, or others lacking capacities Wolterstorff thinks essential to fully-fledged personhood. As I say, the first feature of natural rights is that they are much more like human rights than human-person rights. They are natural in belonging to people simply in virtue of their being human. They aren't earned or achieved, nor bestowed by the state or constructed by society. Even rights that we might think only human-person rights—the right to paid employment, for example—can be viewed in this way. People such as infants or the disabled do not lack them, but only the ability to make use of them. So why is it that humans possess natural rights in this sense, simply in virtue of their being human and without regard for their capacities? Neo-Calvinists would say, with other Christians, it is because all humans are created in the divine image.

Second, natural rights are, as the American Declaration of Independence says, inalienable. An individual cannot lose their natural rights. They cannot be voluntarily given up, nor taken from you by society or the state, or forfeited even as a result of wrong behavior. They are retained even if misused. In this respect, natural rights are like the structure of creation order. Recall that neo-Calvinists believe all created things retain their structure even when misdirected as a result of the fall. The created structure of individuals and institutions is inalienable, we might say. So, too, are their natural rights.

Third, and most importantly, natural rights are objective. The idea of objectivity is that of norms that apply regardless of what the people to whom they apply think of them. Objective rights are rights all are obligated to respect, whether or not individuals and societies recognize their obligation. Similarly, objective wrongs are wrongs all are obligated to avoid, whether recognized or not. If oppression is an objective wrong, oppressing a minority group is wrong whether or not society thinks it wrong. If withholding material provision from the needy is objectively unjust, it matters not that some will disagree in the name of property rights. Similarly, if failure to give affected parties political voice is an objective expression of disrespect, then it is wrong no matter a polity's cultural customs or political culture. If there are natural rights to autonomy, a social minimum, and political voice, they are objective and apply regardless of objections.

In positing the objectivity of legitimacy-conditional rights and wrongs, my account is clearly opposed to what might be called the "social recognition" thesis. According to this thesis, "all statements about the existence of rights presuppose the existence of institutions or social practices governed by rules, rules that can be viewed as conferring rights on individual members of the community."[6] I hold that social recognition is not required for individuals to possess basic rights. In supposing that individuals can be wronged even where social institutions do not exist to formally recognize or prosecute these wrongs, my account affirms institution-independent moral rights by which we can judge that individuals have, indeed, been wronged.

In various ways neo-Calvinism suggests that we conceive of the moral conditions for legitimacy in objective terms, whether we focus on objective rights or objective wrongs. One way is the *Imago Dei*. The fact that each person is created in God's image means that each is of equal and inestimable worth. It is this fact, rather than social or institutional recognition, that confers on each person a certain inviolable dignity, such that their God-given value demands they be treated and respected in certain ways. Otherwise, they are wronged. Thus, the *Imago Dei* provides grounds for structural critiques of whole social and legal systems, both past and present, domestically and internationally. It can give, and has given, philosophical justification to powerful movements of social reform, such as America's Civil Rights Movement.[7]

In addition to neo-Calvinist reasons for affirming the objectivity of natural rights, recall the sort of evidence given earlier in the book. Various historical figures and experiences, in our praising or condemning them, reflect the objectivity of moral rights and wrongs. In condemning the injustice of religious intolerance, European imperialism, and slavery, and in praising social reformers such as William Wilberforce and Martin Luther King Jr., we affirm the existence of moral norms that transcend cultural and political contexts. We do the same whenever we condemn the practices of other cultures at present, such as our condemnation of cultures that practice female circumcision or of governments that suppress free speech. At least insofar as we hold ourselves to be rational in making such judgments, in morally evaluating persons and events from contexts not our own we presuppose the existence of rights and wrongs that apply across contexts as well.

While I am emphasizing here the objectivity of natural rights, neo-Calvinism says something else novel and important about natural rights: institutions can, and do, possess such rights, not only individuals. While talk of institutional rights is not altogether uncommon, they are commonly viewed, I think, in instrumental or pragmatic terms. In this respect, they are thought asymmetrical to basic individual rights, which are viewed as more principled and deontological. Neo-Calvinism resists this undervaluing of institutional rights, however. The tradition gives institutional rights truly principled grounds, primarily by understanding them in terms of divine creation order and modal ontology. In using the language of natural rights to characterize institutional rights, I am taking my cue from writings inspired by neo-Calvinism.[8]

As I will explain later, the implications for legitimacy that we can draw from the idea of objective natural rights and wrongs, considered by itself, are actually limited—even when we recognize that institutions, including the state, have natural rights alongside individuals. The objectivity of legitimacy-conditional rights and wrongs cannot, by itself, explain why they are legitimacy-conditional. For there are objective wrongs which it seems inappropriate to legally proscribe (e.g., a broken promise between friends). There may also be objective wrongs which, while being fit objects of legal enforcement, likely needn't be prevented as a condition of legitimacy (e.g., tax evasion by the rich using offshore bank accounts). So the question is raised: which objective wrongs are legitimacy-conditional? In other words, which natural rights, of all the natural rights individuals and institutions might possess, are legitimacy-conditional? Answering these questions requires the second big idea of neo-Calvinist legitimacy, that of basic human flourishing.

But even if, by itself, the idea of objective, natural rights is insufficient to explain why legitimacy-conditional rights are legitimacy-conditional, it is a necessary part of the explanation. In brief, it is necessary for the following reason. Were legitimacy-conditional rights and wrongs not objective, then legitimate legal coercion could only come by consent. But natural rights are objective, and their objectivity at least makes it possible for legal coercion absent consent to be legitimate, as we sometimes believe it is. Chapter 8 will expand on this line of reasoning.

BASIC HUMAN FLOURISHING

The proposition that legitimacy-conditional wrongs are violations of natural rights leaves much to be filled in. For instance, I just mentioned the question of how we are to discriminate between those natural rights that are legitimacy-conditional and those that are not. But there is a still more fundamental question. Where, philosophically, does the content of these rights and wrongs come from? Since I aim at a general framework for understanding legitimacy, I am not as interested in fixing the specific content of legitimacy-conditional rights as I am in explaining how we might go about doing so. So the foregoing discussion of natural rights leaves two gaps which I now want to fill in.

The second big idea of neo-Calvinist legitimacy, that of basic human flourishing, speaks to both these issues. I will first address the more fundamental question of where the content of rights comes from. Then I will address the second question of how to distinguish between rights that are and aren't legitimacy-conditional.

Where the Content of Legitimacy-Conditional Rights Comes From

So how, philosophically speaking, do we go about filling in the content of these basic rights and wrongs? What conceptual category might yield a clear philosophical picture of what we are doing when we fill in this content? One more way of putting the question is this: legitimacy may depend upon protecting a list of basic rights, but how philosophically is this list to be drawn up?

What I suggest is that we cannot answer this question, and fill in the content of legitimacy-conditional rights and wrongs, except with reference to a view of human flourishing. Your view of human flourishing may differ from mine, but the present point is that, in either case, a person must have some such view in order to generate a list of basic rights in a non-arbitrary way.

First let me try and clarify the claim. My claim that legitimacy-conditional rights and wrongs are tied to basic human flourishing has two senses, a weaker and stronger. While I advance both as true, I will spend more time explaining and defending the weaker version of the claim. The stronger builds on the weaker, though, so I hope my explanation and defense of the weaker will indirectly make the stronger more plausible also.

Primarily, the claim is that, conceptually, any account of rights presupposes a view of human flourishing. One might think this is a fairly obvious and uncontroversial point, and might also notice that there is nothing distinctively neo-Calvinist about it. Still, it is a point worth making because it's one badly obscured by JL's proceduralist apparatus, and one that I think is underappreciated even if evident upon reflection. The other, stronger sense of the claim that rights are tied to human flourishing emerges from the distinctively neo-Calvinist idea of public justice. In this sense, the claim is more about the type of account of human flourishing one ought presuppose and how one ought use it in evaluating legitimacy. In sum, the stronger claim is that we cannot properly weigh any rights claim except in light of the interconnected flourishing of society as a whole, including both its individual and collective social actors. I will say a little more about this stronger sense later, but first let us examine the weaker sense.

To illustrate that basic rights always make assumptions about human flourishing, albeit assumptions we usually make unwittingly, consider the examples of three familiar rights: the right to bodily integrity, the right to material subsistence, and the right to personhood before the law.

The right to bodily integrity assumes that control over one's own body contributes to a flourishing human life. It is not simply the fact that people do, in fact, object to violations of their bodily integrity that establishes this right. We can see this by asking whether someone could establish a right to an inviolable five-meter radius of personal space simply by complaining whenever this radius was transgressed. Why would this complaint carry little weight, while claims to bodily integrity carry much weight? It is because we are assuming that for embodied beings such as ourselves, bodily integrity really is essential to a flourishing human life, but that a five-meter radius of personal space is not. We assume bodily integrity is, indeed, required for human flourishing, either as itself partially constitutive of this flourishing or as a precondition for achieving some further end with which human flourishing is identified.

Likewise, the right to the material necessities of life, but not plovers' eggs,[9] assumes that such things as food, clothing, and shelter are necessary for a flourishing human life. In denying a basic right to plovers' eggs we are assuming that humans can flourish with or without plovers' eggs. Basic rights are basic in virtue of the fundamental importance of the interests and dignity they protect. There is no basic right to plovers' eggs, for they are not a human interest of fundamental importance, neither as a necessary part or precondition for human flourishing.

Similarly, why do we affirm personhood before the law as a basic right, but not a right to being addressed with "Sir," "Madam," "Esquire," or another honorific? It is because the former is a fundamental expression of respect for people who possess inviolable dignity, while the latter is not. The former, but not the latter, is partially constitutive of, or at least a condition of, a flourishing human life.

Now any of these cases might be judged differently were we beings of a different sort or possessed less value than we do. Things would be different, say, if we were disembodied minds; or if we had hyper-sensitive sensory organs that left us feeling assaulted whenever our five-meter radius of personal space was transgressed; or if we had no more value than dandelions. But we are the beings we are, with certain interests and value. As such, certain ways of living (e.g., enjoying bodily integrity, material sufficiency, and personhood under the law) are part or precondition of a flourishing life. And other ways of living, being neither a fundamental part nor precondition of a flourishing life, are either unnecessary (e.g., enjoying a five-meter radius of personal space), optional (e.g., having plovers' eggs), or obviously harmful (e.g., being denied standing under the law).

Charles Taylor also helps us see that rights presuppose wider value systems. Summarizing the relevant points from Taylor's work, Lister writes:

> We cannot simply count the number of laws or forbidden actions in order to assess the level of coercion associated with a particular policy, for the same reasons that we cannot arrange our basic liberties so as to maximize liberty *tout court*. We should not say that there is less coercion in a society with no traffic lights and no freedom of conscience than in a society with freedom of conscience and heavily regulated traffic, despite the greater number of discrete acts of interference in the latter case . . . we need to assess the value of the liberties or opportunities that laws deny people, or create.[10]

The point is that the freedoms we are prepared to recognize as a matter of basic right are freedoms that we value. They score high on a qualitative, if not quantitative, scale. And on what grounds do we value them? Taylor's illustrations suggest that we value certain freedoms in light of broader presuppositions about what's valuable in life. In this way, we normatively ground the freedoms that need protecting, and the wrongs that need to be prevented, as a matter of basic justice. This grounding allows us to discriminate between wrongs that are more or less serious. Of course, as Lister notes, which freedoms and wrongs are of fundamental significance "will often be the subject of reasonable disagreement."[11] But that we must make such judgments to simply work out basic rights in a non-arbitrary way remains true. In Taylor's example, the value judgment is that freedom to live without regulation of one's religious beliefs is more important than freedom to live without regulation of traffic. Consequently, religious freedom is rightly regarded as a demand of basic justice, but not traffic freedom. So basic freedoms presuppose wider value systems, and as I read Taylor the lesson to be learned is that basic rights in general presuppose views of human flourishing.

In both my examples and Taylor's assumptions about human flourishing are being made, as they are in all cases of basic rights, if only we look for them. In sum, I think it is as Michael Sandel says: "Justice is inescapably judgmental. Whether we're arguing about financial bailouts or Purple Hearts, surrogate motherhood or same-sex marriage, affirmative action or military service, CEO pay or the right to use a golf cart, questions of justice are bound up with competing notions of honor and virtue, pride and recognition. Justice is not only about the right way to distribute things. It is also about the right way to value things."[12] Similarly, our views of basic justice are always bound up with notions of the human good and what it requires.

Consider now briefly the stronger sense of the claim that legitimacy is tied to human flourishing, which emerges from the idea of public justice (tenet 8). In our discussion of public justice last chapter, I identified three ways in which public justice is distinctive as a conception of justice. Public justice gives each their due by weighing and balancing rights claims against one another; it views both individuals and institutions as making valid rights claims; and it balances such claims for the common good. These ideas are relevant here also. Regarding the type of account of human flourishing legitimacy-conditional rights presuppose, it ought be a view of flourishing that takes seriously both individuals and institutions. Not only individual humans matter. Collective social actors do also, such as cultural communities, as does the environment itself. The account of flourishing presupposed should also be a genuine account of flourishing, not merely of freedom. As public justice aims at the common good and not only rights, so our accounts of human flourishing should incorporate dimensions of social well-being other than the autonomy of social actors. Their freedom is important, but not wholly determinative of societal flourishing. Following Zuidervaart, I add here, too, that we must recognize the interdependence of social actors.[13] We should recognize not only the full variety of social actors, but their many interconnections, and our view of flourishing need also recognize the interconnections between humans, other creatures, and the environment. Social actors are not atomistic, but interdependent.

Regarding how we ought use such views of flourishing, this is where the idea of balancing is again important. To tie natural rights to human flourishing is to weigh rights claims against one another. The idea is this: we cannot know the weight of any claim, and subsequently whether any claim represents a genuine right, except in light of social flourishing as a whole. We cannot know so except in light of other individuals' and institutions' distinctive purposes, structures, and legitimate interests. In a sense, this point is similar to Rawls' that our freedom is limited by that of others; we are, Rawls says, only entitled to that freedom which is compatible with like freedom for all. Unlike Rawls, though, we ought not only weigh the claims of individuals, but also of institutions. Moreover, our goal is not only freedom, but flourishing. And as a result of these differences, it is inappropriate to conceive of the limits on our freedom as resulting from a process in which individuals essentially compete with one another to maximize their own bundle of social goods. We weigh rights claims against others' claims and interests, but we do so in light of interconnected, social flourishing as a whole.

So my neo-Calvinist account ties legitimacy to flourishing in both these ways, both the weaker and stronger. While only the latter is unique to neo-Calvinism, it assumes and builds on the former.

The theme of flourishing has been more prominent in the work of subsequent neo-Calvinists than in that of Kuyper, Dooyeweerd, and Vollenhoven, and it is especially prominent in that of Zuidervaart. "The social order I envision," Zuidervaart writes, "would promote the interconnected flourishing of all Earth's inhabitants."[14] This flourishing includes the environment, too, as the goal is the "interconnected flourishing of all human beings and the Earth they inhabit."[15] Institutional pluralism is not an end in itself, but must be evaluated against the standard of societal flourishing. We must "ask to what extent and in which respects the current array of differentiated levels and macrostructures supports, promotes, hinders, or prevents the interconnected flourishing of human beings and other creatures." This last quote indicates that nonhuman animals are also to be included in our conception of social well-being. Flourishing is even part of Zuidervaart's very definition of truth, including religious truth. Religious truth-claims that lead to just and kind actions are true. Those that compromise flourishing are false.[16]

Their greater willingness to recognize a positive rather than only negative role for the state also reflects contemporary neo-Calvinists' greater emphasis on flourishing. The operative question is no longer—if it ever was—the negative question of whether a sphere or institution is remaining within its boundaries, but the more positive question of whether it is promoting human flourishing consistent with its own distinctive nature and those of others. Contemporary neo-Calvinists have more a "directive" than merely "remedial" view of the state.[17] While seeing a very positive role for the state, though, neo-Calvinists will be quick to point out that a flourishing society requires more than just the state. This qualification is a crucial neo-Calvinist insight. Neo-Calvinism endorses a positive role for the state, but not statism.

To conclude this subsection, the main idea has been that we presuppose views of human flourishing in filling out the content of basic rights and wrongs, but theorists are perhaps loathe to admit doing so, and we often do so unwittingly. To achieve a "clear and uncluttered" view, then, of what legitimacy is about, we must be willing to recognize these underlying views for what they truly are, to wit, views of human flourishing.

How to Distinguish Legitimacy-Conditional Rights from Other Rights

In fact, I don't think neo-Calvinism has much to say directly to this question. Perhaps this is because neo-Calvinists haven't, as I said early on, tackled the question of legitimacy as formulated in contemporary political theory. So what might neo-Calvinists say regarding the distinction between natural rights that are legitimacy-conditional from those that are not? More importantly, what ought we say? Both to extend the neo-Calvinist tradition and help answer the normative question of legitimacy, I will mention two neo-Calvinist thoughts that might indirectly help and then will summarize what I think is the proper way to draw this distinction.

In his discussions of societal evil and systemic deformations, Zuidervaart offers a couple pointers that might help us distinguish between rights that are and aren't legitimacy-conditional. He defines societal evil as "institutions as well as patterns that seem most oppressive and trends that seem most destructive to interconnected flourishing."[18] Perhaps here is how to draw the distinction. Violations of legitimacy-conditional rights are especially oppressive or are especially destructive to interconnected flourishing, whereas violations of other rights may be oppressive or destructive but are less so. As well, Zuidervaart defines systemic deformations as, basically, societal structures that "fundamentally violate[] human life before the face of God."[19] Alternatively, then, perhaps we draw the line here. Violations of legitimacy-conditional rights fundamentally violate human life, while violations of other rights may fail to fully respect human life but do not fundamentally violate it. These pointers represent two questions we might ask in drawing the distinction. Is a right especially needed to prevent oppression and promote flourishing? Does a right protect the fundamental, God-given dignity of human life? If we answer these questions affirmatively, the right in question is legitimacy-conditional.

Wolterstorff identifies another condition on those natural rights that legitimate states can and must protect. It may be that individuals or institutions have certain rights violation of which would compromise social flourishing. If, however—and this is Wolterstorff's condition—protecting those rights would require measures that compromise other still more important rights, then the state should not try to protect them.[20] At least, the state should not try to do so directly through coercion. So the condition is this: legitimacy-conditional rights must be ones the state can protect without thereby committing an even greater injustice. This condition suggests, then, that legitimacy-conditional rights will be more basic than nonbasic. This is because in protecting basic rights, given that they are basic, there is little risk of threatening more important rights even if lesser ones may be.

With these points in mind, I propose this is how we ought discriminate between natural rights that are and aren't legitimacy-conditional: legitimacy-conditional rights are basic, and legitimacy-conditional, in virtue of the fundamental importance of the interests they protect and in virtue of the way they express a fundamental respect for the dignity of rights-holders. Similarly, wrongs are basic and legitimacy-conditional given the great violence they do to persons' interests and dignity. As I use the terms, legitimacy-conditional rights correspond to legitimacy-conditional wrongs. Protecting the former prevents people and institutions from suffering the latter. Likewise, basic rights correspond to basic wrongs. Furthermore, protecting these rights and preventing these wrongs constitute the most elementary demands of justice. So we might interchangeably speak of legitimacy, on my neo-Calvinist account, as a function of "preventing basic wrongs," "protecting basic rights," and "upholding basic justice."

Moreover, it is in light of the great importance of the interests and dignity protected by basic rights (or that are violated by basic wrongs) that the state is justified in using coercion to ensure that these rights are protected (or that these wrongs are prevented and prosecuted). The state is to uphold public justice, which it utterly fails to do if such rights go unprotected. Neo-Calvinism would agree with Allen Buchanan when he writes, "Notice first that there is a conceptual link between justice and coercion: in principle the need to satisfy the demands of justice provides a powerful reason for coercion, perhaps the most powerful reason."[21] Are there not echoes in what Buchanan says of the thought that the state is necessary only "by reason of sin"?

Finally, remember, too, the type of concept that legitimacy is, and how it works in our moral experience. Legitimacy operates as a threshold concept, setting a bar that is lower than that of full justice. It makes sense, then, to equate legitimacy with only meeting the basic demands of justice, rather than with meeting all of its demands.

In sum, considerations from both within and without neo-Calvinism suggest we should distinguish natural rights that are legitimacy-conditional from those that are not in terms of the fundamental importance of the former. Consequently, with respect to the views of human flourishing presupposed by basic rights, basic rights correspond, in particular, to the basic elements of the views of human flourishing they presuppose. In other words, legitimacy-conditional rights are tied to basic human flourishing. It is helpful to consider what Steven Wall says about two different ways in which an ideal of human flourishing can "inform conceptions of political morality."[22] On the one hand, such an ideal may be invoked as an aim the state should promote. On the other, it may simply be invoked as a way of underwriting the elementary demands of a political morality. The idea of basic human flourishing my account involves is meant in the second of these ways. It speaks to the question of "whether an adequate account of concepts such as justice, rights, obligation can be given without appeal to some ideal of human flourishing,"[23] and its answer is no.

Before moving ahead, I add one further clarification. Even if we grant that legitimacy is a function of protecting basic rights or, in other words, of upholding basic justice, whose account of basic justice will it be? As Alasdair MacIntyre has asked, *Whose Justice? Which Rationality?*[24] In response, the question presupposes a category mistake. In postulating that legitimacy is about basic justice, my point is that however we might fill in the content of basic justice, that legitimacy is a function of basic justice and basic rights is an idea without which we cannot make philosophical sense of our legitimacy-related CCs. These include our conviction that there are certain basic rights that are legitimacy-conditional, and that much legal coercion is legitimate even amidst disagreement between reasonable persons. My neo-Calvinist account remains agnostic about exactly how the content of basic rights and basic justice should be fixed, yet it insists we need conceive legitimacy in terms of upholding basic rights and basic justice, which, in turn, can only be sensibly judged in light of some or another view of human flourishing.

BASIC WRONGS AS EXOGENOUS STANDARD

The third idea of neo-Calvinist legitimacy is that the basic rights on which legitimacy is conditional constitute an exogenous normative standard. This third idea has been implicit in much of what has already been said, and my present discussion will be relatively brief. The relevance of this idea to legitimacy will be revisited at greater length in chapter 10, where I will suggest that it can help us avoid the sort of structural paternalism that JL seems to involve.

First, a disclaimer. I am wary here of wading too deeply into meta-ethical waters. My primary intention is not to speak to any meta-ethical debates, let alone settle them. Rather, it is the more modest goal of developing a framework that makes sense of our legitimacy-related CCs. But for this task, I think it helpful to say something more about the kind of moral standard our convictions seem to presuppose, and it seems to be an exogenous standard.

I will begin by explaining the term "exogenous." I appropriate this term from science. Exogenous phenomena contrast with endogenous phenomena. Something is endogenous if it is "produced or synthesized within the organism or system."[25] Conversely, something is exogenous if it is "introduced from or produced outside the organism or system."[26] So in the present context, in characterizing the moral standard constituted by basic rights as exogenous, neo-Calvinist legitimacy is saying something about the source of this standard. An exogenous standard is not one that is created by human beings. Rather, its source is independent of human beings. An exogenous standard is one that imposes itself on human beings, not one that human beings impose on themselves.

In particular, an exogenous standard is directly opposed to the Kantian ideal of the self-legislating moral agent, an ideal enthusiastically embraced by JLs[27] and constructivists. This Kantian notion is something neo-Calvinists explicitly reject. It, or something similar, is what Kuyper seems to have in mind when he writes, "The Calvinist is led to submit himself to the conscience" but "not as to an individual lawgiver." Instead, we are to submit ourselves to the conscience, and thereby the moral law, insofar as it is through the conscience that "God himself stirs up the inner man, and subjects him to his judgment."[28] Koyzis, too, distances himself from this Kantian way of thinking, arguing that freedom is not being a self-legislator of laws but exercising an authority-bearing office granted by God. To emphasize, this authority is not original to human beings, but granted by God.[29] Authority has a "transcendent origin"[30]—transcendent, like God, not immanent, like ourselves.

The idea of exogenous normativity is implicit in many neo-Calvinist ideas as well. The divine image is imprinted on us by God. In this way it is not, properly speaking, intrinsic to us, much less of our own creation. We are issued the cultural mandate by God. We are very much the recipients, not the authors, of the mandate. Creation order in general is ordered by God, not by us, including the creation norms for society's various institutions. Also consider tenet 9 in particular. It is God, not humans, that ultimately establishes human governments. Despite the endogenous appearance of governments, their structure and norms are, in fact, exogenous according to neo-Calvinism.

It is also true that, on neo-Calvinism, humans positivize creation norms for culture and society, and contemporary neo-Calvinists emphasize the historical-contextual nature of norms much more so than, say, Dooyeweerd who characterized them as timeless and invariant. The contextual, positivizing role neo-Calvinists ascribe to humans may seem in tension with the idea of exogenous normativity.

I don't think it is, however. Notwithstanding recent emphases on the historical-contextual nature of norms, traditionally the primary thrust of neo-Calvinist thought is God-given norms, given in the creation, in line with a high view of divine sovereignty. Even if positivization is emphasized more, positivization is still just that: not the creation of norms, but their concretization (or positivization) in particular contexts. And even for someone like Zuidervaart, who officially rejects the notion of positivization altogether,[31] it remains true that humans act in response to an external stimulus. That is, humans respond to a divine call, a divine call to love. "[H]uman beings have responded to God's gift and call—the call to love God, themselves, fellow human beings, and all creation—and have given responses within their cultural practices and social institutions."[32] He rejects creation norms as timeless and immutable, but prefers "to speak of God's will as divine instruction and invitation and guidance."[33] "Norms are," Zuidervaart says, "dynamic and historically unfolding guidelines that require human responses in order to have effect."[34] There are different points of emphasis, yes, between Dooyeweerd and Zuidervaart. But the call to which humans respond remains exogenous. At a minimum, it seems that the norm of love is exogenous as well. Fundamentally, then, neo-Calvinists concur that God is the prime mover and we the responders. Normativity is fundamentally exogenous, then, however exactly we understand God's action as prime mover and our actions as responders.

Characterizing basic moral norms in terms of an exogenous standard also fits well with the phenomenology of these demands. It has been observed that, "in moral experience, we apprehend moral values and duties which impose themselves as objectively binding and true."[35] We experience these demands as forcing themselves on us, as non-optional, and as constraints on the free exercise of our will rather than as the expression of it. Thus, the phenomenology of basic rights and wrongs also suggests an exogenous source.

Now it is true that, on one reading of Kant, the Kantian directive to understand ourselves as self-legislators is compatible with the sort of exogenous normativity I am describing. Similarly, it might be thought that JL itself should be read this way, in a way compatible with exogenous moral norms. So read, in representing the demands of justice as the outcome of a hypothetical procedural, JL simply re-presents moral norms that obtain whether or not we engage in the proceduralist thought experiment. However, I think a stronger reading of JL is appropriate, according to which JL does not simply re-present humans' moral duties but posits humans as the very source of these duties. Such a reading is more in keeping with the general tenor and internal logic of the JL position that emphasizes popular sovereignty. This matter of how to interpret JLs' representing social norms as the product of popular sovereignty, whether to interpret it weakly or strongly, is one I take up at greater length in chapter 11.

But even if I am right that constructivism is incompatible with exogenous normativity, it's not that the concept of an exogenous standard necessarily involves a metaphysical commitment to God's existence—there are secular alternatives, even if constructivism isn't one of them. For instance, one might believe that morality is a kind of natural fact. As such, basic rights and justice *qua* natural facts would impose themselves on us in much the same way that gravity is an escapable fact for us.

That said, the idea of an exogenous standard does seem to fit more naturally into a theistic framework, such as neo-Calvinism. It is implicit in neo-Calvinist thought in myriad ways, such as those above, and neo-Calvinists also explicitly reject the notion of endogenous normativity. Furthermore, a theistic framework such as neo-Calvinism also has a ready answer to the question of how an exogenous standard might exist, namely, God.

CONCLUSION

In conclusion, the central insight of neo-Calvinism regarding legitimacy is that legitimacy is a function of preventing basic wrongs. Additionally, we have drawn three other ideas from neo-Calvinist thought to help us explicate this view of legitimacy, of which the first two are especially important. First, legitimacy is a matter of natural rights, a key feature of which is their objectivity. Acknowledging that legitimacy-conditional rights and wrongs apply to all regardless of the objections of some is a necessary first step toward understanding legitimacy. Second, what count as basic rights and wrongs can only be determined in light of basic human flourishing. Legitimate rights claims can only be determined in light of societal flourishing, as claims are weighed against the legitimate interests and prerogatives of society's full variety of social actors. Basic rights represent the most important aspects of this flourishing. A third idea is that the kind of standard constituted by basic rights is an exogenous one, one that originates outside of humans.

Putting them together, neo-Calvinist legitimacy says that legitimacy is a function of preventing basic wrongs: that is, preventing (a) violations of individual and institutional natural rights, that (b) are tied to basic human flourishing, and that (c) represent an exogenous normative standard. I have reconstructed this framework for legitimacy out of the conceptual resources afforded us by the neo-Calvinist tradition of social thought. My thesis is that it offers a superior set of categories for making sense of legitimacy, categories that fit and illuminate our legitimacy-related CCs.

Note certain strengths and limitations of this account. As a response to my guiding question—what is legitimacy about?—what it primarily does is shed light on the type of considerations we should bear in mind when discussing and debating specific conditions of legitimacy. While it is an approach built up out of a religious tradition of thought, it is no part whatsoever of the approach to impose a sectarian view on others.

What the theory does not do is provide us with a list of specific conditions that can be readily applied. Does this limitation impugn the theory's significance? Hardly, I think. For, among other reasons, I take it to be very philosophically informative. I also believe that this theory provides a firmer foundation for whatever specific rights we do wish to defend. It secures them by perspicuously formulating the normative grounds on which they stand. Further explanation of how neo-Calvinist legitimacy provides firmer philosophical grounds for basic rights than JL does awaits us in chapter 9.

NOTES

1. See Aristotle's *Politics*, Book I, Chapter V.
2. Hence, the criticism that Mill's ethics aren't compatible with his politics, the aggregate utility-maximizing logic of his ethics with the sort of individual rights he defends in *On Liberty*.
3. Romans 13:4-5 (*The Holy Bible*, 948).
4. Cf. Wolterstorff, *The Mighty and the Almighty*, 99.
5. Wolterstorff, *Understanding Liberal Democracy*.
6. Alistair M. Macleod, "Rights and Recognition: The Case of Human Rights," *Journal of Social Philosophy* 44, no. 1 (Spring 2013): 70 n1.
7. Richard Wayne Wills argues that the *Imago Dei* was central to this movement. Consider this quote from a Martin Luther King, Jr. sermon:

> You see, the founding fathers were really influenced by the Bible. The whole concept of the *imago dei*, as it is expressed in Latin, the 'image of God,' is the idea that all men have something within them that God injected. Not that they have substantial unity with God, but that every man has a capacity to have fellowship with God. And this gives him a uniqueness, it gives him worth, it gives him dignity. And we must never forget this as a nation: There are no gradations in the image of God. Every man from a treble white to a bass black is significant on God's keyboard, precisely because every man is made in the image of God. One day we will

learn that. We will know one day that God made us to live together as brothers and to respect the dignity and worth of every man. This is why we must fight segregation with all of our nonviolent might.

See Richard Wayne Wills, *Martin Luther King, Jr., and the Image of God* (New York: Oxford University Press, 2009); Timothy Keller, *Generous Justice: How God's Grace Makes Us Just* (New York: Penguin Group [USA] Inc., 2010), 86–87.

8. From Chaplin and Wolterstorff specifically.

9. I borrow this well-known example from Dworkin, who, in turn, attributes it to Kenneth Arrow. Ronald Dworkin, "What Is Equality? Part 1: Equality of Welfare," *Philosophy and Public Affairs* 10, no. 3 (Summer 1981): 185–246; Ronald Dworkin, "What Is Equality? Part 2: Equality of Resources," *Philosophy and Public Affairs* 10, no. 4 (Autumn 1981): 283–345.

10. Lister, "Public Justification and the Limits of State Action," 160; Taylor, "What's Wrong with Negative Liberty," 211–29.

11. Lister, "Public Justification and the Limits of State Action," 160.

12. Michael J. Sandel, *Justice: What's the Right Thing to Do?* (New York: Farrar, Straus and Giroux, 2009), 261.

13. E.g., Zuidervaart, *Religion, Truth, and Social Transformation*, 243.

14. Ibid., 271.

15. Ibid., 243.

16. Ibid., 251 cf. 281.

17. These terms are from Jonathan Chaplin, "Conclusion: Christian Political Wisdom," in *God and Government*, ed. Nick Spencer and Jonathan Chaplin (London: Society for Promoting Christian Knowledge, 2009), 223–24.

18. Zuidervaart, *Religion, Truth, and Social Transformation*, 18.

19. Ibid., 233.

20. Wolterstorff, *The Mighty and the Almighty*.

21. Buchanan, "Political Legitimacy and Democracy," 704.

22. Wall, *Liberalism, Perfectionism and Restraint* (New York: Cambridge University Press, 1998), 12.

23. Ibid.

24. Alasdair MacIntyre, *Whose Justice? Which Rationality?* (Notre Dame, IN: University of Notre Dame Press, 1988).

25. http://www.merriam-webster.com/dictionary/endogenous.

26. http://www.merriam-webster.com/dictionary/exogenous?show=0andt=1362000632.

27. Cf. Nagel, "Moral Conflict," 220–21.

28. Kuyper, *Lectures on Calvinism*, 59.

29. See chapter 3, "Authority and Autonomy," in Koyzis, *We Answer to Another*, 59–92.

30. Ibid., 13.

31. Zuidervaart, *Religion, Truth, and Social Transformation*, 262.

32. Ibid., 261.

33. Ibid., 256.

34. Ibid., 229.

35. William Lane Craig, in "Is Faith in God Reasonable? A Debate with William Lane Craig and Alex Rosenberg." Debate hosted by Purdue University, West Lafayette, IN, USA, February 1, 2013. Accessed online at www.youtube.com.

Part III

JL and Neo-Calvinist Legitimacy in Dialogue

Chapter Eight

Is Consent Needed to Justify Coercion?

We now come to part III, in which I will bring JL and neo-Calvinist legitimacy into dialogue with one another. Chapter 6 presented neo-Calvinism in its own terms. Then in chapter 7 I reconstructed my account of neo-Calvinist legitimacy. What I want to do now is bring JL back into the conversation and compare it directly with my account. In particular, I will examine neo-Calvinist legitimacy in light of the unacceptable consequences of JL discussed in part I. I hope to show how it avoids these very consequences, and, in so doing, makes better sense of our legitimacy-related CCs. Recall that in chapter 2 the desideratum I laid out for our best theory of legitimacy was making sense of these CCs. Thus, I will ultimately conclude that neo-Calvinist legitimacy provides a better framework for understanding legitimacy than JL based on its ability to make sense of those three CCs on which JL foundered in part I. The present chapter deals with the first of these CCs, arguing that neo-Calvinist legitimacy makes better sense than JL does of our CC that coercion amidst disagreement is legitimate.

Straightaway I expect that my title for this chapter will be cause for concern. To court the idea that consent is unnecessary for legal coercion is a veritable return to the dark ages, isn't it? Isn't one of the triumphs of the modern era our realization that, as stated in the American Declaration of Independence, governments derive "their just powers from the consent of the governed"? At least on the face of it, suggesting consent is unnecessary for coercion seems a recipe for oppression.

I certainly expect JLs to be among those concerned by the title of this chapter. For as we saw in chapter 3, consent is a central category to JL. Back in chapter 3 I did not explicitly identify consent as being the operative concept in that chapter's critique of JL, focusing instead on the unanimity condition. But for all intents and purposes, consent was primary. JL de-legitimizes all legal coercion as a result of its unanimity condition, and JL's unanimity condition, in turn, embodies the importance of consent. It reflects the belief that the consent of all affected parties, even if only their hypothetical consent, is needed for legitimacy. So the first unacceptable consequence of JL results from consent being a category of central importance to the JL framework.

However, in this chapter I will explain why consent isn't actually needed to justify coercion, at least not certain instances of legal coercion. To accomplish this, I will draw on David Estlund's idea of the nullity of nonconsent. The apothegm that just rule depends on the consent of the governed contains a great deal of truth, but, unless qualified, it is overly general and fails to reckon with considered judgments we hold that point in the opposite direction, that is, judgments that suggest legitimacy does not require consent. In due course I will explain what this apothegm has right, but mostly I will emphasize what is wrong with focusing on consent. Without consent, a regime's descriptive legitimacy may suffer, but whether or not this is so does not concern me. My concern is understanding normative legitimacy, and for this consent is unhelpful.

What is the alternative? By the end of this chapter, I will only get as far as arguing that the alternative is understanding legitimacy in terms of protecting the natural rights of individuals and institutions. Rather than consent, legitimacy is a matter of certain rights and duties that apply to all regardless of objections, given the objectivity of natural rights. In making this argument, I will refer again to the case of the Bakuninist discussed in chapter 3.

The previous chapter signaled a limitation of my argument in this chapter. While I will argue that legitimacy is a matter of preventing natural rights violations, I will say nothing about which of these rights are legitimacy-conditional. I spoke to this issue last chapter with reference to, among other things, Zuidervaart's notion of societal evil and Wolterstorff's condition that protecting rights mustn't violate more important rights, but I will take it up again in chapter 9. However, if we simply go as far as theorizing legitimacy in terms of objective natural rights and wrongs, we will have paved the way for an alternative to a consent-emphasizing account. For if legitimacy-conditional rights are objective—both those of individuals and institutions, including the state—then it is at least possible that consent is unnecessary for their legitimate legal enforcement. On the other hand, without the objectivity of natural rights, it seems that legitimate coercion could only come by consent.

I doubt I will fully assuage the concerns raised by this chapter's title. But what I do hope to show is that we are already committed to denying the necessity of consent. Now if I can persuade readers that they are already committed to its denial, then perhaps readers can also be persuaded that it is possible to both deny the necessity of consent and avoid any untoward consequences of doing so. Our CCs reflect both sides of this equation, and, ultimately, I believe neo-Calvinist legitimacy gives us a framework for integrating both.

JL AND CONSENT

Consent is central to JL's characterization of legitimacy. JL requires that legitimate legal coercion be based on reasons that command the assent of every reasonable person. This is JL's unanimity condition. Consent is given in terms of finding the reasons for coercive proposals acceptable or non-rejectable. All these points are part and parcel of the core JL principle, that legitimate legal coercion is based on reasons that all reasonable persons can accept. The concept of consent is present in this formula, even if the actual word is not.

Of course, the sort of consent JLs have in mind is hypothetical consent. The parties envisioned by JL's agreement scenario are hypothetical, as is the consent they give. The parties are meant to represent real-world persons. However, the consent relevant to JL is not that of actual persons, but that of their hypothetical counterparts.

Even keeping in mind the hypothetical nature of this consent, though, the category of individual consent undoubtedly remains central to JL legitimacy. JL would still have us understand and conceptualize legitimacy in terms of consent.

Another important point is that JL is more concerned with individual consent than simply with democratic decision-making. Despite certain commonalities, these represent distinct approaches to the justification of legal coercion. On the former, we can legitimately coerce person p only if an idealized p would consent to the coercion. On the latter, we can coerce p just so long as the coercion is licensed by a democratic process in which p has equal opportunity to participate. Now as I say, JLs' approach is the former. Majoritarian democratic procedures will not do. Acceptance by each and every affected party is required. In sum, the consent emphasized by JL is no less than the unanimous consent of all individuals.

But is it appropriate and helpful for us to think in terms of this category as we conceptualize legitimacy? To begin with, one reason for thinking not is that in JL it leads to the unacceptable consequence of de-legitimizing all legal coercion. This was the argument of chapter 3. This it does together with JL's thin criteria for reasonable persons and the reasonable multi-interpretability of vague political concepts. But we need not, and should not, conclude that legal coercion is never legitimate. Rather we should call the consent requirement into question.

Now let us consider further reasons why consent should not be central to our understanding of legitimacy, with special emphasis on a reason inspired by Estlund's work. I emphasize that among our CCs is the conviction that withholding consent is insufficient to de-legitimize many uses of legal coercion. If so, consent is unnecessary for legitimacy after all, and we have reason to consider my neo-Calvinist alternative that emphasizes objective natural rights rather than consent.

ESTLUND AND NULL NONCONSENT

It is widely believed that coercion requires consent. For example, speaking of coercion in general, Audi writes that "we can coerce people to do only what they would autonomously do if appropriately informed and fully rational."[1] This widely held belief is akin to what Estlund calls the "libertarian clause," which states, "Without consent there is no authority."[2] JLs share this view.

Taken at face value, this proposition would mean that one can evade coercion simply by withholding consent. But even if consent is conceived along JL lines—hypothetically, in idealized circumstances—it means that coercion is de-legitimized just so long as even one person can withhold consent on reasonable, public grounds. However, an insight of Estlund implies that very often we cannot, in fact, de-legitimize legal coercion simply by withholding consent. This being the case, it seems untrue that legitimacy necessarily requires consent.

Estlund's insight is what he calls the "nullity of non-consent." This notion is counterpart to the more familiar phenomenon of null consent. The latter occurs, for instance, when a promise is made under duress, or on the basis of grossly inaccurate information. In such situations, though consent is given, normatively the situation remains as if it had never been given. In such contexts, consent lacks its typical normative import. Comparably, Estlund points out there are situations in which withholding consent also lacks its typical normative import. Normally, the effect of withholding consent is avoidance of some responsibility one would rather not assume.[3] But if Estlund is right, not all responsibilities can be avoided in this way. There are situations where, though consent is withheld, extenuating moral considerations mean that consent should have been given. Due to these extenuating considerations, individuals who withhold consent nonetheless occupy the same normative position they would have occupied had they given consent.

Why should we accept the nullity of nonconsent? The example Estlund provides is the case of "despicable Joe."[4] Despicable Joe is aboard a flight that crashes. In the aftermath of the crash, a flight attendant issues an order to Joe which, in the judgment of the qualified and knowledgeable flight attendant, will help the maximum amount of injured persons. The question is this: is Joe under an obligation to submit to the authority of the flight attendant? Estlund answers affirmatively, believing it would be wrong of Joe to refuse the flight attendant's orders and, moreover, believing that Joe cannot escape the duty to submit to the flight attendant's orders simply by refusing to consent. If you agree with Estlund's analysis, then you are committed to the nullity of nonconsent. For, at least in this case, you acknowledge that consent is not, in fact, a necessary condition for being under authority. Extenuating moral considerations place Joe under authority even though Joe withholds consent.

Now while Estlund thinks the moral of this story is relatively narrow,[5] applying only to the issue of authority but not legitimacy, I suggest that the implications of Estlund's insight are much wider than he supposes. Why not also apply the concept of null nonconsent to the issue of legitimacy? And why not to a broader range of our moral obligations? We should. For the notion of null nonconsent helps explain a broad spectrum of our actual moral experience and practice, in which we often hold people responsible for wrongdoing even though they would rather go unpunished. We force libertarian-minded citizens to pay taxes needed to fund social services. We press criminal charges against polygamists in spite of the different values they hold. We intervene militarily where regimes fail to uphold human rights. In all such cases, the coerced parties have hardly consented to the coercion to which they are subject, yet we take their nonconsent to be null and void. In fact, whenever we believe ourselves justified on moral grounds in using legal coercion against unwilling others, we affirm the nullity of nonconsent.[6] Given the broad spectrum of our moral experience explained by null non-consent, we should apply the concept not only to authority, but also to basic rights and wrongs more generally, as well as to legitimacy at least insofar as legitimacy requires upholding basic justice.

The point is that in many ways, we already accept coercion without consent. This isn't to say that consent is never required for coercion to be fully justified. I have yet to distinguish between cases where consent is and is not relevant. But our normal experience and practice do suggest that there are cases where consent is not needed, where coercion can be legitimate without consent. Estlund prefaces his discussion of null nonconsent by observing, "Moral obligations can simply befall us."[7] Similarly, it appears that legitimate legal coercion can also "simply befall us," depending upon the extenuating moral considerations at work.

It's true that many real-world cases where we regard nonconsent as null are cases where JLs would say people's objections are unreasonable. Nonetheless, the examples are at least suggestive. Similarly, you might think our experience only suggests that actual consent is unnecessary for legitimacy, whereas JL requires hypothetical consent. But it is far from clear that our experience doesn't also suggest that hypothetical consent is unnecessary. Were our conviction in null nonconsent our only guide, we would have little reason to think consent is always necessary for legitimacy. We might have reason to think consent is sometimes needed, but little to think that it is always needed. In other words, we would have little to reason to think that consent, actual or hypothetical, is a necessary condition for legitimacy.

In fact, the idealizations with which JL preserves the facade of consent actually give us another reason to de-center consent from our legitimacy accounts. Since actual consent is unreliable, JLs can preserve the link between consent and legitimacy only by way of a series of idealizations that remove actual persons ever further from the hypothetical persons who are said to represent them. But in light of the tenuous link that consequently exists between actual and hypothetical consent, we might wonder, along with Estlund, whether JLs are "being fickle—granting something to voluntarism, but then not really honoring it."[8] What the idealizations precisely show is that consent isn't important, which they show by legitimizing coercion without real-world persons' consent. As I think Dworkin has noted, consent is precisely the sort of thing that needs to be real in order to be normatively significant. How can I be bound by a promise I've never made? Or as Kuyper rhetorically asks, "What binding force is there for me in the allegation that ages ago one of my progenitors made a '*Contrat Social*,' with other men of that time?"[9] If actual consent isn't required or important, consent simply isn't important.

Either of the following two points might still be made in defense of consent. One, it might be thought that so long as we criticize hypothetical consent, consistency demands we embrace actual consent in its stead. It does not. For we might simply reject both hypothetical as well as actual consent, as I do. Criticizing hypothetical consent might also simply be a way of challenging an account's internal consistency, of pointing out that an account endorses consent without really honoring it. Two, it might also be thought that I am, in fact, not arguing for less idealization, but more. But I am not asking people to imagine what beliefs they might hold were they omniscient and morally perfect. Instead, I am inviting people to reflect on the implications of the beliefs they themselves now hold. Both these last gasp attempts to preserve consent are unsuccessful.

In sum, among other reasons, there are two primary angles from which we can see that we should de-center consent from our understanding of legitimacy. An account that emphasizes consent, such as JL, leads to the unacceptable conclusion of de-legitimizing all uses of legal coercion. As well, in practice we seem already convinced of the nullity of nonconsent. At least sometimes, coercion is legitimate against unwilling others, and cannot be de-legitimized simply by the absence of consent.

A CATEGORY SHIFT TO OBJECTIVE NATURAL RIGHTS

In light of the nullity of nonconsent, consent should not be central to our understanding of legitimacy. Instead of consent, according to the first companion idea of neo-Calvinist legitimacy, legitimacy is a function of preventing violations of natural rights, rights that, in part, are objective by nature. According to JL, legitimacy-conditional rights are the product of consent and agreement. On neo-Calvinist legitimacy, though, legitimacy-conditional rights are held to be objective, morally binding regardless of consent given or withheld.

So exactly how would thinking in terms of objective natural rights solve the problem caused by JL's emphasis on consent? In chapter 3, we identified this problem as the de-legitimization of all legal coercion. Let me now look at this problem in two slightly different ways.

First, think of the problem in terms of the objecting individual. The problem with consent is that it effectively allows parties to escape obligations that we think should be respected and enforced. I don't mean people who might try to escape by pulling a self-interested trick or by gaming the system. Such objections would be unreasonable and, thus, inadmissible on JL. Rather, my point is that there are certain obligations we seem sure everyone has, even if there are individuals who might put forward reasonable objections to them. According to orthodox, Rawlsian JL, if an individual has a reasonable objection, a social agreement is blocked for everyone, including the objecting individual. It has been proposed, though, that perhaps JL should only grant exemptions on an individual-by-individual basis. On such a model, JL's focus on consent allows only the individual objector to avoid coercion; it wouldn't serve to de-legitimize an agreement for society as a whole. On either model, though, so long as an objector has a reasonable objection, one expressible in public terms and plausibly acceptable to all, the individual escapes. Within the JL framework, nonconsent certainly is not null.

Second, think of the problem in terms of society as a whole. On Rawlsian JL—leaving aside the proposal that JL grant exemptions on an individual-by-individual basis—reasonable objections do not simply grant the individuals who object exemptions from otherwise generally applicable laws. Instead, the reasonable objection of anyone means a law is illegitimate for everyone. Thus JL consent means, for example, that not only the libertarian evades taxes, but his reasonable objections de-legitimize egalitarian redistribution for all. Absent an objector's consent, the standard of no reasonable rejection goes unmet and the social agreement is vetoed for all.

Both these related problems can be illustrated with reference to the Bakuninist discussed earlier. Recall that the Bakuninist has a reasonable objection to centralized states, namely, that such states threaten freedom and equality given that "social life could easily take on an authoritarian character through the concentration of power in a minority of specialists, scientists, officials, and administrators."[10] Now on the one hand, you and I might feel strongly that it is legitimate for the state to exercise legal coercion over the Bakuninist individual. But JL means it is not. By advancing a public reason against the centralized state and thereby withholding his consent, the Bakuninist escapes any duty to support political institutions that preserve public order and enforce basic property rights. Consent withheld, the Bakuninist escapes. On the other hand, given our convictions, we seem sure that centralized states are legitimate, legitimate ways of at least preserving public order and enforcing basic property rights, if nothing more. Such states are imperfect to be sure, but legitimate surely. However, the Bakuninist's objection also means that no one has a duty to support such institutions. We all escape. Legally coercive measures to preserve public order and basic property rights are illegitimate for all.

It might be thought, as Lister does, these problems affect only versions of JL that require consensus on particular measures rather than versions that only require consensus on a framework for deliberation.[11] But they affect both versions. As already explained in chapter 3, they affect both because on either version, the JL requirement for legitimate coercion—consensus—goes unmet just so long as one person reasonably objects. Even if there isn't unanimous support for state inaction, that doesn't mean that there is unanimous support for any state action. Consent is problematic for all versions of JL.

How might the idea of natural rights help solve the problem? In general, it helps because, in virtue of natural rights' objectivity, people are duty-bound to respect them whether or not they want to. We have seen this is the nature of objective moral values and duties; they apply to individuals and societies regardless of objections. The objectivity of natural rights thus gives us grounds for saying that individuals have certain obligations whether or not they consent. The normative force of such obligations is not generated by consent, nor is it blunted by consent withheld. Objectivity explains the phenomenon of null nonconsent. By making natural rights central to our understanding of legitimacy, we can thereby displace the idea of consent from centre stage.

Moreover, neo-Calvinists' particular understanding of natural rights also helps explain the legal enforceability of rights as neo-Calvinists view both individuals and institutions as holding natural rights. This includes the state itself, which has a natural right and duty to enforce public justice. Therefore, if protecting the natural rights of individuals or of other institutions is necessary for public justice, we cannot interfere in the state's doing so. A bridge is required between objective moral norms and their legal enforceability. After all, it's possible there are objective moral norms, but that it is illegitimate to try to legally enforce them. The bridge is provided in part, though, by recognizing the fundamental importance of the interests and dignity protected by certain rights. And we can also bridge morality and legality by recognizing that institutions, too, including the state, have natural rights of their own. Given its right and duty to do public justice, the state can legally enforce certain natural rights pursuant to this goal.

So the idea of natural rights, especially as theorized by neo-Calvinists, solves both the problem of the individual escapee and the problem of legal coercion de-legitimized for all. Even if an individual has a plausible objection, their consent withheld doesn't divest them of their objective moral duties nor others of their natural rights, nor does their consent withheld render measures illegitimate for society as a whole. If the state itself has a natural right to do public justice, it certainly also has the right to exist.

By way of illustration, let us once more revisit the case of the Bakuninist, but now from a neo-Calvinist approach. The problem for JL is that the Bakuninist can de-legitimize laws it seems perfectly legitimate to enforce, even de-legitimize the state itself. This happens by the Bakuninist withholding consent, objecting that the centralized state actually jeopardizes freedom and equality. Neo-Calvinist legitimacy, though, does not direct our attention to consent, either that of the Bakuninist or anyone else, but to extenuating justice-related considerations that bear on the legitimacy of the centralized state. These are considerations such as the basic human interests that would be served by a state that maintained public order and basic property rights. From a neo-Calvinist perspective, these interests represent natural rights, which are objective. So the Bakuninist cannot deny that others have genuine rights claims. The state, too, has a natural right to pursue public justice, and protecting the vital interests basic rights represent is required by public justice. So neither can the Bakuninist protest that he will respect others' rights but absent the state. For he would then be denying the state's natural right to enforce public justice. (Indirectly, he would also jeopardize individuals' natural rights, as they would be left without legal protection.) Consequently, neo-Calvinist legitimacy helps us understand why we are justified in coercing the Bakuninist without his consent: we are justified in doing so because his lack of consent does not nullify the objectivity of these natural rights.

Still, there is a gap here. Significant gains are made by the neo-Calvinist idea of natural rights. It explains why the basic demands of justice must be respected by all. It explains why their applicability is unaffected by consent given or withheld. It also explains why the state itself is legitimate, insofar as the state's right to exist is presupposed by the state's natural right to pursue public justice. What it does not explain, however—as mentioned earlier—is which natural rights are needed for legitimacy. All legitimacy-conditional rights will be, I think, natural rights, but not all natural rights will be legitimacy-conditional. Similarly, the idea of natural rights presented so far does not explain which rights should be most important to the state seeking to do public justice, and which rights, if left unprotected, de-legitimize even the state who claims to be doing public justice.

My argument in this chapter, though, should not be judged a failure on account of the gap remaining. It would be a problem if the gap still remained at the end of my overall argument, but the present chapter gives but one part of how my neo-Calvinist approach theorizes legitimacy. The gap was partially addressed in chapter 7 by my discussion of basic human flourishing, and I revisit it in chapter 9. In short, my account will say that legitimacy is not only a function of protecting natural rights, but of protecting ones that are tied to basic human flourishing, ones that correspond to basic human interests and dignity.

So one might ask: what good is the idea of natural rights if it leaves this gap unaddressed? The answer is that natural rights are objective, and that objectivity is needed to justify legal coercion where consent is absent. Objectivity provides at least a possible basis for coercion where consent is absent, even if it does not specify which objective wrongs warrant a coercive response. In other words, it is a necessary condition of understanding legitimacy, even if not a fully sufficient one. Without objectivity as a possible basis for legitimate coercion, consent seems all that's left, and coercion reduces to brute force if the basis is neither of these.

WHAT, THEN, OF CONSENT?

So far, I hope to have persuaded the reader that it is easier to make sense of our legitimacy-related convictions if we begin with the notion of objective, natural rights than if we begin with consent. I am arguing that the idea of consent should not be central to our understanding of legitimacy, neither actual consent nor hypothetical. As much is suggested by the nullity of non-consent in our actual moral experience.

But in other ways, doesn't our lived experience also indicate the great importance of consent? At the risk of sounding contradictory, I answer: it certainly does. And it is these indications, I think, that make JL so attractive in the eyes of so many. Put another way, our experience tells us that consent is important, a fact that JL takes to mean that consent is of overriding importance. But might JL go too far and exaggerate its importance? (My answer can be anticipated easily enough.) Whether or not it does, I grant that I share many consent-emphasizing intuitions, and that often legal coercion is not fully justified if coercion is absent.

How, then, are we to reconcile these conflicting sets of intuitions—those that suggest the importance of consent (which motivate JL) and those that do not, such as the nullity of non-consent (which motivate my account)? On my view, how do I see these fitting together? And what do I take to be the real import of each?

Taking into account the full range of our intuitions—both consent-emphasizing and consent-bypassing—what they suggest is a crucial asymmetry between two types of legal coercion. On the one hand, it seems that consent is not necessary to legitimize legal coercion when it is a basic right that's at stake. On the other, when legal coercion is used to pursue some further demand of justice or some other social goal, consent is necessary. Thus, my proposal for reconciling our consent-emphasizing and consent-bypassing intuitions is a threshold model. Below the threshold, consent is unnecessary. Above, it is necessary.

This is the general model I propose for reconciling our consent-emphasizing and consent-bypassing convictions. Let me now add a few points of clarification.

First, to speak more precisely, above the threshold consent is necessary in the sense that it is necessary for further legal coercion to be fully justified or fully just, though it is not necessary for legitimacy. I understand legitimacy to be a predicate that primarily attaches to regimes, and only secondarily to individual laws. On my view, it is a property possessed by regimes who satisfy the condition of upholding basic justice, or, in other words, of protecting natural rights tied to basic human flourishing. Moreover, such regimes retain this property however else they may authorize the use of, and exercise, legal coercion. Included in this allowance, such regimes retain legitimacy whether or not authorization of legal coercion for further purposes involves obtaining the consent of those who will be affected by further measures. This may seem an implausible picture unless we bear in mind that a regime may at no point jeopardize basic justice itself. If it does, legitimacy is forfeited. For, as per my account, legitimacy consists in preventing violations of basic rights. Remember the condition Wolterstorff suggested above: a state may not enforce a right, even a natural right, if doing so threatens other, still more important rights. Also bear in mind that I am talking about legitimacy in particular, not full justice, and bear in mind the sort of concept that legitimacy is. It is a concept that identifies legal coercion which, while falling short of full justice, nonetheless remains morally credentialed in a relevant way.[12] On the model I propose, I readily grant that many measures going beyond basic justice which I am prepared to deem legitimate will fall short, perhaps far short, of full justice. However, they remain morally credentialed being part of a set of laws which, as a whole, uphold basic justice and protect essential natural rights.

Second, following from what has just been said, here is a clearer statement of how I think we ought view coercive measures above the threshold: above the threshold of basic justice, consent should be sought and justice is not fully served unless consent is given. Contrast the situation below the threshold. There, consent needn't be sought and basic justice is served whether or not consent is given. Below the threshold, it is still preferable, morally and practically, to reinforce otherwise legitimate laws with the consent of affected parties. But the legitimacy of laws that protect basic rights should not be regarded as captive to the consent of affected parties. Conversely, it is appropriate to regard laws above the threshold as captive to the consent of affected parties. Though such laws, absent consent, are not illegitimate, neither are they fully justified.

In sum, the idea here is that consent is not necessary for legitimacy, but it is for full justice. Legitimacy is a function of meeting the basic demands of justice, but these are not understood as including a consent requirement.[13]

Third, note again the level of generality at which my proposal is aimed. As with my neo-Calvinist account developed in chapter 7, my current proposal puts forth the general categories in terms of which we can successfully reconcile our consent-emphasizing and consent-bypassing convictions. I take it that no one, including JLs themselves, can make sense of their convictions without appealing to some threshold of the kind that my model involves.[14] For everyone has certain convictions about basic justice on which they are unwilling to budge, certain rights they would be unwilling to make vulnerable to democratic procedures. Everyone has such convictions, though what is considered nonnegotiable will vary somewhat from person to person. Moreover, everyone also has certain convictions about all the other stuff that is the fodder of politics, albeit convictions they hold more loosely. These other matters, important though they might be, are not the stuff of basic justice. That they are not is reflected by the fact that they are negotiable. Similarly, in contrast to matters of basic justice, there is also a greater willingness to subject these other issues to democratic adjudication.

My model, then, reflects this common category distinction between issues that we are and issues that we are not willing to subject to democratic procedures. Accordingly, I propose we make sense of this category distinction in terms of a threshold below which consent is not required for legitimate coercion and above which consent is required. The model does not say which specific uses of legal coercion fall into one or the other category. On this we should expect disagreement. But, with an eye to the issue of legitimacy, it suggests that we reconcile our consent-emphasizing and consent-bypassing intuitions in terms of these general categories. On this we should find common ground.

It shouldn't go unnoticed that there is also very much a consent-emphasizing dimension of neo-Calvinism. A powerful democratic impulse courses throughout the ideals and writings of the tradition. It is evident in the intensity with which neo-Calvinists affirm the equality of all citizens. Kuyper declares, "No man has the right to rule over another man. . . . As man I stand free and bold, over against the most powerful of my fellowmen."[15] To reject any natural hierarchy among citizens is to place all on equal footing: "To have placed man on a footing of equality with man, so far as the purely human interests are concerned, is the immortal glory which incontestably belongs to Calvinism," so says Kuyper.[16] As summarized by tenet 1 of my outline of neo-Calvinism, people are naturally equal and free, and ultimately accountable only to God. This democratic impulse is also evident in neo-Calvinists' sensitivity to all forms of oppressive government. Kuyper urges vigilance with which we "must ever watch against the danger which lurks, for our personal liberty, in the power of the state."[17] Oppression lurks where "no constitutional rights" are recognized "except as the result of princely favor."[18] As we have seen, contemporary neo-Calvinists are also sensitive to the hegemonic tendencies of technology and, especially, the capitalist economy. Furthermore, neo-Calvinists' democratic impulse is seen in the ever greater diffusion of power that attends the process of societal differentiation.

These recurrent themes of democracy, individual liberty, and constitutional checks against overreaching governments all suggest that consent is important. On my wider view, it does, indeed, have a vital, even if circumscribed, role to play in a just social order. And, remember, the only real qualification I am putting on consent is that it is unnecessary when legitimacy-conditional basic rights and wrongs are at stake.

In sum, consent is no part of my neo-Calvinist account of legitimacy. However, that consent plays an important role in any fully just polity is a value that also can, and should, be appropriated from neo-Calvinist thought.

CONCLUSION

While a democratic impulse courses through neo-Calvinism, my focus in this chapter has been how we ought not exaggerate the importance of consent in our political philosophy, particularly regarding the issue of legitimacy. I have made this point by highlighting how, in our actual moral experience, we regard coercion as legitimate even without consent. As suggested by Estlund, we are convinced of the nullity of non-consent. Taken generally, this idea captures our sense that, at least concerning the basic demands of justice, individuals cannot escape coercion simply by withholding consent. When extenuating moral considerations demand the use of legal coercion, coercion may be used with or without consent. The first idea of neo-Calvinist legitimacy—that of objective, natural rights—helps explain these phenomena. Moreover, on neo-Calvinism both individuals and institutions, including the state, possess natural rights, which helps explain the legal enforceability of natural rights.

So, is consent needed, as the title of this chapter asks? Drawing on the idea of null nonconsent, I hope to have persuaded readers that they are, in fact, committed to answering this question negatively in at least some instances. I explained that consent would play a role within my broader view. However, contrary to the impression one receives from sweeping statements such as that governments derive "their just powers from the consent of the governed," this role has definite limits.

Lastly, we also saw that by replacing the idea of consent with that of objective natural rights and wrongs, neo-Calvinist legitimacy is able to avoid the first unacceptable consequence to which JL leads. This was exemplified by our reassessment of the Bakuninist case. Hence, while JL de-legitimizes all uses of legal coercion, my neo-Calvinist account does not.

NOTES

1. Audi, "The Place of Religious Argument," 689.
2. Estlund, *Democratic Authority*, 119.
3. Cf. "Appeals to hypothetical consent can seem to miss the point of consent. Often, it is a source of freedom and power to be able to refuse to consent to something and thereby prohibit certain actions of others. This is a value that hypothetical consent theories might be charged with ignoring" (Ibid., 125).
4. Ibid., 124.
5. Estlund thinks null nonconsent does not inform the question of when it is legitimate to legally coerce others. ("Normative consent . . . can establish authority even if it cannot establish legitimacy.") That is, he thinks it a separate question whether it is permissible to issue legal commands, even if one is required to obey any commands that might be issued. For my part, I fail to see how the same moral considerations that obligate one to support legal coercion cannot at the same time legitimize the use of that coercion. On my view, the need to uphold basic natural rights both obligates and legitimates. For instance, in Estlund's own example of despicable Joe, wouldn't the same considerations that require him to submit to authority also legitimize the use of force to compel Joe to respect the flight attendant's orders? Such considerations include the high stakes involved—namely, the needs of those injured—and the fact that the flight attendant is well-positioned to meet these needs.

Estlund would also reject the sort of legitimacy account I propose. For despite the concept of null non-consent, consent still factors into Estlund's account insofar as we are to treat people as if they had consented where nonconsent is null. Consent plays no role, though, in the sort of "urgent task theory" that I propose, and for this reason he would reject it. However, I would argue that the lesson of null nonconsent is not, in fact, the importance of counterfactual consent, but the unimportance of either actual or counterfactual consent regarding our basic rights and duties. Accordingly, I don't think it any strike against urgent task theories that they are not based on consent.

See Ibid., 127, 130–31.
6. Cf. Will Kymlicka, "The Ethics of Inarticulacy," *Inquiry* 34, no. 2 (1991): 173–74.
7. Estlund, *Democratic Authority*, 117.
8. Ibid., 130.
9. Kuyper, *Lectures on Calvinism*, 69.
10. Bakunin, *Bakunin on Anarchy*, 7.
11. Andrew Lister, "Public Justification of What? Coercion vs. Decision as Competing Frames for the Basic Principle of Justificatory Liberalism," *Public Affairs Quarterly* 25, no. 4 (October 2011): 349ff.
12. "Thus, legitimacy is a weaker idea than justice. . . . At some point, the injustice of the outcomes of a legitimate democratic procedure corrupts its legitimacy, and so will the injustice of the political constitution itself. But before this point is reached, the outcomes of a legitimate

procedure are legitimate whatever they are. . . . Legitimacy allows an undetermined range of injustice that justice might not permit" (Rawls, *Political Liberalism*, 428 [emphasis mine]).

13. So I agree with Arneson that there is not a basic right to a democratic say. See Richard J. Arneson, "The Supposed Right to a Democratic Say," in *Contemporary Debates in Political Philosophy*, ed. Thomas Christiano and John Christman (Blackwell Publishing Ltd., 2009), 197–212. A right above the threshold? Yes. Below the threshold? No.

14. Rawls' comments quoted earlier this chapter in a footnote reflect such a threshold, his emphasis on procedures belying what he demonstrably thinks. He says that "[a]t some point" procedural outcomes become so unjust that legitimacy is compromised. But he alleges that "before this point is reached" it is procedures that make for legitimacy. Instead, it seems to me that what Rawls has done is identify a substantive threshold. Below it, even procedures cannot suffice for legitimacy. (Rawls, *Political Liberalism*, 428.)

15. Kuyper, *Lectures on Calvinism*, 69.

16. Ibid., 19.

17. Ibid., 68.

18. Ibid., 84.

Chapter Nine

The Human Flourishing Tie

My account says legitimacy is a function of protecting natural rights that are tied to basic human flourishing. What is this tie to human flourishing? As outlined in chapter 7, the tie is twofold, having a weaker and stronger sense. In the former, any account of basic rights conceptually presupposes some or another view of human flourishing. Otherwise, it is arbitrary. In the latter, human flourishing is tied to natural rights in that we cannot weigh any rights claim except in light of societal flourishing as a whole. As in chapter 7, I will focus here more on the former. Primarily I will explain how understanding the inevitable dependence of natural rights on some or another account of human flourishing yields a clearer picture of rights' philosophical grounds. I will focus less on the stronger sense in which rights are tied to flourishing, but this stronger sense does depend on the weaker that I will defend at some length.

If I am successful, what sort of difference should the reader expect? The reader should not expect that the idea of basic human flourishing will make it any easier to make specific legitimacy judgments. Not necessarily, at least. In many cases, doing so will still be difficult and will require a great deal of practical wisdom and judgment. However, I do intend to make clearer the sort of philosophical assumptions that we do make, and should make, when discussing and debating legitimacy. In other words, I share Rawls' goal of achieving a "clear and uncluttered" understanding of the issue at hand.[1] Such an understanding of legitimacy, I hope to show, requires us to appreciate how our legitimacy-related convictions are tied to views of human flourishing.

As I shall explain, human flourishing is counterpoint to JL's idea of proceduralism. Rather than making clear the philosophical presuppositions of our legitimacy convictions, JL's proceduralism obfuscates them. This is the Humean point to which I referred earlier. JL's proceduralist framework foregrounds the fact of agreement, but obscures the normative significance of the reasons for the agreement. But we should not follow Hume in replacing proceduralism with a utilitarian approach. Justifying rights in terms of aggregate utility is, I take it, a nonstarter.[2] Instead, the needed replacement for JL-style proceduralism is basic human flourishing.

Moreover, in chapter 4 we saw that JL's proceduralism leads to the unacceptable consequence of undercutting legitimacy-conditional basic rights. It does so, I argued, by conflicting with key characteristics of real-world basic rights. Whereas actual rights are procedure-independent, have definite content, and are impervious to popular opinion, JL delivers rights that are fundamentally procedure-dependent, the product of a contentless proceduralism, and contingent on group consensus. I explained that, at root, these mischaracterizations of basic rights result from JL's commitment to proceduralism.

So how is basic human flourishing the antidote to proceduralism? In short, an account of human flourishing provides content where JL-proceduralism does not. Thus, by understanding legitimacy in terms of human flourishing, my neo-Calvinist account makes clear what lies at bottom of our legitimacy-related convictions, including those of JLs. That is, it makes clear the type of philosophical presupposition that lies at bottom. For even JLs themselves must ultimately rely on views of human flourishing to operationalize their procedures. This final and inescapable need for human flourishing is a point badly obscured by JL's proceduralist framework.

Moreover, if we conceive of rights as tied to basic human flourishing, we can make sense of the characteristics real-world rights have. For the content and importance of these rights is determined by their contribution to human flourishing, and not by procedures and group consensus. Thus, human flourishing is the appropriate replacement for proceduralism since it does not undercut basic rights in the way that JL's proceduralism does.

In the course of the following discussion, I hope to again make clear the level of abstraction at which my account aims. My point is that whatever our preferred account of human flourishing may be, that we must rely on some such account is inevitable. I begin by reviewing JL's problematic proceduralism. Then I highlight the human flourishing tie, emphasizing how rights presuppose views of human flourishing.

JL'S PROBLEMATIC PROCEDURALISM REVISITED

The problems with proceduralism, including JL proceduralism, may not be readily apparent. Indeed, fair procedures present themselves as a wholly appropriate way of resolving many real-world disagreements. Thus, it is unsurprising, and even laudable, that philosophers have tried to use proceduralism in their theories to deal with various issues within political philosophy.

As attractive as the idea might initially seem, however, we have seen that relying too heavily on philosophical proceduralism leads to problems of the sort we reviewed in chapter 4. For one, it is JLs' proceduralist aspirations that lead to what I called the "vacuity of the reasonable"—how JL passes the buck to hypothetical contractors without telling us which of their reasons or agreements are reasonable—or what Estlund calls the "flight from substance."[3] The internal logic of JL demands that the category of the reasonable be emptied of determinate content. This demand is made in the name of popular sovereignty. *Ex hypothesi*, it is the procedure's participants who themselves provide the needed content. JLs are also committed to the vacuity of the reasonable since stipulating what counts as reasonable would merely beg the question on behalf of whatever social arrangements a theorist favors[4] and would rob the procedure of any genuine heuristic value in explicating the demands of justice or legitimacy.[5] Furthermore, I explained in chapter 3 why JL logic demands that reasonableness primarily apply to persons rather than to reasons or proposals. Concerning the reasonableness of persons, the flight from substance is evident in Rawls' Spartan twofold criteria for reasonable personhood.[6] These criteria provide scarcely any more content than to require that persons respect reciprocity as well as the reality of reasonable pluralism. The vacuity of the reasonable; the flight from substance; or think, too, of Hegel's critique of Kant, that the categorical imperative is a merely formal principle bereft of the substance provided by concrete, historical institutions. All point to the same problematic phenomenon: the lack of content provided by philosophical theories that are overly procedural.

A second problem with proceduralist theories is that they lend credence to the idea that something is right just because it is popular. Yet we know this idea to be certainly false.[7] A unanimity condition is essential to JL. The procedure that determines the principles of justice and legitimacy must culminate in social arrangements on which all agree. The justification of social arrangements depends on the fact of agreement itself. Of course JL's contractors are hypothetical, not real. But at the same time they are also intended to be not so very different from real-world persons. Otherwise they could not serve as meaningful proxies for real-world persons. Hence JL, indirectly, if not directly, implies that the demands of justice and legitimacy are determined by popular opinion.

Taken together with the asymmetry between the procedure-dependence of JL rights and the procedure-independence of basic rights, these concerns lead to the more general problem that JL undercuts the basic rights we regard as necessary for legitimacy. How so? It portrays them as procedure-dependent, not procedure-independent. It portrays them as lacking content in the absence of political deliberation, whereas actual basic rights have definite content given humans' interests and dignity. It also portrays their justification as dependent on group consensus, even though something isn't right just because it is popular. Thus, JL undercuts legitimacy-conditional basic rights by conflicting with characteristics we experience these rights as having. We experience these rights as the prerequisites of fair procedures. But on the JL hypothesis, they are the products of fair procedures instead.

Remember that proceduralism causes one other noteworthy problem, which I regard as more a philosophical than normative failing. Proceduralist approaches obscure the considerations that really justify any justifiable social arrangement. For any proposal to which all parties agree, we may ask a further question: why did they agree to the proposal? It is those considerations which seem to really justify a social arrangement. Or to put this point in the idiolect of JL, there is always the further question of why an agreement is reasonable. What considerations make it reasonable or unreasonable to accept? It is these considerations that seem to justify a JL agreement, not the fact of agreement itself. Hume leveled this very critique against the social contract theories of his day,[8] and it remains relevant to proceduralist theories of today, including JL. This criticism doesn't mean that proceduralist thinking ought not play any role in our practical reasoning whatsoever. But it does mean that, at most, its usefulness is as a mere heuristic, or as a kind of decision-procedure. It also means that, *qua* philosophical theory, proceduralism does not yield the "clear and uncluttered" view that we seek. A truly clear and uncluttered view would, instead, bring to light the nature of the substantive considerations that make reasons and proposals worthy objects of unanimous agreement.

By way of reminder, then, the foregoing are the problems JL faces in virtue of its proceduralism. In what follows, I hope to lay bare the nature of the considerations that truly underwrite our judgments of legitimacy. By doing so, I also hope to place the basic rights we cherish on a firmer philosophical foundation.

THE NEED FOR HUMAN FLOURISHING

To understand our legitimacy-related convictions, we must understand that in holding them we presuppose some or another view of human flourishing. JL suggests that we can make sense of our convictions while eschewing such substantive views, but we cannot. To answer the pressing question of why an agreement is made, or of what makes it reasonable rather than unreasonable, we must appeal to some such view. It is views of human flourishing, whether or not they are recognized as such, that provide the content needed to operationalize a proceduralist approach. As Estlund might say, the flight from substance must end in substance.[9] And this substance is given by views of human flourishing. This point requires unpacking.

As a preliminary point, it is crucial to appreciate that views of flourishing can vary in their specificity and yet remain views of flourishing. Some views will endorse a rather specific ideal of flourishing. Others will allow a greater range of individual choice. But both relatively narrow and relatively permissive views nonetheless pertain to human flourishing. In what sense? Let us borrow again from Charles Taylor. That both narrow and permissive views concern human flourishing is seen in the fact that both presuppose ways of being that are, either explicitly or implicitly, "strongly evaluated" to be superior to alternative ways of being.[10] Even views that allow a great range of individual choice strongly evaluate living autonomously as superior to guiding one's life by external religious or social rules.

Also by way of background, consider some representative views of human flourishing. Aristotle and Aquinas provide paradigm cases. According to Aristotle, human flourishing consists in the exercise of practical wisdom as a member of a self-governing polity. According to the latter, in the beatific vision. But views of human flourishing need not be so parochial. As I say, they will vary in the specificity of their demands. So, for instance, in elaborating the "diversity of goods" with which our political theory must reckon, Taylor lists the life of "personal integrity," that of Christian agape love, that of self-direction, and that of utilitarian rationality as four recognizable "modes of life" that find adherents in contemporary Western society.[11] Each of the ends Taylor lists would allow a wider range of individual freedom than either Aristotelian or Thomistic accounts of human flourishing, but each is nonetheless a view of human flourishing. Each holds forth a given way of living as qualitatively superior to alternatives, not as a matter of mere taste, but of moral fact. The life of personal integrity is judged superior to that of mere "conformity to established standards which are not really one's own."[12] Or take the life of self-direction, which "sees the dignity of human beings as consisting in their directing their own lives, in their deciding for themselves the conditions of their own existence, as against falling prey to the domination of others, or to impersonal natural or social mechanisms which they fail to understand, and therefore cannot control or transform."[13]

Here, then, we have six examples of views of flourishing: flourishing *qua* exercise of practical wisdom, *qua* beatific vision, *qua* personal integrity, *qua* agape love, *qua* self-direction, and *qua* utilitarian rationality. Some have more the appearance of "comprehensive doctrines,"[14] others less so. Some are more narrow, others more permissive. But we should not miss that all are views of flourishing.

In contrast to the proceduralism of JL, let us now reflect on the ways in which views of human flourishing deliver substance.

The examples just given help illustrate that views of human flourishing, whatever their other traits, are essentially contentful. This means that any such view specifies human flourishing in terms of concrete ways of being, whether narrow or general. On one view, flourishing is the exercise of practical wisdom; on another, it is self-expression; on still another, it is the exercise of autonomy; and so on. The content of each may be different, but each is, indeed, contentful.

In turn, each of these concrete ways of being requires certain material conditions for its realization. That is to say, there are particular political, economic, and social conditions that must be in place for the realization of each. Now the required conditions will vary depending on the way of living to be realized. For instance, those required by collective self-governance will likely differ from those needed for a life of self-direction. The latter sort of life may well require relatively strong individual property rights, in comparison to the relatively strong forms of public ownership that would seem conditions of the former. And the conditions for both collective self-governance and self-direction would be different again from those needed for the cultivation and exercise of utilitarian rationality. A thoroughgoing education in science would certainly be needed for the latter, though not for the former two, or at least not needed to the same degree. Having wide space for a personal prerogative may be needed for maintaining personal integrity, but is anathema to strict utilitarian impartiality. My point here is that, while the conditions for various ways of being will vary, each way of being will nonetheless require certain concrete conditions for its realization. These concrete conditions are then part of the determinate content provided by a given view of flourishing.

Moreover, views of flourishing are contentful in that they specify particular functionings that ought be achieved. Flourishing consists not merely in having the opportunity to function in certain valuable ways, but in the actual functioning itself. Here I have in mind Nussbaum's distinction between "capabilities" and "functionings." Whereas capabilities are merely capacities for functioning in various ways, functionings involve the actual exercise of capabilities. In other words, then, my present point is that the views of flourishing we presuppose are never simply about capabilities. All such views have functionings they prefer—even relatively permissive, liberty-emphasizing views—because for any opportunity we think it important to have, we can ask the further question of why it is important. It may be that an opportunity is important because of the functioning enabled by the opportunity. Then it is that functioning, which is enabled by the opportunity, that is valued by the presupposed view of flourishing. For instance, why is the opportunity to freely associate with others significant? Plausibly because association with others is a basic good of human life. Alternatively, it may be said that an opportunity is important simply because it enables and maximize freedoms;

certain opportunities are important, it is claimed, regardless of functionings. However, as Taylor's insight discussed in chapter 7 helps us see, this explanation will not do. It is patently implausible to talk in terms of "maximizing" freedom.[15] We must make judgments about which freedoms are morally significant. But making these judgments inevitably raises the question of why this freedom rather than that. And to answer this further question, we must suppose that certain functionings—that is, exercising free choice over some matters rather than others—are of greater moral significance than other functionings.[16] JLs themselves recognize that some freedoms are more significant than others.[17] Thus, the views of flourishing presupposed by basic rights, whether autonomy-emphasizing or not, always involve functionings and never only capabilities or opportunities.

Likewise, we should understand that a view of flourishing may intrinsically value the exercise of freedom, and not only instrumentally value freedom for the sake of some further good. But such a view is no less about flourishing for doing so. And in all likelihood, a view of flourishing will involve some combination of both these elements. Some rights and opportunities will be valued instrumentally and others intrinsically.

Note also that we cannot say that a freedom is morally justified just because of convergence, without saying anything about its role in human flourishing. That is, we cannot say it is important simply because diverse people converge on and agree on its importance. JLs say this, but they should not. We cannot because the normative significance of the convergence stands to be scrutinized. If we judge that convergence on only certain rights or opportunities is significant, or that only convergence of certain viewpoints is significant—if, in other words, we are unwilling to accept convergence on just anything—then it seems it is moral criteria external to the fact of convergence that is truly normatively significant. We should then look to that external criteria for what rights and freedoms are morally important and for their justification.

Nor can we avoid presupposing some or another view of flourishing by attempting to justify the importance of a right or opportunity in terms of a hypothetical procedure. For we cannot escape asking why it would be reasonable for parties to make a given agreement. We cannot answer this question without recourse to judgments about the importance of various functionings, even if these functionings value only the exercise of free choice rather than the making of particular choices.

In sum, there are various ways in which an account of human flourishing provides content to basic rights, ways which also serve to make content available where the contentless proceduralism of JL does not. We have just covered several such ways. Content is made available by the particular concrete ways of life such views explicitly or implicitly deem superior. Moreover, it is actually achieving these ways of life, these functionings, that is held to be significant, not merely having opportunities. This being the case, these views furnish us with more content than if it were possible to theorize opportunities in the abstract apart from functionings. Further content is derivatively given by the conditions needed to achieve these functionings or ways of being. Such will include the political, economic, and social conditions required for achieving them. In these ways views of flourishing provide substantive content where empty proceduralism does not.

Let me now consider a major objection to the notion that philosophers need appeal to some or another view of human flourishing to explain political legitimacy. The objection is this: isn't it obvious that you and I will disagree over what counts as human flourishing? Disagreement over human flourishing is endemic to contemporary pluralistic societies; reasonable pluralism seems an inescapable fact. This raises the question of how we can legitimately exercise political power amidst disagreement over conceptions of human flourishing, and appealing to any one particular conception seems a maladroit answer.

In response, disagreement over flourishing does not, in fact, impugn my suggestion that human flourishing is necessary to understand legitimacy. The following two points help us see why it does not.

First, the issue of legitimacy is separable from multi-perspectival acceptability, and neo-Calvinist legitimacy does not take multi-perspectival acceptability as a condition of legitimate legal coercion. In Rawls' wake, it is sometimes assumed the concept of legitimacy, by its very essence, addresses itself to a variety of viewpoints. But there is no need for this assumption. Instead, the concept of legitimacy in its most general sense is simply that of a threshold which, while falling short of full justice, is nonetheless morally credentialed in some way. Multi-perspectival acceptability is one way of spelling out the moral credentials possessed by legitimate legal coercion, but certainly not the only way. Protecting basic rights, for instance, is another. Moreover, if my argument of chapter 3 is correct, then understanding legitimate coercion in terms of a unanimity condition actually de-legitimizes all legal coercion, giving us reason to reject such a condition. And my account does reject the condition. Thus, even if a particular view of flourishing falls afoul of a multi-perspectival acceptability requirement, my appeal to flourishing is not impugned since such a requirement is neither a helpful nor necessary way of theorizing legitimacy.

Second, despite disagreement over flourishing, my appeal helps illuminate legitimacy by highlighting the sort of philosophical presuppositions involved in any non-arbitrary account of legitimacy conditions. No one, I think, can make philosophical sense of their legitimacy-related convictions without presupposing some view of flourishing at a conceptually fundamental level. I challenge any and all to philosophically account for their convictions without an appeal to human flourishing, and believe this is a challenge none can meet. The content of the basic rights one believes in must ultimately come from somewhere, and ultimately it comes from a view of human flourishing that is either wittingly or unwittingly presupposed. This is an inescapable fact of how we reason about rights, and, in turn, legitimacy, whether or not these underlying views are obscured by an overlay of proceduralism.

In chapter 4 I argued that the unacceptable consequence of JL's proceduralism was its undercutting of legitimacy-conditional basic rights. To conclude this section, how does the appeal to flourishing help place basic rights on a firmer philosophical foundation? It does so by making clearer the philosophical grounds on which they stand, as it is explicit about where the content of natural rights comes from. It is not as though it is left up to contractors, hypothetical or otherwise, to give to basic rights whatever content they wish, but this content is delivered by the elements of human flourishing. JL's proceduralism does not deliver rights that are procedure-independent, contentful, and impervious to popular opinion. But my neo-Calvinist alternative, with its appeal to flourishing, does.

THE BASICS OF HUMAN FLOURISHING

In understanding our legitimacy-related convictions, it is important to come clean about the views of flourishing they presuppose. It is also important, though, to only focus on the basics of this flourishing. Why is this? Explaining why will help fill the gap left at the end of chapter 8, that of explaining which natural rights are legitimacy-conditional, and which are most important to public justice. Thinking in neo-Calvinist terms, we could reframe the current question as follows: which of the demands of public justice are legitimacy-conditional? Neo-Calvinists have long recognized that the state has a natural right to pursue public justice, but let's now ask, assuming the state will never meet all the demands of public justice, which demands it must uphold to be legitimate. The answers to these questions—why focus on the basics of human flourishing and which rights or demands of public justice are legitimacy-conditional—are related.

We already saw in chapter 7 some pointers from neo-Calvinism suggesting we focus only on natural rights that are basic. Based on Zuidervaart's notion of societal evil, I proposed we isolate legitimacy-conditional rights violations as those that are especially oppressive or destructive to social flourishing. Or based on his notion of systemic deformation, we might understand legitimacy-conditional rights violations as those that fundamentally disrespect humans' God-given dignity. Wolterstorff's condition that protecting rights mustn't threaten more important rights also implied that the state should focus on relatively basic rights. I now want to simply extend this account somewhat, and draw the conclusion that we need only, and should only, focus on the basics of human flourishing in theorizing legitimacy. So why focus only on the basics of human flourishing?

Here is one way of understanding why: while I've presented human flourishing as an antidote to JL's content-free proceduralism, flourishing will still appear to be the wrong sort of antidote unless we qualify it in some way. This is because views of human flourishing often, if not always, involve requirements that go far beyond those we think legally enforceable. We think the purview of the state is restricted, restricted to only certain demands of justice or morality but not all. Now what we want to explain are the natural rights that are necessary for legitimacy, but human flourishing seems the wrong category insofar as views of flourishing often purport to explain much more.

We focus only on the basics of human flourishing, then, to ensure that views of flourishing provide us with the right kind of content for explaining legitimacy-conditional rights. The right content is content that corresponds only to the natural rights needed for legitimacy. It is not content that extends to the whole host of rights that a perfectly just regime might uphold.

Here is another way of understanding why we focus only on the basics of human flourishing, which we have seen before and which I reiterate now: we focus only on the basics because there are certain interests humans have, and certain ways their dignity ought be respected, that are of fundamental importance to human flourishing. These interests and dignity are of fundamental importance to human beings given the sort of beings that we are, with the worth we intrinsically possess. For instance, given that our bodies require nutrition and maintenance, rights to material provision and healthcare are essential. Given that humans represent discrete centers of consciousness in discrete bodies, each having their own will, rights to bodily integrity and autonomy are fundamentally important. And as another example, impartial application of the law is a fundamental expression of respect for the equal moral worth of all persons. In general, given humans' inviolable dignity, their basic rights should be respected and accorded overriding importance. Created in the image of God, humans have a unique worth: "Look at the birds of the air: they neither sow nor reap nor gather into barns, and yet your heavenly Father feeds them. Are you not of more value than they?"[18] So why should we consider any of these rights to be basic? Rights to such goods as material provision, healthcare, bodily integrity, autonomy, and fair application of the law? It is not, as JL would have it, because no one could reasonably reject such rights. Rather, these rights are basic given the fundamental importance of the interests and dignity they protect given the sort of beings that we are.

In making these judgments regarding humans' fundamental interests and dignity, notice that we cannot help but presuppose certain views of human flourishing. Whatever one's view of flourishing, there will be certain elements of the view that stand out as basic and whose fundamental importance justifies their legal enforcement. Various views of flourishing will, of course, understand the sort of beings we are in varying ways, what our interests are and what our dignity demands. But for any such view, its views on our interests and dignity will inform its account of the interests and dignity that correspond to the natural rights that must be protected for legitimacy. My point here is not to defend any one account of basic flourishing. Rather, it is to outline the terms in which we should understand any account of legitimacy-conditional natural rights. For any account of basic rights to be nonarbitrary, these are the sort of philosophical presuppositions and categories the account must involve.

One last point. It should be clear that my aim is not to promote any account of flourishing in full using political institutions. Rather, my aim is simply to marshal the philosophical resources necessary for making sense of the basic rights we consider necessary for legitimacy.

ILLUSTRATIONS

The main difference made by the appeal to basic human flourishing is that it helps us explain the content and urgency of basic rights with much greater philosophical clarity than JL. So let me now sketch, briefly yet, I hope, suggestively, how appealing to human flourishing makes possible a different sort of justification of basic rights.

For example, what justifies redistribution that ensures all receive a social minimum? It is well-known that justifying redistribution is a challenge for JL. There evidently are reasonable objections to coercive redistribution, such as those put forward by libertarians. Hence, it falls short of JL's unanimity condition. If we are quite sure, though, that such redistribution is justified, how else might it be justified?

Alternatively, we might justify it in terms of basic human flourishing. Since humans are embodied beings with physical needs, achievement of basic physical health is of fundamental importance to their well-being. Therefore, provision for these basic physical needs is also of fundamental importance, material assistance that ensures adequate nutrition and shelter. (A right to public healthcare could be justified along similar lines.) These considerations justify a natural right to a social minimum, and insofar as this natural right represents a fundamental human interest, it also represents a basic demand of public justice and one which, as such, is legally enforceable. JL struggles to make sense of a legitimacy-conditional right such as this. But a neo-Calvinist approach, emphasizing the basics of human flourishing, can readily make sense of it, and does so with philosophical clarity.

Or what justifies the right to basic education? As JLs would have it, universal education is justified because no one could reasonably reject it. But does such an explanation really get at the moral considerations that are operative in the justification of public education? It seems not. If anything, what justifies a right to basic education is not hypothetical unanimity but the moral importance of intellectual development for beings such as ourselves. The further facts that schooling nurtures young people's capacity for individual agency and prepares them to assume productive places in society also seem eminently relevant to a proper justification of the right to education.

In explaining why universal education cannot be reasonably rejected, JLs will presumably point to considerations such as these. But on the JL justification of universal education, it is not these considerations that are primary. Rather it is the fact of agreement itself. So even if JL can justify a right to basic education, it doesn't seem to do so with reference to the operative moral considerations. On the other hand, neo-Calvinist legitimacy would justify it, and, again, with greater philosophical clarity. It would be justified not on the basis of a hypothetical agreement, but in light of the basics of individual and social well-being. It is easy to see education as a basic component of human well-being, and universal primary and secondary education as a basic component of social well-being as a whole. In turn, these considerations correspond to a basic right to education.

To take one more example, what justifies the right to religious freedom? At least at first glance, a JL justification seems able to protect religious freedom. Despite the rise of secularism in the West, most people still consider the choice to be religious or not important for the exercise of individual autonomy. Given these mores, JL deems it reasonable to reject any proposal that would significantly restrict traditional religious practice. Religious freedom still seems safe.

However, given the rising tide of scientism[19] in Western society, one wonders just how secure this defense of religious freedom is. For a vocal segment of the population regards religious belief as patently unreasonable, and this segment seems to be growing in influence. Religious belief is regarded as intellectually dubious, even positively retrograde. The so-called "new atheists" give voice to this antipathy toward traditional religion.[20] On this view, it might be thought perfectly reasonable to deny religious freedom, since religious beliefs are considered false and as obstacles to moral and intellectual advancement. In fact, it would not be surprising if secular theorists came to think there was a principled basis for denying religious freedom even if a majority of the population was, in fact, religious. It would be unsurprising since this is already the posture JLs seem to take toward the issue of young-earth creationism.[21] So it is not unthinkable that a JL approach would censure religious practice, or judge religious freedom unimportant to individual autonomy. As traffic freedom is deemed insignificant,[22] so might religious freedom one day be deemed insignificant.

Conversely, assuming that there is in fact a basic right to religious freedom, how might it be justified with reference to human flourishing? Depending on one's view of flourishing, religious freedom might be understood as fundamental in one of basically two ways. It might be that religious practice itself is viewed as significant. Or it might be that religious choice itself, regardless of which religion is chosen or whether any religion is chosen at all, is viewed as significant to individual autonomy. But whether religious practice is thought valuable or not, a view of human flourishing can justify religious freedom in a clear and parsimonious way. Furthermore, since the right is a component of basic human flourishing, its normative justification remains unaffected by the rising tides of secularism and scientism.

My hope is that these three examples we have briefly considered—rights to a social minimum, to education, and to religious freedom—point, in a fairly vivid way, to the difference made by understanding legitimacy-conditional rights in terms of human flourishing. In contrast to JL's putative justifications of these rights, human flourishing allows them to stand on clearer, firmer, more satisfying philosophical grounds.

NEO-CALVINISM AND HUMAN FLOURISHING

All that's been said so far in this chapter pertains to the weaker sense in which legitimacy is tied to human flourishing. But there is a stronger sense as well, informed by a view of flourishing that is more distinctively neo-Calvinist. Before concluding this chapter, then, let me just remind the reader of the stronger sense in which neo-Calvinism suggests legitimacy-conditional natural rights are tied to human flourishing.

According to this stronger sense, natural rights don't only conceptually presuppose some or another view of human flourishing, but they also can only be determined in light of a particular type of view of human flourishing. It must be a view that accounts for institutions' natural rights as well as for individuals. It must be a view that isn't only concerned with the freedom of social actors, but that is concerned more broadly with social flourishing. Not only freedom, but flourishing, matters. Similarly, it must incorporate a concern for the common good. Only in light of the common good can individuals' and institutions' rights be properly discerned. It should be a view that doesn't conceive of social actors atomistically, but should appreciate their deep interconnectedness. This includes their interconnectedness with non-human animals and the environment, the flourishing of which should also be promoted.

This stronger sense of the tie to human flourishing also says something about how we are to use a view of flourishing, namely, by weighing and balancing the rights claims of social actors in light of social flourishing as a whole. It is not by a hypothetical procedure in which distinct individuals, with conflicting views of flourishing, compete to maximize their respective bundles of social goods. We weigh rights claims against one another in light of our interconnected flourishing and the common good, being sensitive to the distinctive natures, purposes, and legitimate interests of both individuals and society's varied institutions and collective social actors. This idea of weighing and balancing claims is part of the neo-Calvinist notion of public justice.

We've noted that this weighing and balancing isn't an exact science. The process follows no easy algorithm. But what neo-Calvinism says about the type of view of human flourishing we ought use, and how we ought use it, highlights the relevant considerations to consult in doing public justice. These ideas raise the right questions, even if they don't provide easy answers. In this way, the stronger sense in which legitimacy is tied to human flourishing is much like my project as a whole. My neo-Calvinist account seeks to improve and reframe the questions we ask about legitimacy, even though it doesn't provide a checklist of specific legitimacy conditions.

CONCLUSION

Of the three ideas of my neo-Calvinist account, the second may be the most important to a clear philosophical understanding of legitimacy. Why does a neo-Calvinist approach theorize legitimacy in terms of the negative task of preventing wrongs? It is because these wrongs are violations of basic rights, rights that correspond to interests and dignity that call out for protection with particular urgency. And, philosophically speaking, where does the content of these basic rights and wrongs come from? It is given by some or another view of basic human flourishing. By illuminating where the content of basic rights comes from, this second idea is especially valuable in making philosophical sense of our legitimacy-related convictions. By making clearer the philosophical grounds on which basic rights rest, neo-Calvinist legitimacy avoids the unnecessary philosophical shuffle involved in contractarian theories such as JL, justifying them in terms of their vital contribution to human interests, dignity, and flourishing.

In comparison with the content-free proceduralism of JL,[23] basic human flourishing delivers rights that are procedure-independent, contentful, and not beholden to group consensus. It thereby also avoids the unacceptable consequence of undercutting actual basic rights, which themselves are procedure-independent, contentful, and not determined by popular opinion.

NOTES

1. Rawls, *Justice as Fairness*, 176.
2. Are we justified in killing an innocent person to quell a race riot? Certainly not, though utilitarianism, on grounds of aggregate utility, would seem to sanction this flagrant rights violation. That utilitarianism would permit rights violations of this sort I regard as fatal to the theory. For this famous example, see H. J. McCloskey, "A Non-Utilitarian Approach to Punishment," *Inquiry* 8 (1965): 249–63.
3. Estlund, *Democratic Authority*, 85–97.
4. Here think again of what Fabienne Peter calls the "political egalitarian's dilemma," discussed in chapter 4.
5. Estlund, *Democratic Authority*, 247.
6. Rawls, *Political Liberalism*, 48–58.
7. JLs themselves "never suppose that our thinking something is just or reasonable, or a group's thinking it so, makes it so." "Note that the standard is not what principles or institutions people will *actually accept*." See Ibid., 111; Nagel, "Moral Conflict," 221 (emphasis in original).
8. See Hume, "Of the Original Contract," 164–81.
9. Cf. "deep deliberative democratic theory represents itself as wholly proceduralist, and as eschewing procedure-independent standards" but "it invokes independent standards after all." (Estlund, *Democratic Authority*, 85ff.)
10. Taylor's idea of "strong evaluation" refers to the practice of distinguishing between higher and lower ways of living, and we make such distinctions in various ways. For instance, we admire certain ways of life while holding others in contempt. As well, we hold certain human activities and achievements in "awe," others not. Taylor's point is that all such modes of strong evaluation are genuinely moral judgments, and yet they go beyond a narrow focus on the permissibility or impermissibility of discrete actions. [Charles Taylor, "The Diversity of Goods," in *Philosophy and the Human Sciences: Philosophical Papers 2*, by Charles Taylor (New York: Cambridge University Press, 1985), 230–47.] Going as they do beyond a narrow focus on discrete actions, these judgments reflect the belief that a given way of being is morally superior to others, and that it ought be pursued while others avoided.
11. Ibid., 234–36.
12. Ibid., 234.
13. Ibid.
14. Rawls, *Political Liberalism*, 12–13.
15. Think here also of H. L. A. Hart's early critique of Rawls' initial formulation of the liberty principle. Or think of G. A. Cohen's discussion of the freedoms and un-freedoms involved in the case of Mr. Morgan's yacht, and of the relative importance of some of these and of the relative unimportance of others.
16. Take Locke as an example of the inevitability of valuing certain liberties over others. "Equal political rights are then not among the inalienable liberties; Locke was a liberal but not a democrat" (Freeman, *Rawls*, 20).
17. See Rawls, *Political Liberalism*, 335; Audi and Wolterstorff, *Religion in the Public Square*, 4; Lister, "Public Justification and the Limits of State Action," 160.
18. Matthew 6:26 (*The Holy Bible*, 811–12).
19. Of course, there is already widespread respect for science in our society—as I agree there should be. But *scientism* is the more radical view that holds that science, and science alone, can deliver truth and knowledge. However, while philosophically more radical, scientism is gradually becoming more culturally mainstream, as endorsed by prominent public intellectuals such as Lawrence Krauss and Alex Rosenberg.
20. Among the leading figures in this movement are Richard Dawkins, Sam Harris, Daniel Dennett, and the late Christopher Hitchens.
21. Freeman, *Rawls*, 387.
22. Think again of the Taylor material discussed in chapter 7, from which the traffic freedom example comes.
23. To review the ways in which JL is content-free, refer back to chapter 4.

Chapter Ten

How to Steer Clear of Paternalism

As I suggested in chapter 5, JL seems to involve a problematic, albeit unusual, form of paternalism. If so, this would be a third unacceptable consequence to which JL leads. JL seemingly involves paternalism by posing a question of self-interest that is not answered by affected parties themselves, but by their hypothetical counterparts.

In chapter 5 I also identified the key distinction on which my charge of paternalism turns, the difference between enacting coercion for people's good and doing so for the sake of justice. My suggestion was that JL falls on the wrong side of this divide, by making a question about people's good central to its justification of coercion. Let me state upfront that, once again, this is the basic intuition that drives my argument in the present chapter, that there is an important difference between interest-based and justice-based justifications.[1] It also lies behind my contention that my neo-Calvinist account justifies coercion in relevantly different terms that avoid paternalism.

Yet I acknowledge that it is difficult to delineate these justifications' different philosophical territories. The difficulty arises since, in some sense, interests also seem to factor into approaches that would foreground rights and justice (such as neo-Calvinist legitimacy). In this chapter, then, I take up again the issue of how interests factor differently into interest-based and justice-based justifications. The fact that I admittedly make only partial progress on the issue is one reason why my argument here is more provisional than those of chapters 8 and 9, and a second is that, as noted in chapter 5, the paternalism I allege may be thought insignificant even if JL is guilty as charged.

Now our question in this chapter is this: how would neo-Calvinist legitimacy steer clear of the paternalism to which JL leads?

My answer will be that a neo-Calvinist approach avoids paternalism because it explains legitimacy in terms of an exogenous normative standard addressed to real persons rather than in terms of a self-legislated law produced by hypothetical persons, as JL does. Paternalism is a function of the type of question asked and of who provides the answer. Given JL's constructivist commitment to representing legitimate laws as the product of popular sovereignty, JL asks whether a proposal is acceptable to each citizen in light of their self-interest considered severally. It asks a question of self-interest. But to answer this question, JL does not direct us to actual citizens, but to their hypothetical counterparts. Conversely, neo-Calvinist legitimacy understands the relevant normative standard not as a product of human self-legislation, but as exogenous. Thus, the operative question concerns the basic demands of this standard vis-à-vis our treatment of others in society, individuals as well as institutions and groups. The need for hypothetical persons does not even arise within a neo-Calvinist framework. Since the question is not one of self-interest, we need not mitigate factors that might distort or bias people's answers to a question of that sort.

I have already discussed, in chapter 5, the factors that conspire together to produce JL's paternalistic implications. I will review them here only briefly. After that, I will explain my neo-Calvinist alternative and how it can help us make sense of legitimacy while steering clear of paternalism. Related to this alternative, we will consider how it incorporates a concern for people's interests in a way that seems relevantly different from JL. Given the lesser importance of this chapter to my overall argument, I will move relatively quickly through these steps. I hope to say enough to make a provocative, pregnant, and plausible suggestion, but not more.

RECAPPING JL'S POSSIBLE PATERNALISM

Recall how JL leads to paternalism.

JL takes the first step down this path when it pursues constructivism. JLs are committed to representing the demands of legitimacy as the product of human legislation. Their commitment is not merely to proceduralism as a heuristic or decision-procedure. It is clear that the procedure itself and the fact of agreement are of crucial importance to their position.[2] The reasons for agreement and the arrangements agreed upon may also be important, but they are not foundational to the view. If they were, JLs could treat the proceduralist apparatus as a mere aid to discovery, and eliminable. But JLs do not regard their proceduralism in this way. Rather, JLs regard constructivism as the only appropriate mode of justification given citizens' free-and-equal status. The spirit animating JL's constructivism is the aspiration to make political communities wholly sovereign over the norms that govern them.[3] Although our moral experience strongly suggests that moral duties can, indeed, "simply befall us,"[4] constructivism denies they can. Norms of legitimacy and justice do not simply befall us, but are the product of popular sovereignty in one sense or another. They hold onto this commitment even if it means appealing to hypothetical contractors and hypothetical acts of self-legislation.[5]

In our earlier discussion of JL's possible paternalism, I mentioned, but did not emphasize, that the category of self-legislation lies at root of the problem. So I emphasize it now. As far as JL's possible paternalism is concerned, we can ultimately trace the problem back to JL's insistence that we understand legitimacy in terms of self-legislated norms.

Given this commitment to self-legislation, JLs ask what hypothetical contractors might legislate for themselves in a procedure requiring unanimity. In the procedure, each citizen evaluates proposals in terms of their self-interest as seen from their distinctive viewpoint. Unanimity is required by citizens' free-and-equal status. It is assumed that citizens hold different comprehensive views, but also that no citizen can be legitimately coerced by a majority decision she cannot accept.

Logic also demands that the question posed to citizens be one of self-interest. Or, at least, it demands that it not be a question of justice or legitimacy. If it were either of the latter, JLs would simply be asking the hypothetical contractors the very same question that JLs themselves are trying to answer. Making the question one of self-interest avoids this potential circularity.[6]

In sum, the picture that emerges is of a procedure that resembles real-world voting processes in various ways. It involves persons occupying diverse standpoints; who have some sympathy toward others and the common good[7]; but who each decide how to cast their vote chiefly on the basis of their own self-interest, as they themselves perceive it.

However, despite these resemblances, JL ultimately directs us to hypothetical rather than real persons in assessing the multi-perspectival acceptability of a proposal. Why? Because actual persons cannot be counted on to discern their own reasonable self-interest. They cannot given the moral, epistemic, and economic obstacles they face. These obstacles distort how real-world persons perceive their self-interest and they bias social arrangements. It might be thought that JLs mean only to prevent bias and do not presume that individuals misunderstand their own self-interest. However, there are strong indications in JL writings that suggest otherwise. For instance, Barry justifies a public system of employment insurance by asking, "[U]nder what conditions would it be rational for someone dependent on employment for an income to decline insurance[?]" Barry thinks it obvious that unemployment insurance serves one's self-interest, and irrational to judge one's self-interest otherwise.[8] Also, Freeman's defense of Rawls' inclusion of "the pleasures of a deeper understanding of the world" among the political values of public reason, as compared to "spirituality" which is excluded, seems aimed at misperceived self-interest. Not only might religion bias social arrangements. Additionally, citizens are wrong to think spirituality important to the development of their two moral powers, but right to think science important to their development.[9] So, idealizing the hypothetical contractors corrects both for moral and epistemic shortcomings. The idealizations prevent both biased social arrangements as well as misperceptions of self-interest. JL means to correct both types of defects that keep real-world persons from realizing their own reasonable self-interest. Throughout, whenever I speak of JL's concern with self-interest, I have in mind self-interest freed from both types of defects.

But while proceduralism might have the noble aim of realizing fairness, the effect, I suggest, is perverse. For by transmuting actual persons into hypothetical ones, we render the actual persons unable to speak for themselves. We substitute in the judgment of hypothetical persons and substitute out that of actual persons. And because the hypothetical parties are presumed to speak concerning a question of actual persons' self-interest, paternalism results.

THE NEO-CALVINIST EXOGENOUS ALTERNATIVE

How does neo-Calvinist legitimacy steer clear of this possible paternalism?

As I have explained, the root cause of JL's paternalism is JL's insistence on popular sovereignty. JLs insist that we understand ourselves to be the authors of the basic norms that govern our societies, even if this means appealing to hypothetical persons. The solution proposed by neo-Calvinist legitimacy cuts off the problem at its root. Instead of insisting upon a self-legislated standard, a neo-Calvinist approach explains legitimacy in terms of an exogenous normative standard.

As explained in chapter 7, exogenous is a scientific term meaning "introduced from or produced outside the organism or system."[10] Likewise, an exogenous moral standard is one that is not constructed by humans. It impresses itself upon human polities, but originates outside of them. Positing such a standard is consistent with acknowledging one or another decision rule as a helpful tool in discerning the demands of this standard. Indeed, I would regard both the Golden Rule as well as counterfactual contractarian scenarios in this vein. But positing an exogenous standard is inconsistent with holding such heuristic devices to be of primary or essential normative significance. It needn't necessarily be possible to represent exogenous norms in constructivist terms. Being exogenous, such a standard would obtain whether or not decision procedures such as the Golden Rule or contract scenarios were available to us as shortcuts for discerning its demands.

We saw in chapter 6 that neo-Calvinists would clearly recommend this first move, of replacing the JL starting point of popular sovereignty with something like an exogenous standard. In an introduction to Kuyper's Stone Lectures, McKendree R. Langley writes, "The notion that people themselves create basic norms (that is, popular sovereignty) is rejected."[11] Kuyper himself describes the political theorist's insistence on popular sovereignty in the most pejorative terms: "And herein lies its self-abasement . . . from the standpoint of the sovereignty of the people, the fist is defiantly clenched against God, while man grovels before his fellowmen, tinseling over this self-abasement by the ludicrous fiction that, thousands of years ago, men, of whom no one has any remembrance, concluded a political contract, or, as they called it, '*Contrat Social*.'"[12] Similarly, in reference to Dooyeweerd's views, one commentator writes, "What then is the secular state? The secular state is that state which denies any transcendental claim upon itself."[13] To deny "any transcendental claim upon" oneself is, in my terminology, to deny an exogenous standard and insist on self-legislation.

An implication of understanding legitimacy in terms of an exogenous normative standard is that legitimacy does not depend on how persons subjectively perceive their own self-interest. This is a notion JL accepts, postulating as it does that legitimacy results from each person accepting a proposal in light of how they subjectively perceive their self-interest, that is, in light of how they themselves perceive their self-interest as opposed to how their interests might be judged from an impersonal viewpoint. *Ex hypothesi*, each person evaluates their self-interest reasonably, such is the effect of JL's idealizations (moral, cognitive, and economic). But each person also does so from a distinctive viewpoint. Conversely, neo-Calvinist legitimacy makes no use of the idea of multi-perspectival acceptability based on subjective self-interest.

Thus, on neo-Calvinist legitimacy, we are not forced to justify coercive laws with reference to the question of whether person x should regard a proposal as being in x's reasonable self-interest. This is a question we are wise to avoid in our philosophical account, since once it is posed we must determine who will answer it. Will it be person x herself, or someone else? Paternalism results if we prefer someone else's evaluation of x's interests to x's own evaluation and justify coercion on this basis. Better just to altogether avoid this dilemma of who speaks for x.

Instead, on my proposal we justify coercive laws with reference to the question: does this law prevent violations of basic natural rights? In other words, does this law uphold basic justice? (Again here I speak interchangeably of preventing basic rights violations and of upholding basic justice.) This is the heart of the subsidiary question we should ask.[14] Such demands, on neo-Calvinism, constitute an exogenous normative standard. Thus, it makes little sense to try to understand these demands in terms of self-legislation. In turn, it also makes little sense to try to understand them in terms of how persons severally perceive their self-interest. Neo-Calvinist legitimacy's subsidiary question concerns basic rights, not self-interest.

To help discern and uphold basic rights, I suggest we ask this further question as well: does this right correspond to basic human interests and dignity or basic social well-being in such a fundamental way that we feel we have no choice but to coerce others to respect it, with or without their consent? Answering it will, I think, help us zero in on the basic demands of an exogenous normative standard. My contention is that this and the last are the right questions to ask and the questions that we must ask if we are to steer clear of the structural paternalism that JL would seem to involve. They are the right questions for making philosophical sense of our legitimacy-related convictions.

So, on a neo-Calvinist approach, there is simply no need to appeal to hypothetical persons since the question put to us is not one of self-interest. The justification of legitimacy conditions does not depend upon persons' subjective self-interest. Thus, we need not worry about correcting for distorted perceptions of self-interest. Rather, neo-Calvinist legitimacy puts to us a question of basic rights, a question which can be ably investigated without appeal to hypothetical persons. We consider actual persons simply as they are, with the interests and dignity they objectively have, given the sort of beings they are. And we consider institutions, too, with their distinctive purposes, norms, structures, and interests. The normative standard to which we appeal is one under which we all stand as equals, and the conversation to which theorists are invited is in terms of the fundamental demands of this standard. It is an exogenous standard that imposes itself on us in spite of our subjective self-interest, not because of it.

Therefore, I propose a trade. Once we trade conceptual categories, self-legislation for that of an exogenous standard, a solution to the threat of paternalism comes available. I suggest neo-Calvinists can help show us the way forward.

But, it may be asked, why should we believe that such a standard exists? To respond, we needn't take up deep questions of theology or meta-ethics. One reason is simply this: only if we posit the existence of such a standard can we ostensibly account for our legitimacy-related CCs.[15] These include the conviction at hand, namely, that it is illegitimate to coerce others on paternalistic grounds. Postulating an exogenous standard, we seem able to steer clear of the structural paternalism in which JL entangles us. Without it, we are faced with JL and its starting point of popular sovereignty, and with the paternalism that results from it.

INCORPORATING INTERESTS WHILE STEERING CLEAR OF PATERNALISM

To some, the neo-Calvinist alternative I have presented here may not look any better. It may be objected that all theories, include my own, are paternalistic insofar as all justify coercion based on people's interests. After all, don't I tie legitimacy to the interests involved in basic human flourishing? Don't I understand basic rights in terms of basic interests and dignity? It might seem that wherever we turn, we must ultimately give an interest-based justification of coercion. And if such justifications are paternalistic, it might seem that we are all doomed to paternalism, neo-Calvinists included.

Earlier I suggested that while all accounts of legitimacy—both those that offer interest-based justifications and those that offer justice-based ones—do incorporate human interests in some sense, there are different ways in which this can be done. Some of these ways involve paternalism, and some do not. My response to the present objection is to grant that neo-Calvinist legitimacy takes human interests into account in a certain way, but deny that it is relevantly similar to the way that JL does. In the following comments, I hope to make clearer this distinction between how interests factor into justice-based as opposed to interest-based justifications of coercion.

Consider two seemingly relevant differences between how interests factor into the two types of justification, and, accordingly, how interests factor differently into neo-Calvinist and JL legitimacy. I admit the following comments are incomplete. But the intuitive difference between coercion for people's good and for the sake of justice remains compelling, and, as such, I think it worth my pursuing even if I do so imperfectly.

First, though JL and neo-Calvinist legitimacy answer the same primary question, the subsidiary question asked by each is different. Recall Estlund's aforementioned distinction between an account's primary and subsidiary questions.[16] To review, a subsidiary question is one that is asked to help answer the primary one. Consequently, the nature of the subsidiary question shapes the way answers to the primary question are justified. Now both JL and neo-Calvinist legitimacy are ultimately concerned with the same primary question, namely, what coercive forms of legal coercion are legitimate even if imperfect? But their subsidiary questions are importantly different. While JL's subsidiary question is one of perceived self-interest, the neo-Calvinist question is not.

In this chapter we have already reviewed what JL's subsidiary question is. Each party is asked whether a proposal serves their reasonable self-interest. Answers to the primary question—that a proposal is or isn't a legitimate use of legal coercion—are justified in terms of this subsidiary question. A proposal is legitimate only if, and precisely because, everyone would regard it as being in their reasonable self-interest. Everyone would view the reasons on which it is based as acceptable.[17]

Conversely, the subsidiary question on a neo-Calvinist approach asks whether a proposal respects or violates basic rights. Here, a proposal is legitimate, if legitimate, because it respects the basic rights of individuals and institutions. Now to answer this subsidiary question, I also offered a variation on the question that might serve as a helpful heuristic. Does a proposal protect conditions so basic to human flourishing, both that of the individual and that of society, that we feel we have no choice but to coercively enforce them, regardless of consent?

While it is true that I spell out basic flourishing in terms of humans' and institutions' basic interests and dignity, notice that on a neo-Calvinist view interests do not enter the picture in terms of the subsidiary question, as they do on JL. I think this more than merely a verbal point. For this difference in subsidiary questions allows us to characterize JL and neo-Calvinist approaches in strikingly different ways. On JL, something is a basic right because it serves people's reasonable self-interest. By contrast, on my neo-Calvinist account, something can serve people's self-interest only if it respects basic rights. The former is true of JL since its subsidiary question is one of self-interest. The latter is true of neo-Calvinism since its subsidiary question is one of basic rights and since it views social actors' flourishing as being deeply interconnected.[18] JLs might pay lip service to the notion that people ought only pursue their self-interest within the limits of justice. However, to determine what justice requires, at a conceptually more fundamental level, JLs resort to the notion of people's reasonable self-interest. More than merely a verbal point, then, the difference between JL and neo-Calvinist subsidiary questions seems to indicate that interests play a more foundational role in JL than in neo-Calvinist legitimacy.

Now consider a second way of seeing the difference between JL's and neo-Calvinism's incorporation of interests. Both approaches are concerned with citizens' interests in some sense, but the vantage points from which they presume to evaluate these interests are rather different. JL incorporates the interests of individuals as judged from their own subjective viewpoints. Hence, the multiplicity of perspectives involved in multi-perspectival acceptability. Conversely, a neo-Calvinist approach considers the interests of individuals as judged from an impersonal, third-person point of view. The divine creation order, of which legitimacy-related norms are a part, is objective and applies to all. It determines what constitutes human well-being apart from humans' subjective opinions on the matter. So, we can see the contrast between JL's and neo-Calvinism's incorporation of interests in this difference between first- and third-person viewpoints.

I think this difference also helps illuminate why JL leads to possible paternalism while neo-Calvinist legitimacy does not. Consider the following.

Were legal coercion used against a rights violator because he had violated basic rights, it seems mistaken to label this a case of paternalism. There might be other reasons to object to the coercion. For instance, perhaps the law is overbroad or the punishment draconian. But given the type of justification proffered for the coercion, it seems it cannot be criticized as paternalistic. On the other hand, were we to legally coerce a rights violator to benefit the rights violator himself, I think we'd rightly be accused of paternalism.[19] Why the difference? Perhaps the reason we judge these cases differently with respect to paternalism is because the former justification averts to a third-person perspective (i.e., a moral standard regarded as universal) while the latter to a first-person perspective (i.e., to the good of the coerced rights violator). Similarly, since a neo-Calvinist approach takes interests into account from an objective, impersonal perspective, whereas JL takes them into account from multiple first-person perspectives, JL seems liable to paternalism in a way that neo-Calvinist legitimacy does not.

In sum, I believe that while interests play a role in both JL and neo-Calvinist justifications of legitimate coercion, the role they play is relevantly different. I have suggested two angles from which this difference can be appreciated. First, the subsidiary question of JL directly involves persons' self-interest, whereas the subsidiary question of neo-Calvinist legitimacy does not. The latter does so only indirectly. Second, JL incorporates interests by way of multiple, first-person perspectives, whereas neo-Calvinism would have us conceive of basic human interests from an impersonal, third-person perspective.

Let me conclude this section's reflections by clarifying their import, as I see it. While they represent only a partially adequate account of the difference between JL's and neo-Calvinism's incorporation of interests, taken together I believe they strongly suggest that such a difference does exist, and that it has differential implications for paternalism. In light of these considerations, we can more readily see how an exogenous normative standard helps us toward justice-based rather than interest-based justifications of coercion. For an exogenous standard accounts for interests differently than JL does.

CONCLUSION

So why would neo-Calvinist legitimacy not lead to paternalism in the way JL seems to do? I have answered this question in several steps. First, I explained the meaning of an exogenous standard. A neo-Calvinist approach explains legitimacy in terms of such a standard. This category contrasts with that of popular sovereignty, on which JL insists. Second, we saw that using an exogenous standard thereby avoids making the subsidiary question one of self-interest. For its part, JL appeals to subjective self-interest, interests relative to idiosyncratic viewpoints as opposed to the objective human good. Third, we also saw that in light of its different subsidiary question, neo-Calvinist legitimacy has no need for hypothetical persons. As such, we mitigate the threat of paternalism for we are not required to represent actual persons' self-interest in terms of how hypothetical persons would view them.

My proposal in this chapter has been somewhat tentative. But while JL's paternalism is, I grant, only a possible paternalism, it seems wise to altogether steer clear of it. I hope to have shown how we might do just that, by taking a neo-Calvinist approach instead. There is a difference between coercion for people's good and for the sake of justice. JL at least runs the risk of being on the wrong side of this divide. Better to be safely on the right side.

One last word. My critique of popular sovereignty in this chapter may give rise to a certain misunderstanding. What I have rejected in this chapter is not the right of real-world political communities to govern themselves. They do have such a right, and we have seen earlier in the book that a powerful democratic impulse courses through neo-Calvinist thought. What I have rejected is the insistence that, philosophically, we understand even the most basic norms of justice in terms of popular sovereignty. Ironically, this very insistence leads to paternalism.

NOTES

1. Again cf. Gutmann and Thompson, "The paternalist claim is not that the conduct is morally wrong but that it is harmful to the citizen herself. . . . Legal paternalism is the restriction by law of an individual's liberty for his or her own good." (Gutmann and Thompson, *Democracy and Disagreement*, 261.)

2. The whole thrust of Freeman's argument is that the social contract is not an unnecessary philosophical shuffle because the fact of agreement itself is significant. See Freeman, "Moral Contractarianism," 57–76.

3. In reading JL as well as the broader secular liberal tradition of which it is part, one also senses the aspiration, shared with Marx, to bring philosophical concepts and justifications down from heaven to earth. This seems also to be an underlying motivation of JL.

4. Estlund, *Democratic Authority*, 117.

5. This issue of how to interpret JLs' constructivism, whether strongly or weakly, is one to which I return in chapter 11.

6. For discussion, see Estlund, *Democratic Authority*, 245–48. Also, see discussion in chapter 5.

7. As per Rawls, JL's contractors are neither egoists nor altruists.

8. Brian Barry, "Chance, Choice and Justice," in *Contemporary Political Philosophy: An Anthology*, ed. Robert E. Goodin and Philip Pettit. Hoboken, NJ: Blackwell Publishing, 2006, 233.

9. Freeman, *Rawls*, 390–93.

10. http://www.merriam-webster.com/dictionary/exogenous?show=0andt=1362000632.

11. Abraham Kuyper, *Christianity: A Total World and Life System* (Marlborough, NH: Plymouth Rock Foundation, Inc., 1996), ix.

12. Kuyper, *Lectures on Calvinism*, 75.

13. This quote is from Rousas John Rushdoony's introduction. (Dooyeweerd, *The Christian Idea of the State*, xi.)

14. To be precise, the subsidiary question includes an additional clause. As explained in chapter 8, a law can be legitimate even if it does not represent a demand of basic justice provided it is enacted by a regime that, as a whole, upholds basic justice. For simplicity's sake, though, I do not include that clause here.

15. Recall that in saying this I am not necessarily supposing that an exogenous standard can only be conceived religiously. At least at this stage of the argument, I remain open to the possibility of secular accounts of exogenous morality. A view that regarded morality as a natural property would be one such account.

16. Estlund, *Democratic Authority*, 245–48.

17. To be sure, JLs never explicitly say something as bald as, "Proposal x is legitimate because x is for your own good." Nor do they intend to say this. As I acknowledged in chapter 5, JLs' intention is clearly to explain legitimacy in terms of fairness-related considerations. My point here, though, as it was earlier, is about what JLs are committed to saying, about what their logic amounts to. Despite their official or intended position, they tie legitimacy to self-interest as seen by the subsidiary question they ask. Such is how we ought reconstruct JL logic.

18. I am indebted to Zuidervaart for his strong emphasis on the interconnected nature of our flourishing.

19. Given the high stakes involved in rights violations, we might actually accept paternalistic coercion in this case. But even if we did, wouldn't it still be basic justice that ultimately legitimizes the coercion? Paternalism might be the subjective motive of the coercers, but it seems the objective considerations that legitimize the coercion pertain to basic justice nonetheless.

Chapter Eleven

Conclusion

My guiding question has been this: what is the best framework for a philosophical understanding of legitimacy? We recognize that coercive political power may be legitimate even if imperfectly exercised, and yet the concept of legitimacy is not well understood. My concern has not been to formulate a list of specific legitimacy criteria. Rather, it has been to explain how we ought to go about formulating such a list. To further our understanding of legitimacy, I have sought to identify the most apt conceptual categories for theorizing legitimacy at a higher level of generality.

JL represents one response to my guiding question. It does not elaborate a list of specific legitimacy conditions so much as it provides a way of conceptualizing legitimacy and of formulating specific conditions. According to JL, legitimate legal coercion is based on reasons that all reasonable persons can accept. JLs explicate this core principle with reference to a hypothetical procedure. Legal coercion is legitimate when it would receive unanimous support in such a procedure. Thus, on a JL framework, legitimacy is understood in terms of consent, procedures, and self-legislation.

Alas, JL leads to consequences that are unacceptable insofar as they conflict with CCs we hold about legitimacy. I explained how JL unacceptably de-legitimizes all legal coercion, principally owing to its consent-emphasizing unanimity condition. We saw how JL also undercuts legitimacy-conditional basic rights, conflicting with the characteristics of procedure-independence, substance, and objectivity that real-world rights have. As well, we considered the possibility that JL structurally involves paternalism in the way it justifies coercion. If this is right, JL runs counter to our conviction that coercion on paternalistic grounds is illegitimate. Failing as it does to make sense of these convictions, we should reject JL in search of an alternative. Even theorists sympathetic to JL such as Bohman and Richardson[1] have already rejected the category of "RACAs"[2] and parted ways with versions of JL that focus on RACAs, as mainstream, Rawlsian versions do. My critiques of JL provide further reason to part ways with the traditional JL paradigm.

The alternative I suggest, though, is rather different from Bohman and Richardson's, as I suggest we turn to the neo-Calvinist tradition of social thought to develop a better framework for legitimacy. First I outlined the tradition by way of nine general tenets, advancing it as a rich fund of conceptual insights and resources. Then out of these resources I reconstructed a neo-Calvinist theory of legitimacy. The main insight I draw from neo-Calvinism concerning legitimacy is that legitimate legal coercion is a function of preventing basic wrongs. Coercive political power is necessary only "by reason of sin." I explicated this main insight in terms of three companion ideas, of which the first two are especially important. Legitimacy is a function of preventing wrongs that are (a) violations of individuals' and institutions' natural rights, rights that are (b) tied to basic human flourishing, and that (c) represent an exogenous normative standard. So formulated, my neo-Calvinist account does not advance a list of specific conditions, like Nussbaum's list of capabilities[3] or Henry Shue's three basic rights.[4] But only in this way can it stand on all fours as an alternative to JL and aptly respond to my guiding question.

Most recently, in part III, I have argued that a neo-Calvinist approach can help us at those very points where JL is inadequate. Why doesn't a neo-Calvinist approach de-legitimize all legal coercion the way JL does? By replacing consent with natural rights as a category of central importance, it prevents consent withheld from de-legitimizing otherwise justifiable coercion given natural rights' objectivity. Why doesn't a neo-Calvinist approach undercut basic rights the way JL does? It does so in virtue of the determinate and appropriate content made available by views of basic human flourishing, in contrast to the content-free proceduralism of JL. And if, indeed, JL structurally involves a problematic form of paternalism, how might neo-Calvinism help us avoid it? Whereas JL's emphasis on self-legislation leads to interest-based justifications of coercion, understanding legitimacy in terms of an exogenous normative standard instead leads to justice-based justifications of coercion that account for human interests in a relevantly different way. Such was the suggestion of chapter 10. In sum, since it makes better sense of our CCs, I conclude that a neo-Calvinist account provides a superior framework for understanding legitimacy.

In this chapter, I will conclude by executing three final tasks. First, I will consider a couple more objections. I cannot, of course, hope to respond to all the objections that might be made to my account. But I would like to answer what I take to be a couple of the more serious questions that may linger, and that pertain to the project overall rather than to any specific part of it. Second, I will say a word concerning future directions that further development of

OBJECTIONS AND REPLIES

Objection: JL and CR legitimacy are more compatible than it seems.

Reply: It might seem that JL is perfectly compatible with certain neo-Calvinist ideas, in particular those of natural rights' objectivity and an exogenous standard. Both these ideas point to moral obligations that persons have regardless of their *de facto* views. That actual persons have such obligations is something JLs recognize.[5] Indeed, the irrelevance of *de facto* views is reflected in JLs' abstracting away from actual to idealized persons. Throughout objective values and duties have been characterized as binding individuals and societies whether or not they recognize them. So, it seems that JLs would readily concur with a neo-Calvinist understanding of the objectivity of natural rights, if not also with the idea of an exogenous standard.

Furthermore, the objection might not only be that I have exaggerated certain differences between JL and neo-Calvinism. It might also be that I have misinterpreted JL and its constructivism. JLs are constructivists in their commitment to representing the demands of justice or legitimacy as the product of a suitable procedure. Now the question arises how most appropriately to interpret this commitment. Previously I indicated it might be given either a strong or a weak reading. That is the issue I will now take up at greater length. For the purveyor of the current objection likely interprets JL's constructivism weakly, in which case JL does appear much more compatible with the ideas of objective natural rights and exogenous norms. Correspondingly, the objector would likely regard my strong reading as a misinterpretation. So how best to understand JL's constructivism?

Let me first clarify what I mean by weak and strong readings. On a weak reading, JLs' procedural representation of legitimate social norms is just that, simply a re-presentation of moral demands that obtain quite apart from the procedure.[6] A procedural representation does not make a given principle obligatory. It simply reveals it to be obligatory. On a weak reading, the procedure is interpreted as a mere heuristic. It may be a helpful decision procedure, but maybe not. And, in any case, it is nowise essential to the normative justification of the principles in question.

By contrast, according to a strong reading of JL's constructivism, a procedural representation does make a principle obligatory. It does not simply reveal it to be such. The procedure is not a mere heuristic, for apart from a procedural representation a putative principle is held to be unjustified. This is a strong reading in the sense that constructivism so interpreted involves a stronger commitment to the normative significance of JL's hypothetical procedure. Without the procedure, norms are unjustified.

Though I have not so far defended it, throughout I have operated with a strong reading of JL's constructivism. Indeed, I think this the most appropriate interpretation of JL's constructivism. Now why do I read JL this way?

Let me canvass multiple ways of responding to this question.

First, many explicit statements can be gleaned from JL texts indicating a strong reading. For instance, Nagel says of enforceable moral principles that "their rightness will not be demonstrable independent of th[e] possibility" of representing them as the product of an appropriate procedure.[7] So as to distance himself from procedure-independent moral criteria, Rawls writes, "Once more I stress that there is no criterion of a legitimate expectation, or of an entitlement, apart from the public rules that specify the scheme of cooperation."[8] And in resisting Habermas' criticism that he is insufficiently procedural, Rawls responds,

> In justice as fairness, these basic [i.e., constitutional] liberties are not in a prepolitical domain; nonpublic values are not viewed, as they might be in some comprehensive doctrine (such as rational intuitionism or natural law), as ontologically prior and for that reason prior to political values. . . . In my reply I have simply observed that from within that political conception of justice, the liberties of the moderns do not impose the prior restrictions on the people's constituent will as Habermas objects.[9]

If one looks hard enough, it is certainly possible to also find countervailing statements in the JL corpus. Nonetheless, JLs seem to hold a strong commitment to constructivism at least insofar as they affirm statements such as those quoted here.

Quite apart from proof-texts, though, there are additional, more robust philosophical considerations weighing in favor of a strong reading.

One such reason is that JLs seemingly interpret free-and-equal personhood in a way that involves a strong constructivism. For JLs, people's free-and-equal status is denied unless they can see themselves as joint authors of the social norms to which they are subject. "It is part of citizens' sense of themselves, not only collectively but also individually, to recognize political authority as deriving from them and that they are responsible for what it does in their name."[10] So apart from procedural representations of political authority free-and-equal citizens cannot properly understand themselves. Similarly, Freeman explains that constructivism involves "an idealization of moral agency where free persons are conceived as autonomous, responsible not only for their actions and ends but also for the very rules and principles by which they regulate their actions and pursue their ends."[11] If, then, JLs wish to retain these conceptions of freedom and equality, it seems they must attach significant normative weight to their procedural representations of legitimate laws.

Another consideration favoring a strong reading is that JL seems to lose much of its philosophical distinctiveness if we treat the procedure as mere heuristic. If it is mere heuristic, then it seems altogether possible that there are other ways of reasoning out and philosophically justifying legitimate social arrangements. These other ways might involve neither a procedure nor social agreement. But, it seems to me, JLs would be swift and firm in their rejection of this possibility. For instance, Freeman defends contractarianism as a basis for morality on the grounds that such an approach alone justifies moral principles in the right way, namely, "*in a way that is reasonable or fair to everyone.*"[12] The contract or procedure is essential on this view, for only the contract ensures fairness. As proceduralism is essential to Freeman's contractarianism, so it would seem essential to JL. Without it, not only might there be other nonprocedural ways of reasoning out and justifying social arrangements, but JLs' aim to fairly arbitrate between competing comprehensive views would be undermined. In light of these costs, a strong reading seems most appropriate.

So much can be said in favor of interpreting JLs to be strongly committed to constructivism. But even if they are not so committed—and I grant the point is disputable—I still regard my thesis as relevant and instructive. How so?

It would remain pertinent given my fairly general aim of urging a shift in categories in our understanding of legitimacy. Even if, strictly speaking, there is no conceptual incompatibility between JL and key features of neo-Calvinist legitimacy—such as the ideas of objective natural rights and exogenous norms—it is certainly true that JL emphasizes certain conceptual categories more than others. Moreover, these are different from neo-Calvinist points of emphasis. It is certainly true, in other words, that JL foregrounds concepts such as consent, procedures, and self-legislation, while a concept such as objective natural rights, if indeed present, is distant in the background. My thesis has traction, then, insofar as I am urging that the ideas of natural rights, basic human flourishing, and exogenous normative standards ought be central to our understanding of legitimacy. The centrality of these concepts JL definitely does deny, even on a weak reading.

That said, for the aforementioned reasons I do think JL is best interpreted as strongly committed to constructivism. As such, JL's conceptual categories (consent, procedures, self-legislation) contrast more sharply with those of neo-Calvinist legitimacy (natural rights, basic human flourishing, exogenous normative standard). The two are not as compatible as the objector seems to think.

Objection: The neo-Calvinist tradition is superfluous.

Reply: I have suggested that we turn to the neo-Calvinist tradition of social thought for an alternative to JL, and I have reconstructed my own account of legitimacy with the tradition's general premises in mind. To reiterate, my account is constituted by the following propositions: that legitimacy is a function of preventing basic wrongs; that legitimacy-conditional wrongs are violations of natural rights; that legitimacy-conditional rights presuppose views of human flourishing; and also that these rights and wrongs constitute an exogenous normative standard.

In light of my reconstruction, though, one might wonder whether it is possible to simply translate all that I have said about neo-Calvinist thought into secular terms. This question gives rise to the present objection, the objection that the tradition itself is superfluous. It is superfluous both to the legitimacy account I have advanced and, more broadly, to any worthwhile ideas that might be gleaned from the tradition. I take it this objection pertains more to my secondary aim concerning comparative political theory than to my primary aim concerning the normative issue of political legitimacy. Recall that one of my secondary aims is to put forth the neo-Calvinist tradition as a rich source of conceptual insights that can be brought to bear on various issues within political theory, both by neo-Calvinist as well as secular theorists.

All the tradition's worthwhile ideas are translatable into secular terms, so this second objection goes, and as such the neo-Calvinist background is expendable. The propositions constituting my account contain no references to God or other conspicuously religious concepts. As they stand, they exemplify secular translations of ideas originally overlaid with unnecessary religious language. As the objection was once put to me, the neo-Calvinist tradition seems neither necessary nor sufficient to my neo-Calvinist account.[13] It is not necessary, for we can simply begin with the propositions in their secular formulations. Nor is it even sufficient, for reconstructing my account has required me to selectively interpret the tradition and omit distinctively religious elements. It might seem, then, that there is little use in either secular or religious theorists mining the neo-Calvinist tradition for conceptual insights, *pace* my suggestion. Political philosophers can carry on perfectly well without it.

Unlike the contract metaphor of JL, I do not think that the appeal to the neo-Calvinist tradition is an unnecessary philosophical shuffle. In response to this second objection, I will make two main points.

First, the background is not superfluous inasmuch as it provides a wider conceptual context for any specific propositions that pertain to political theory. This wider context gives philosophical depth to these propositions, drawing connections—so far as such connections are of interest—between them and concepts from other philosophical fields that bear on them. To illustrate this point, let me highlight two ways in which the wider neo-Calvinist background gives philosophical depth to specific propositions of neo-Calvinist legitimacy. These correspond to two challenges with which JLs, or other secular theorists, are left should they try to appropriate the propositions apart from the wider background.

For one, the neo-Calvinist background gives us a way of ontologically grounding the objective values and duties involved in the idea of natural rights. It is, of course, possible to simply start from the assumption that legitimacy-conditional wrongs are morally objective wrongs. So far as one is exclusively interested in political theory, it may be reasonable to simply take their objectivity as a primitive fact. However, the idea of objective values and duties clearly raises a question of moral ontology, which, while going beyond the purview of political theory, is nonetheless a relevant and important philosophical question. The wider neo-Calvinist background offers a ready answer to the question of moral objectivity's ontological grounding: objective values and duties are grounded in God and in the divine creation order. *Qua* tradition of social thought, the neo-Calvinism I have presented offers a ready answer but does not develop it at length. Nonetheless, it makes available a deeper philosophical reading of moral objectivity than is possible if the idea is simply considered on its own. The corresponding challenge left for JLs and other secular theorists is to find alternate grounds for the objective values and duties that bear on the issue of legitimacy. Some JLs, such as Rawls, articulate a constructivist conception of moral objectivity,[14] but it remains an open question whether such a conception adequately addresses the issue of morality's ontological grounding.

Two, the wider neo-Calvinist background also gives us a way of understanding the unique, equal, and surpassing value of all human beings. This is a dignity that all humans possess regardless of their level of development or capability, and that no nonhuman animal possesses. Neo-Calvinism provides a way of understanding this universal human dignity with its concept of the *Imago Dei*, buttressed by its concept of the cultural mandate as a divine call issued universally and uniquely to humans. Conversely, as Wolterstorff explains, the phenomenon of human dignity—as something equally possessed by all humans regardless of their capacities, and as something uniquely human and greater than the dignity possessed by any nonhuman animal—is not easily explicable on metaphysical naturalism.[15] On metaphysical naturalism, it is very difficult to see why disabled humans should be viewed as having the same dignity as able humans, and why certain nonhuman animals, such as dolphins or the higher primates, shouldn't be viewed as having dignity equal to that of certain humans, such as infant or disabled humans. Wolterstorff's own explanation of human dignity is idiosyncratic,[16] but I think his criticisms of naturalistic explanations are cogent and would be widely shared by neo-Calvinists. The main neo-Calvinist explanation of human dignity is, as I say, the *Imago Dei*, which God has imprinted on all humans. The divine image has significant political implications—for political equality, rights, dignity, freedom—but can only be fully appreciated in a broader theological, ontological, and normative context.

There is also a second reason for retaining the neo-Calvinist background. While I have brought the tradition to bear on the question of political legitimacy, it may also be helpful in addressing other normative questions within political theory. The idea here is quite simple. We have found the tradition helpful once, and we might find it helpful again. It will not do, I think, to grant that the tradition might be helpful again, but to assume that whatever help it might provide can equally be found by pursuing some other philosophical path. It might not. Moreover, in advancing the tradition as a fund of conceptual insights and resources, I have emphasized that these might be brought to bear on any number of issues within political theory. I wonder, for instance, how the neo-Calvinist idea of the positivization of creation norms might inform the longstanding debate between natural law and legal positivism. Or I wonder how the distinction between structure and direction, and neo-Calvinists' affirmation of structure's persistence even when misdirected, as well as the concept of common grace, might bear on discussions of reasonable pluralism and reasonable disagreement. The idea here is that every line of rational inquiry is necessarily tradition-bound,[17] and that when theorists encounter difficulty they may benefit from approaching an issue from an altogether different perspective. They might benefit from approaching it as it would be approached by a different tradition. Such has been my attempt here, to approach the issue of legitimacy from a neo-Calvinist perspective in light of the difficulties encountered by JL and its secular backdrop. Since it might be comparably helpful in addressing other issues, the wider neo-Calvinist background is not merely superfluous.

Moreover, we cannot guarantee in advance that the ideas we find helpful in neo-Calvinism will be translatable into secular terms. I think the foregoing examples—of moral objectivity and human dignity, which neo-Calvinism more readily grounds than secular naturalism—call into question the possibility of doing so. It is certainly possible simply to assert bare propositions that, stripped of any religious language, appear entirely secularized. Yet underlying such propositions are distinctively theistic claims, such as that moral objectivity is grounded in God and that human beings are made in the image of God. Surely these deeper claims are not translatable.

In sum, the neo-Calvinist tradition may seem neither necessary nor sufficient to my account, but only, I think, if we view matters rather narrowly. The tradition is unnecessary only if we regard the relevant propositions in their barest form, without concern for the deeper philosophical issues underlying them. The tradition is insufficient only in the sense that it takes some philosophical work to appropriate its insights. It does not, as it were, wear on its sleeve a theory of legitimacy formulated in the terms of contemporary analytic philosophy. However, the tradition is, indeed, sufficient insofar as it possesses all the raw conceptual materials needed to reconstruct the theory, and it may well be necessary for deeper philosophical analyses of concepts deployed by political theorists.

Finally, even if the impossibility of translating neo-Calvinist insights into secular language is granted, it might still be asked why a neo-Calvinist approach is necessary as opposed to a theistic approach more generally. I recommend neo-Calvinism in particular because it is much more amenable to certain CCs of the modern era than other theistic approaches. For instance, by emphasizing sphere sovereignty it is more amenable to our convictions concerning religious freedom and church-state separation. I think other political theologies—Roman Catholic, Lutheran, Muslim—are less so. My claim is not that these traditions, as they now stand, remain incompatible with religious freedom and church-state separation. Hardly. For instance, I already noted in chapter 6 that since Vatican II Roman Catholicism has officially endorsed church-state separation. But these concepts seem to fit more naturally within neo-Calvinism than within the others, given its distinctive themes of institutional rights and institutional pluralism. Thus, I suspect neo-Calvinism makes distinctive claims that cannot be entirely captured by secular translations, nor by alternate theisms.

FUTURE DIRECTIONS

There are various directions further work on neo-Calvinist legitimacy might take. Here I mention just two, corresponding to two important challenges I face.

The first challenge is to move from the high level of generality at which my account operates to a concrete set of specific legitimacy conditions. I regard the account I've developed as very philosophically informative. That said, what it informs is how we ought go about formulating specific legitimacy conditions. Thus, much of the practical pay-off of the project would come in eventually formulating a list of these conditions.

The account assumes that we cannot philosophically justify a whole host of basic rights without presupposing that humans have been designed to flourish in particular ways. Discussion in chapter 9 briefly illustrated how this reasoning from basic human flourishing to basic rights might go, particularly with respect to the elements of flourishing that might justify rights to a social minimum, to education, and to religious freedom. But what else must we presuppose about basic human flourishing, at both individual and social levels, in order to philosophically justify a fuller set of fundamental rights? And what might a set of fundamental institutional rights look like? The latter is a particular lacuna in the current political philosophy literature. We need a fuller account of basic human flourishing in order to adjudicate disputes over the fundamental rights individuals possess, such as possible rights to leisure or to newly emerging technologies, and to determine the fundamental rights that institutions possess. In other words, we need not only the category of basic human flourishing. We also need that particular view of flourishing which is best suited to underwrite basic rights and adjudicate such disputes. Further work is required to discover and work out the specific features of this view, and, in so doing, to move from a general level to a set of specific legitimacy conditions.

The second challenge is to more fully explain how neo-Calvinist legitimacy, positing as it does the need for particular views of human flourishing to justify basic rights, comports with the reality of pluralism. This is an especially poignant challenge given that JL theorists often emphasize the need to abstract away from such views. Views of flourishing of the sort I say are necessary are, so far as legitimacy is concerned, typically seen as part of the problem rather than as part of the solution. To the contrary, my neo-Calvinist account asserts that a morally appropriate and politically legitimate approach to pluralism cannot be philosophically justified apart from presuppositions of the sort my account identifies, including presuppositions about flourishing. Much would be required to fully work out and evaluate this claim. Similarly, in Rawls' wake multi-perspectival acceptability is often seen as part of the very concept of legitimacy. A fuller explanation is required of why a neo-Calvinist account rejects this assumption, and of how a neo-Calvinist conception of legitimacy can address diverse views within pluralist societies. Further work is also needed on a neo-Calvinist appraisal of the so-called fact of reasonable pluralism, and on a neo-Calvinist appraisal of the burdens of judgment and reasonable disagreement. All these varied issues seem implicated in reconciling neo-Calvinist legitimacy with pluralism.

If I am right, the neo-Calvinist tradition offers myriad research possibilities as its insights are brought to bear on various issues within political theory. Here I have mentioned but two, concerning issues raised by my own account of legitimacy that is indebted to neo-Calvinism.

FINAL REFLECTIONS

What is legitimacy about? This has been my guiding question.

My response to this question has been offered at a relatively high level of generality, and my hopes for the project are fairly general as well. While my overall argument has been comprised of various specific ideas, my hope is that the collective force of these ideas will have the following general effect. That is, they are intended to give us pause to reconsider the categories in terms of which we, under the influence of the regnant JL approach, theorize legitimacy. My goal is a framework for understanding our convictions about legitimacy. To this end, I have urged on us a shift in categories: from conceiving legitimacy in terms of consent, procedures, and self-legislation, to conceiving it in terms of natural rights, basic human flourishing, and an exogenous normative standard. If the collective force of my arguments has made this category shift at all plausible, I count this philosophical progress.

Throughout, I have been motivated by, and remained tethered to, certain key ideas. And here I do not mean the formal ideas that I developed as part of my official account. Rather, I mean more informal ideas which have made periodic appearances while influencing my thinking throughout. Perhaps chief among these is the Humean point that parties to a social agreement have reasons for agreeing, and that it is these reasons that are most normatively significant. Similarly, if a reason or social arrangement is deemed reasonable, there must be independent grounds for doing so and it is these grounds which are most important. As well, I regard the nullity of nonconsent as crucial, as a normative reality with which legitimacy theorizing must reckon. As political actors, we all seem ready to coerce others regarding what we consider to be justice's most basic demands, even as we each have different ideas of what these demands are. A striking feature of our convictions about real-world legitimacy is a certain indifference to those who would disagree with us.

Another of these informal ideas is that views of flourishing—or comprehensive views, or conceptions of the good, or some such thing—are always operative in the background of political theories.[18] I suspect this goes both for theories where the background views are explicit as well as for theories where they are only implicit. This suspicion is akin to one of Reformational philosophy's most distinctive claims: that no philosophy is truly autonomously. Dooyeweerd speaks of the "'pretended autonomy' of theoretical thought."[19] All theorizing and rational inquiry, including philosophy, is dependent on presuppositions that are ultimately spiritual, or religious, in nature.

A last idea worth mentioning, that has shaped my thinking throughout and that also can be drawn straight from the neo-Calvinist tradition, is this: that political coercion is necessary "by reason of sin." To my ears, that legitimacy is fundamentally about preventing basic wrongs rings true "all the way down"[20] as we seek to achieve reflective equilibrium between various levels of legitimacy-related convictions and propositions.

It is ideas like these that convince me that the JL framework fails to capture what legitimacy is about. Neo-Calvinism, with its affirmation that coercion is only necessary "by reason of sin," seems a more apt starting point for understanding legitimacy. My account, and the arguments I offer in its defense, is the fruit of reflecting upon these ideas and attempting to formulate them in ordered, analytic terms, all the while drawing inspiration and insight from the neo-Calvinist tradition.

I think it bears emphasizing one last time that what I have presented here is primarily a philosophical account. I have been arguing that as theorists we cannot make good philosophical sense of our legitimacy convictions without the sort of presuppositions identified by neo-Calvinist legitimacy. Without them, we cannot account for our convictions in an internally consistent way, convictions such as the legitimacy of much actual legal coercion, the necessity of basic rights for legitimacy, and the illegitimacy of paternalism. That said, it is no part of the view defended here that, in our political engagement, we should seek to base laws on specifically theistic or Christian premises. Such would be a bad misinterpretation of my argument. Ironically, it would also be an utter mischaracterization of the very neo-Calvinist tradition I suggest we turn to, for central to this tradition are notions of sphere sovereignty and societal differentiation, which include a principled church-state separation and religious freedom (see especially tenets 6, 7, and 8). To ignore the sphere sovereignty of individuals, church, or state is, in a word, illegitimate.

In closing, one further reflection on where, in the final analysis, I believe JL goes wrong.

As it seems to me, the root problem of JL is this: JLs try to ground legitimacy in some version of popular sovereignty, rather than in the character and commands of a sovereign and perfectly good God. Indeed, all of the challenges with JL that I have discussed—those owing to its unanimity condition, those owing to its proceduralism, and any that might owe to its idealized self-legislators—can be traced back to this root issue. Neo-Calvinists will claim that any line of theoretical thought will be misdirected if opposed to God, and it would not be unreasonable, I think, for them to take the unacceptable consequences to which JL leads, and ultimately its failure to explain legitimacy, as vindication of this claim.

In fact, we should regard a high view of God's sovereignty as probably the single most foundational premise for any inquiry conducted along neo-Calvinist lines. Though I have not yet emphasized this point, let me do so now. While I have argued for the conceptual categories of natural rights, basic human flourishing, and an exogenous normative standard, it may be that, in turn, we cannot make sense of these categories apart from theistic premises. Of course, this latter claim has not been part of my present argument. But if such turns out to be the case, we would have still more reason to learn all we can from neo-Calvinism.

However contentious these last reflections might be, I hope the reader will see in my project progress on the important normative issue of political legitimacy.

NOTES

1. Not only Bohman and Richardson, though. See two articles by Chambers, both of which survey the current state of debate over public justification (Chambers, "Theories of Political Justification," 893–903; Chambers, "Secularism Minus Exclusion," 16–21).
2. "RACAs" stands for reasons that all can accept. See Bohman and Richardson, "Liberalism, Deliberative Democracy, and 'Reasons,'" 253–74.
3. Nussbaum, *Creating Capabilities*, 33–34.
4. Henry Shue, *Basic Rights: Subsistence, Affluence, and U.S. Foreign Policy* (Princeton, NJ: Princeton University Press, 1980). Shue prioritizes three substantive basic rights: to subsistence, security, and liberty.
5. Remember, for example, "Note that the standard is not what principles or institutions people will *actually accept*, but what it would be unreasonable for them not to accept, given a certain common moral motivation in addition to their more personal, private, and communal ends" (Nagel, "Moral Conflict," 221).
6. I thank Will Kymlicka for stimulating the discussion here.
7. Nagel, "Moral Conflict," 220–21.
8. Rawls, *Justice as Fairness*, 72.
9. Rawls, *Political Liberalism*, 404–7.
10. Ibid., 431.
11. Freeman, "Moral Contractarianism," 66–67.
12. Ibid., 75 n32.
13. I believe I have Henry Laycock to thank for the essence of this objection.
14. See Rawls, *Political Liberalism*, 110–25; Freeman, *Rawls*, 291–94.
15. Wolterstorff, *Understanding Liberal Democracy*, 186–93, 206–17.
16. Wolterstorff actually rejects the *Imago Dei* as well as a grounding for human rights, and suggests instead that they are grounded in God's desire for friendship with humans. (Ibid., 193–200.)
17. This thesis is developed by MacIntyre in his books, Alasdair MacIntyre, *After Virtue* (Notre Dame, IN: University of Notre Dame Press, 1984); MacIntyre, *Whose Justice?*.
18. Taylor, MacIntyre, Wolterstorff, and Alvin Plantinga each in their own way affirm this point. See Charles Taylor, *Sources of the Self: The Making of the Modern Identity* (Cambridge, MA: Harvard University Press, 1989); MacIntyre, *Whose Justice?*; Nicholas Wolterstorff, "Then, Now, and Al," *Faith and Philosophy* 28, no. 3 (July 2011): 253–66; Alvin Plantinga, "Reason and Belief in God," in *Faith and Rationality: Reason and Belief in God*, ed. Alvin Plantinga and Nicholas Wolterstorff (Notre Dame, IN: University of Notre Dame Press, 1983), 16–93.
19. Zuidervaart, *Religion, Truth, and Social Transformation*, 52.
20. Jeremy Waldron, *Law and Disagreement* (New York: Oxford University Press, 1999), 295.

Bibliography

Alston, William P. *Perceiving God*. Ithaca, NY: Cornell University Press, 1991.
Arneson, Richard J. "The Supposed Right to a Democratic Say." In *Contemporary Debates in Political Philosophy*, edited by Christiano, Thomas and Christman, John, 197–212. Hoboken, NJ: Blackwell Publishing Ltd., 2009.
Audi, Robert. "The Place of Religious Argument in a Free and Democratic Society." *San Diego Law Review* 30, no. 4 (1993): 677–702.
Audi, Robert, and Wolterstorff, Nicholas. *Religion in the Public Square: The Place of Religious Convictions in Political Debate*. Lanham, MD: Rowman & Littlefield Publishers, Inc., 1997.
Augustine. *The City of God against the Pagans*. Edited by Dyson, R. W. New York: Cambridge University Press, 1998.
Bakunin, Michael. *Bakunin on Anarchy*. Edited and translated by Dolgoff, Sam. New York: Random House, Inc., 1971.
Barry, Brian. "Chance, Choice and Justice." In *Contemporary Political Philosophy: An Anthology*, edited by Goodin, Robert E. and Pettit, Philip, 229–39, 2006.
———. *Justice as Impartiality*. New York: Oxford University Press, 1995.
Bohman, James, and Richardson, Henry S. "Liberalism, Deliberative Democracy, and 'Reasons That All Can Accept.'" *The Journal of Political Philosophy* 17, no. 3 (2009): 253–74.
Bratt, James D. *Abraham Kuyper: Modern Calvinist, Christian Democrat*. Grand Rapids, MI: William B. Eerdmans Publishing Co., 2013.
Brettschneider, Corey. *When the State Speaks, What Should It Say? How Democracies Can Protect Expression and Promote Equality*. Princeton, NJ: Princeton University Press, 2012.
Buchanan, Allen. "Political Legitimacy and Democracy." *Ethics* 112 (July 2002): 689–719.
Calvin, John. *Institutes of the Christian Religion*. Edited by McNeill, John T. Translated by Battles, Ford Lewis. 2 vols. London: S. C. M. Press, 1961.
Chambers, Simone. "Secularism Minus Exclusion: Developing a Religious-Friendly Idea of Public Reason." *The Good Society* 19, no. 2 (2010): 16–21.
———. "Theories of Political Justification." *Philosophy Compass* 5, no. 11 (2010): 893–903.
Chan, Joseph. "Legitimacy, Unanimity, and Perfectionism." *Philosophy and Public Affairs* 1 (2000): 5–42.
Chaplin, Jonathan. "Civil Society and The State: A Neo-Calvinist Perspective." In *Christianity and Civil Society: Catholic and Neo-Calvinist Perspectives*. Lanham, MD: Lexington/Rowman & Littlefield, 2008.
———. "Conclusion: Christian Political Wisdom." In *God and Government*, edited by Spencer, Nick and Chaplin, Jonathan, 205–37. London: Society for Promoting Christian Knowledge, 2009.

———. "Dooyeweerd's Notion of Societal Structural Principles." *Philosophia Reformata* 60 (1995): 16–36.

———. *Faith in the State: The Peril and Promise of Christian Politics*. Toronto, ON: Institute for Christian Studies, 1999.

———. *Herman Dooyeweerd: Christian Philosopher of State and Civil Society*. Notre Dame, IN: University of Notre Dame Press, 2011.

———. "Subsidiarity as a Political Norm." In *Political Theory and Christian Vision: Essays in Memory of Bernard Zylstra*, 81–100. Lanham, MD: University Press of America, Inc., 1994.

Cohen, G. A. "On the Currency of Egalitarian Justice." *Ethics* 99 (July 1989): 906–44.

———. *Rescuing Justice and Equality*. Cambridge, MA: Harvard University Press, 2008.

Cohen, Joshua. "Democracy and Liberty." In *Deliberative Democracy*, edited by Elster, Jon, 185–231. New York: Cambridge University Press, 1998.

Constant, Benjamin. "The Liberty of the Ancients Compared with that of the Moderns." In *Benjamin Constant: Political Writings*, edited and translated by Fontana, Biancamaria. New York: Cambridge University Press, 1988.

Dooyeweerd, Herman. *A Christian Theory of Social Institutions*. Edited by Witte, John, Jr. Translated by Verbrugge, Magnus. La Jolla, CA: The Herman Dooyeweerd Foundation, 1986.

———. *The Christian Idea of the State*. Translated by Kraay, John. Nutley, NJ: The Craig Press, 1968.

Dworkin, Ronald. "Liberalism." In *A Matter of Principle*. Cambridge, MA: Harvard University Press, 1985.

———. "What Is Equality? Part 1: Equality of Welfare." *Philosophy and Public Affairs* 10, no. 3 (Summer 1981): 185–246.

———. "What Is Equality? Part 2: Equality of Resources." *Philosophy and Public Affairs* 10, no. 4 (Autumn 1981): 283–345.

Eberle, Christopher J. *Religious Conviction in Liberal Politics*. New York: Cambridge University Press, 2002.

Estlund, David M. *Democratic Authority: A Philosophical Framework*. Princeton, NJ: Princeton University Press, 2008.

Flathman, Richard E. "Legitimacy." Edited by Goodin, Robert E., Pettit, Philip, and Pogge, Thomas. *A Companion to Contemporary Political Philosophy, 2007*. Blackwell Reference Online.

Freeman, Samuel. "Moral Contractarianism as a Foundation for Interpersonal Morality." In *Contemporary Debates in Moral Theory*, edited by Dreier, James, 57–76. Hoboken, NJ: Blackwell Publishing Ltd., 2006.

———. *Rawls*. New York: Routledge, 2007.

Gaus, Gerald. *Contemporary Theories of Liberalism: Public Reason as a Post-Enlightenment Project*. Thousand Oaks, CA: Sage, 2003.

———. *Justificatory Liberalism: An Essay on Epistemology and Political Theory*. Oxford: Oxford University Press, 1996.

———. "On Two Critics of Justificatory Liberalism: A Response to Wall and Lister." *Politics, Philosophy & Economics* 9, no. 2 (May 2010): 177–212.

———. *The Order of Public Reason: A Theory of Freedom and Morality in a Diverse and Bounded World*. New York: Cambridge University Press, 2011.

Gaus, Gerald, and Vallier, Kevin. "The Roles of Religious Conviction in a Publicly Justified Polity: The Implications of Convergence, Asymmetry and Political Institutions." *Philosophy and Social Criticism* 35, no. 1–2 (January 2009): 51–76.

Goudzwaard, Bob. "Christian Politics in a Global Context." In *Political Order and the Plural Structure of Society*, edited by Skillen, James W. and McCarthy, Rockne M. Emory University Studies in Law and Religion. Atlanta, GA: Scholars Press, 1991.

———. *Globalization and the Kingdom of God*. Edited by Skillen, James W. Grand Rapids, MI: Baker Books, 2001.

———. "Globalization, Regionalization, and Sphere Sovereignty." In *Religion, Pluralism, and Public Life: Abraham Kuyper's Legacy for the Twenty-First Century*, edited by Lugo, Luis E., 325–41. Grand Rapids, MI: William B. Eerdmans Publishing Co., 2000.

Gutmann, Amy, and Thompson, Dennis. *Democracy and Disagreement*. Cambridge, MA: The Belknap Press of Harvard University Press, 1996.

Habermas, Jürgen. "Reconciliation Through the Public Use of Reason: Remarks on John Rawls's Political Liberalism." *The Journal of Philosophy* 92, no. 3 (March 1995): 109–31.

"Hanging Gardens of Babylon." *Britannica*. Accessed June 30, 2016. https://www.britannica.com/place/Hanging-Gardens-of-Babylon.

Hume, David. "Of the Original Contract." In *David Hume: Political Writings*, edited by Warner, S. D. and Livingston, D. W., 164–81. Indianapolis, IN: Hackett, 1994.

Jackson, Timothy P. "To Bedlam and Part Way Back: John Rawls and Christian Justice." *Faith and Philosophy* 8, no. 4 (October 1991): 423–47.

Keller, Timothy. *Generous Justice: How God's Grace Makes Us Just*. New York: Penguin Group (USA) Inc., 2010.

Kelly, Thomas. "Evidence." Edited by Zalta, Edward N. *Stanford Encyclopedia of Philosophy*, 2006. http://plato.stanford.edu/entries/evidence/.

Koyzis, David T. *Political Visions & Illusions: A Survey and Christian Critique of Contemporary Ideologies*. Downers Grove, IL: InterVarsity Press, 2003.

———. *We Answer to Another: Authority, Office, and the Image of God*. Eugene, OR: Pickwick Publications, 2014.

Kukathas, Chandran. *The Liberal Archipelago: A Theory of Diversity and Freedom*. New York: Oxford University Press, 2003.

Kuyper, Abraham. *Christianity: A Total World and Life System*. Marlborough, NH: Plymouth Rock Foundation, Inc., 1996.

———. *Lectures on Calvinism*. Peabody, MA: Hendrickson Publishers, 2008.

Kymlicka, Will. *Contemporary Political Philosophy: An Introduction*. New York: Oxford University Press, 1990.

———. "The Ethics of Inarticulacy." *Inquiry* 34, no. 2 (1991): 155–82.

Larmore, Charles. *Patterns of Moral Complexity*. New York: Cambridge University Press, 1987.

———. "The Moral Basis of Political Liberalism." *Journal of Philosophy* 96 (December 1999): 599–625.

———. *The Morals of Modernity*. New York: Cambridge University Press, 1996.

Lister, Andrew. "Public Justification and the Limits of State Action." *Politics, Philosophy & Economics* 9, no. 2 (2010): 151–75.

———. "Public Justification of What? Coercion vs. Decision as Competing Frames for the Basic Principle of Justificatory Liberalism." *Public Affairs Quarterly* 25, no. 4 (October 2011): 349ff.

———. *Public Reason and Political Community*. New York: Bloomsbury, 2013.

Macedo, Stephen. "In Defense of Liberal Public Reason: Are Slavery and Abortion Hard Cases?" In *Natural Law and Public Reason*, edited by George, Robert P. and Wolfe, Christopher, 11–49. Washington, D.C.: Georgetown University Press, 2000.

MacIntyre, Alasdair. *After Virtue*. Notre Dame, IN: University of Notre Dame Press, 1984.

———. *Whose Justice? Which Rationality?* Notre Dame, IN: University of Notre Dame Press, 1988.

Macleod, Alistair M. "Rights and Recognition: The Case of Human Rights." *Journal of Social Philosophy* 44, no. 1 (Spring 2013): 51–73.

Marshall, Paul A., and Gilbert, Lela. *Heaven Is Not My Home: Learning to Live in God's Creation*. Nashville, TN: Thomas Nelson, 1999.

McCarthy, Rockne M., Skillen, James W., and Harper, William A. *Disestablishment a Second Time: Genuine Pluralism for American Schools*. Grand Rapids, MI: Christian University Press, 1982.

McCloskey, H. J. "A Non-Utilitarian Approach to Punishment." *Inquiry* 8 (1965): 249–63.

McGrath, Alister. *Christian Theology: An Introduction*. Cambridge, MA: Blackwell Publishing Ltd., 1994.

Mill, John Stuart. "Considerations on Representative Government." In *On Liberty and Other Essays*, edited by Gray, John. Oxford World's Classics. New York: Oxford University Press, 1991.

Moreland, J. P. *The Recalcitrant Imago Dei: Human Persons and the Failure of Naturalism.* London: SCM Press, 2009.

Mouw, Richard. *He Shines in All That's Fair: Culture and Common Grace.* Grand Rapids, MI: Eerdmans, 2001.

———. "Some Reflections on Sphere Sovereignty." In *Religion, Pluralism, and Public Life: Abraham Kuyper's Legacy for the Twenty-First Century,* edited by Lugo, Luis E., 87–109. Grand Rapids, MI: William B. Eerdmans Publishing Co., 2000.

Mouw, Richard J., and Griffioen, Sander. *Pluralisms and Horizons: An Essay in Christian Public Philosophy.* Grand Rapids, MI: William B. Eerdmans Publishing Co., 1993.

Nagel, Thomas. "Moral Conflict and Political Legitimacy." *Philosophy and Public Affairs* 16, no. 3 (Summer 1987): 215–40.

Nozick, Robert. *Anarchy, State, and Utopia.* New York: Basic Books, Inc., 1974.

Nussbaum, Martha C. *Creating Capabilities: The Human Development Approach.* Cambridge, MA: The Belknap Press of Harvard University Press, 2011.

———. "Perfectionist Liberalism and Political Liberalism." *Philosophy and Public Affairs* 39, no. 1 (2011): 3–45.

O'Donovan, Oliver, and O'Donovan, Joan Lockwood, eds. *From Irenaeus to Grotius: A Sourcebook in Christian Political Thought.* Grand Rapids, MI: William B. Eerdmans Publishing Co., 1999.

Peter, Fabienne. *Democratic Legitimacy.* New York: Routledge, 2009.

Pettit, Philip. *Republicanism: A Theory of Freedom and Government.* New York: Oxford University Press, 1999.

———. *The Common Mind: An Essay on Psychology, Society and Politics.* New York: Oxford University Press, 1993.

Plantinga, Alvin. "Reason and Belief in God." In *Faith and Rationality: Reason and Belief in God,* edited by Plantinga, Alvin and Wolterstorff, Nicholas, 16–93. Notre Dame, IN: University of Notre Dame Press, 1983.

Quong, Jonathan. "Disagreement, Asymmetry, and Liberal Legitimacy." Politics, Philosophy & Economics 4, no. 3 (2005): 301–30.

———. *Liberalism without Perfection.* New York: Oxford University Press, 2011.

Rawls, John. *A Theory of Justice.* Revised Edition. Cambridge, MA: The Belknap Press of Harvard University Press, 1999.

———. *Justice as Fairness: A Restatement.* Cambridge, MA: The Belknap Press of Harvard University Press, 2001.

———. *Political Liberalism.* Expanded Edition. New York: Columbia University Press, 2005.

———. "The Idea of Public Reason Revisited." In *Political Liberalism, Expanded Edition,* 440–90. New York: Columbia University Press, 2005.

Raz, Joseph. "Facing Diversity: The Case of Epistemic Abstinence." *Philosophy and Public Affairs* 19, no. 1 (Winter 1990): 3–46.

"Roman Catholicism." *Britannica.* Accessed June 22, 2013. www.britannica.com/EBchecked/topic/507284/Roman-Catholicism.

Sandel, Michael J. *Justice: What's the Right Thing to Do?* New York: Farrar, Straus and Giroux, 2009.

Scanlon, T. M. "Contractualism and Utilitarianism." In *Utilitarianism and Beyond,* edited by Sen, Amartya and Williams. Bernard, 103–28. Cambridge: Cambridge University Press, 1982.

———. *What We Owe to Each Other.* Cambridge, MA: Harvard University Press, 1998.

Schwartzman, Micah. "The Completeness of Public Reason." *Politics, Philosophy & Economics* 3, no. 2 (2004): 191–220.

Shue, Henry. *Basic Rights: Subsistence, Affluence, and U.S. Foreign Policy.* Princeton, NJ: Princeton University Press, 1980.

Simmons, A. John. *Moral Principles and Political Obligations.* Princeton, NJ: Princeton University Press, 1979.

Skillen, James W. *The Good of Politics: A Biblical, Historical, and Contemporary Introduction.* Grand Rapids, MI: Baker Academic, 2014.

———. "The Pluralist Philosophy of Herman Dooyeweerd." In *Christianity and Civil Society: Catholic and Neo-Calvinist Perspectives*, edited by Schindler, Jeanne Heffernan, 97–114. Lanham, MD: Rowman & Littlefield Publishers, Inc., 2008.

Skillen, James W., and McCarthy, Rockne M., eds. *Political Order and the Plural Structure of Society*. Emory University Studies in Law and Religion. Atlanta, GA: Scholars Press, 1991.

Skinner, Quentin. *The Foundations of Modern Political Thought: The Age of Reformation*. Vol. 2. Cambridge: Cambridge University Press, 1978.

Smart, J. J. C., and Williams, Bernard. *Utilitarianism For and Against*. New York: Cambridge University Press, 1973.

Storkey, Elaine. "Sphere Sovereignty and the Anglo-American Tradition." In *Religion, Pluralism, and Public Life: Abraham Kuyper's Legacy for the Twenty-First Century*, edited by Lugo, Luis E., 189–204. Grand Rapids, MI: William B. Eerdmans Publishing Co., 2000.

Taylor, Charles. *Sources of the Self: The Making of the Modern Identity*. Cambridge, MA: Harvard University Press, 1989.

———. "The Diversity of Goods." In *Philosophy and the Human Sciences: Philosophical Papers 2*, by Taylor, Charles, 230–47. New York, NY: Cambridge University Press, 1985.

———. "What's Wrong with Negative Liberty." In *Philosophy and the Human Sciences: Philosophical Papers 2*, by Taylor, Charles, 211–29. New York, NY: Cambridge University Press, 1985.

The Holy Bible: English Standard Version. Wheaton, IL: Crossway, 2005.

Thoreau, Henry David. *Civil Disobedience and Other Essays*. Mineola, NY: Dover Publications, Inc., 1993.

Tierney, Brian. *The Idea of Natural Rights: Studies on Natural Rights, Natural Law and Church Law 1150–1625*. Atlanta, GA: Scholars Press, 1997.

Vallier, Kevin, and D'Agostino, Fred. "Public Justification." Edited by Zalta, Edward N. *Stanford Encyclopedia of Philosophy*, 2012. http://plato.stanford.edu/entries/justification-public.

VanDrunen, David. *Natural Law and the Two Kingdoms*. Grand Rapids, MI: William B. Eerdmans Publishing Co., 2010.

Vollenhoven, Dirk H.T. *Introduction to Philosophy*. Edited by Kok, John H. and Tol, Anthony. Sioux Center, IA: Dordt College Press, 2005.

Waldron, Jeremy. *Law and Disagreement*. New York: Oxford University Press, 1999.

———. "Theoretical Foundations of Liberalism." *Philosophical Quarterly* 37 (1987): 127–50.

Wall, Steven. *Liberalism, Perfectionism and Restraint*. New York: Cambridge University Press, 1998.

Waluchow, Wilfrid J. *The Dimensions of Ethics: An Introduction to Ethical Theory*. Peterborough, ON: Broadview Press, Ltd., 2003.

Williams, Howard. "Kant on the Social Contract." In *The Social Contract from Hobbes to Rawls*, edited by Boucher, David and Kelly, Paul, 132–46. New York: Routledge, 1994.

Wills, Richard Wayne. *Martin Luther King, Jr., and the Image of God*. New York: Oxford University Press, 2009.

Wolters, Al. *Creation Regained*. Grand Rapids, MI: William B. Eerdmans Publishing Co., 1985.

Wolterstorff, Nicholas. *Justice in Love*. Grand Rapids, MI: William B. Eerdmans Publishing Co., 2011.

———. *Justice: Rights and Wrongs*. Princeton, NJ: Princeton University Press, 2008.

———. *The Mighty and the Almighty: An Essay in Political Theology*. New York: Cambridge University Press, 2012.

———. "Then, Now, and Al." *Faith and Philosophy* 28, no. 3 (July 2011): 253–66.

———. *Understanding Liberal Democracy: Essays in Political Philosophy*. Edited by Cuneo, Terence. Oxford: Oxford University Press, 2012.

———. *Until Justice and Peace Embrace*. Grand Rapids, MI: William B. Eerdmans Publishing Co., 1983.

———. "Why We Should Reject What Liberalism Tells Us about Speaking and Acting in Public for Religious Reasons." In *Religion and Contemporary Liberalism*, 162–81. Notre Dame, IN: University of Notre Dame Press, 1997.

Zuidervaart, Lambert. *Religion, Truth, and Social Transformation: Essays in Reformational Philosophy*. Montreal & Kingston: McGill-Queen's University Press, 2016.

Index

abortion, 52n42, 68, 73
Althusius, Johannes, 111n24
anarchism. *See* Bakuninist thought
Aquinas, Saint Thomas, 91, 157
Aristotle, 86, 116, 157
the arts, 89, 99
associational pluralism. *See* sphere sovereignty
Audi, Robert, 28, 30n1, 140
Augustine, 90
authority, 18, 140–141, 150n5; individual freedom as authority, 86–87, 129; as ultimately derived from God, 102, 108
autonomy. *See* freedom

Barry, Brian, 26, 30n1, 171
Bakunin, Michael, 35, 36, 38, 51n18. *See also* Bakuninist thought
Bakuninist thought, 37, 38–39, 43; on freedom, 37, 42; objection to centralized government, 39, 143
the Bible: Exodus 20:13-16, 54; Genesis 1, 93; Genesis 1:27, 85; Genesis 1:27-28, 88; Matthew 6:26, 162; Romans 2:14-15, 96; Romans 13:1-2, 108; Romans 13:1-5, 117
Bohman, James, 3, 24, 181
Brettschneider, Corey, 21, 28, 29
Buchanan, Allen, 31n9, 127
business, 89, 97, 99–100, 101, 102

Calvin, John, 83, 87, 96
capabilities approach, 54, 158, 182
capitalism, 101, 148
Catholicism, Roman, 82, 99, 104, 189; and Vatican II, 82, 110n6
Chaplin, Jonathan, 4, 84, 91
church. *See* ecclesiology
church and state, separation of, 83, 104; Neo-Calvinist affirmation of, 102–104, 192
civil society, 99
coercion, 1, 2, 7–8, 68, 149
Cohen, Joshua, 21, 28, 30n1
Cohen, G. A., 70, 167n15
common good: in justificatory liberalism, 59, 72, 171; part of neo-Calvinist public justice, 106–107, 124, 165–166
common grace, 96, 188
comparative political theory, neo-Calvinism and, 4, 7, 9, 82, 109, 182, 186, 188
consent, 146–148; centrality of to justificatory liberalism, 46, 137, 139; hypothetical vs. actual, 137, 139; null non-consent, 140, 141–142, 191
consensus, 8, 36, 53, 61, 62, 154, 166. *See also* justificatory liberalism
considered convictions, 19, 57; criteria for best legitimacy account, 19–20, 137, 181; three important legitimacy convictions, 7–8, 20

constructivism. *See* proceduralism
contractarianism, 30n1, 60, 172, 178n2, 185
creation order, 93–95, 97, 175
creation/fall/redemption paradigm, 89, 90, 95
creationism, young-earth, 164
the cultural mandate, 88–90, 91, 95, 130, 187

deliberative democracy, 21, 30n1, 167n9
differentiation, social, 95, 99, 106, 148, 192; and role differentiation in individual lives, 101
direction. *See* structure and direction
disagreement, 46–47, 98, 160
divine right of kings, 86, 116
Dooyeweerd, Herman, 84, 100, 191; government's founding-function, 91, 100
Dworkin, Ronald, 21, 64n18, 133n9

Eberle, Christopher, 20, 23, 31n11, 41, 52n42
ecclesiology, 87, 103–104
education, 7, 89, 97, 99, 106, 164
the environment, 88, 99, 106
equality, conceptions of, 38, 43; Neo-Calvinist equality, 86–87
Estlund, David, 55, 60; null non-consent, 140–141
evil: societal evil, 90, 126, 161
exogeny, 129–130; contrast with self-legislation, 170, 173

fairness, conceptions of, 43
the fall. *See* sin
family, 59; as social sphere, 90, 97, 99, 102, 105, 113n111
Filmer, Sir Robert. *See* divine right of kings
flourishing, 126, 153, 156; basic vs. non-basic, 5, 128, 161–163
freedom, 73; conceptions of, 37, 42; freedom of conscience, 37, 52n32; freedoms of differential importance, 123–124, 158
freedom of religion, 53, 54, 59, 164–165

Freeman, Samuel, 30n1, 171, 178n2, 184–185

Gaus, Gerald, 20, 51n22, 52n50, 75
Golden Rule, 172
God, 108, 192; source of exogenous normativity, 131, 187
Goudzwaard, Bob, 84, 93, 101
government, 90–91, 105, 107, 144–145; coordinating functions, 91, 118; prelapsarian government disputed, 90, 91–92
Griffioen, Sander. *See* Mouw, Richard J.
Gutmann, Amy, 22, 30n1, 69

Habermas, Jürgen, 55, 184
historical unfolding. *See* differentiation, social
Hobbes, Thomas, 117
human flourishing, views of, 157, 158–159; examples, 157
human nature, 91, 94
human rights, 6, 119, 141; Universal Declaration of Human Rights, 54
Hume, David, 60, 153, 156, 191

image of God, 87; as basis for rights, 119, 162, 187; and equality, 85–86, 120
Imago Dei. *See* image of God
institutions, 18, 37, 70, 93; as rights-bearers, 5, 102, 120, 189
institutional pluralism. *See* sphere sovereignty
interests, 69, 76, 162, 175–177; interest-based vs. justice-based justifications, 75–76, 175; justificatory liberalism's question of, 72, 74
Islam, 189

justice: relation to rights and wrongs, 127, 173. *See also* legitimacy, political
justificatory liberalism, 20–21, 29, 54; default position in, 26–27, 48; hypothetical persons in, 72–73, 171–172; individual exemptions version of, 143; main idea, 2, 22, 45; and perfectionist liberalism, 21; and political liberalism, 20; unanimity condition, 22, 44–45, 50, 137, 155

Kant, Immanuel, 42, 44, 55, 131, 155; self-legislation ideal rejected by neo-Calvinists, 87, 129
King, Jr., Martin Luther, 61, 120, 132n7
Koyzis, David T., 4, 84, 91, 93, 94, 97, 99, 103, 105–106, 108, 110n6; individual freedom as authority, 86–87, 129
Kuyper, Abraham, 4, 98, 104, 142, 173; biographical information, 83, 108; differences from contemporary neo-Calvinists, 93, 106, 125; government needed "by reason of sin", 90, 91, 112n48, 118; on sphere sovereignty, 86, 99–100, 101, 107
Kymlicka, Will, 21, 43, 60

legitimacy, framework(s) for: book's main question, 15–16, 27, 76, 109, 116, 132, 148, 154, 181, 190; justificatory liberalism as, 30, 181; Neo-Calvinist legitimacy as, 116, 182
legitimacy, political, 1; context-transcendent, 17, 28–29; distinct from justice, 128, 147; and multi-perspectival acceptability, 160, 190; normative vs. descriptive, 17, 138. *See also* legitimacy, framework(s) for
libertarianism, 33n59, 47, 49; justificatory liberalism's redistribution problem, 36, 143, 163
Larmore, Charles, 32n22
Lister, Andrew, 21, 22, 32n27, 123–124, 144; on higher-order unanimity, 47–48; two framings of justificatory liberalism, 26–27, 33n59, 49
Locke, John, 52n38, 86, 117, 167n16
Luther, Martin, 82

Macedo, Stephen, 21, 27, 56, 57
MacIntyre, Alasdair, 128, 193n17
marriage, 90, 97, 99, 101, 105
Marshall, Paul, 88
mediating structures, 82
Mill, John Stuart, 21, 69, 86
modal ontology, 100, 101, 120
Mouw, Richard J., 97, 99, 103

Nagel, Thomas, 21, 184, 193n5; liberalism's higher-order impartiality, 51n23, 64n10
natural law, 93, 188
natural rights, 5, 9, 143, 144; features of, 119–120. *See also* rights
Neo-Calvinism, 148–149, 185–189; conception of equality, 86–87; and Reformational philosophy, 84; variant of Reformed Christianity, 82, 83
Neo-Calvinist legitimacy, 165, 182, 189–190; preventing wrongs the main idea, 115, 117–118, 191; subsidiary questions of, 173–174, 176; summarized, 115, 132, 182; three big ideas of, 5, 115. *See also* public justice, neo-Calvinist
non-consent, null. *See* consent
norms, creation, 89, 93, 94, 95, 96–97, 101, 106; flexibility in application, 93, 94, 95
Nussbaum, Martha, 24, 42, 54, 158, 182

objectivity, 143, 146; objective rights defined, 53, 61, 119; evidence of, 61, 120
obligation, political, 18, 108

paternalism, 68, 75, 169; in justificatory liberalism, 73, 75, 170–172
Paul, Saint, 91, 108
Peter, Fabienne, 55; the "political egalitarian's dilemma", 55, 167n4
Pettit, Philip, 51n21, 60, 77n5
perfectionist liberalism. *See* justificatory liberalism
political liberalism. *See* justificatory liberalism
positivization, 94, 95, 130, 188
pluralism. *See* reasonable pluralism
political theology, varieties of, 82–83; Anabaptist, 83; Lutheran, 82, 189; Reformed view of church and state, 83, 104. *See also* Catholicism, Roman
popular sovereignty, 131, 155, 170, 172, 173, 177–178, 192
proceduralism: and constructivism, 41–42, 54, 56, 170; idealizations in, 25–26, 73; internal logic of, 40–42, 55, 58, 155,

171; its lack of content, 57–60; obscures why agreement is reasonable, 60, 156, 166; substance vs. procedure distinction, 24–25, 54–56; weak vs. strong interpretation of, 131, 183–185

public justice, neo-Calvinist: distinctive features of, 105–106, 124–125, 165–166; and transnational institutions, 107

public justification: justificatory liberalism' principle of, 27, 29, 41, 54, 76, 115. *See also* public reason

public reason: nature of public reasons, 22–23; relation to public reasons and public justification, 33n42

Quong, Jonathan, 21, 26, 32n32, 33n50, 45, 50, 64n20, 68

Rawls, John, 4, 39, 45; considered convictions and reflective equilibrium, 19, 20, 57, 153; criteria of reasonableness, 24–25, 42, 155; exemplar of justificatory liberalism, 2, 20–21; formulation of the legitimacy issue, 4, 15, 17, 150n12, 160, 190; liberal principle of legitimacy, 22, 41; original position's key question, 70, 74; and proceduralism, 55, 56–57, 184, 187; and public reason, 23, 28, 45, 59, 171

Raz, Joseph, 21, 61–62, 85

"reasonableness", 41; vacuity of, 155. *See also* reasonable persons

reasonable persons, 23–25, 39, 40; basic to proceduralism, 41–42; idealizations of, 26, 46; two criteria for, 37. *See also* Rawls, John

reasonable pluralism, 24, 39, 190

"reasons all can accept". *See* Bohman, James

redistribution. *See* libertarianism

Reformed Christianity. *See* political theology, varieties of

Reformational philosophy. *See* Neo-Calvinism

Richardson, Henry S. *See* Bohman, James

rights, 54, 61; connection to human flourishing, 122–124; legitimacy-conditional rights defined, 11n5; procedure-independence of, 56–57, 155; three characteristics of, 53, 166. *See also* rights, basic

rights, basic: to bodily integrity, 53, 58, 123, 162; to education, 164, 189; equal standing under law, 54, 58, 60, 123; to healthcare, 162, 163; to material subsistence, 123, 163; as opposed to non-basic, 126–127

Rousseau, Jean-Jacques, 29, 44, 50

Runner, H. Evan, 84

same-sex marriage, 68, 124

Sandel, Michael, 124

Scanlon, T. M., 16, 32n27, 70, 71

science, 22, 46, 89, 97, 99, 101, 167n19; and moral powers' development, 171

scientism, 164

self-interest: as conceived in justificatory liberalism, 171, 173, 176

self-legislation, 3, 5, 25, 76, 171

Seerveld, Calvin, 84

Shue, Henry, 182

sin, 89, 98; government necessary "by reason of", 5, 90

Skillen, James, 84, 91, 101, 106

social contract. *See* justificatory liberalism

social pluralism. *See* sphere sovereignty

sphere sovereignty, 99–102, 105, 106, 189, 192; of individuals, 86

the state. *See* government

structure and direction, 89, 95

subsidiarity, principle of, 82, 99

Taylor, Charles, 157, 193n18; liberties' differential importance, 48, 77n4, 123–124, 158

Thompson, Dennis. *See* Gutmann, Amy

Thoreau, Henry David, 51n6

unanimity. *See* justificatory liberalism

utilitarianism, 43, 44, 116, 157, 167n2; differences from neo-Calvinism, 102, 106; rule-utilitarianism and justificatory liberalism, 62

Vollenhoven, Dirk H. T., 84

Waldron, Jeremy, 49
Wall, Steven, 128
Westminster Confession of Faith, 96, 104; Heidelberg Catechism, 104; Westminster Larger Catechism, 113n84; Westminster Shorter Catechism, 96, 113n84
Wolters, Al, 89, 94, 97
Wolterstorff, Nicholas, 4, 30n1, 67, 91, 102, 103, 104, 119, 127, 147, 193n18; critique of metaphysical naturalism, 187; differences from neo-Calvinism, 85, 106, 193n16
wrongs, basic. *See* Neo-Calvinist legitimacy

Zuidervaart, Lambert, 4, 84, 93, 97, 99, 106, 130; on flourishing, 124, 125; on societal evil and transformation, 90, 126, 138, 161
Zylstra, Bernard, 84, 102

About the Author

Philip Shadd is a research associate of the Centre for Philosophy, Religion & Social Ethics (CPRSE) at the Institute for Christian Studies (Toronto, Ontario, Canada). He received his PhD in philosophy from Queen's University (Kingston, Ontario) in 2013, and from 2013 to 2015 he was assistant professor of Philosophy at LCC International University in Klaipėda, Lithuania. Dr. Shadd has served as part-time faculty at Redeemer University College (Ancaster, Ontario), the Institute for Christian Studies, as well as McMaster University (Hamilton, Ontario). His research focuses on the intersection of political theology and Anglo-American political theory, and he has critically examined the notions of public reason and public justification in his published work. Outside of work, he enjoys spending time with his young family, participating in church life, and following all things sport.